COURTING DISASTER

Even if you've never been in a lawsuit, you'll pay more this year for legal costs than for groceries because our country is

COURTING DISASTER

What Runaway Litigation Is Costing You And What Can Be Done To Stop The Fallout

J. WARREN KNISKERN

Foreword by F. LaGard Smith

BROADMAN
& HOLMAN
PUBLISHERS

Nashville, Tennessee

Published by:
Broadman & Holman Publishers
Nashville, Tennessee

4261-62
0-8054-6162-0

Dewey Decimal Classification: 347
Subject Heading: Litigation \ Arbitration and Award \ Legal Ethics
Library of Congress Card Catalog Number: 94-46121

Unless otherwise noted, all Scripture quotations are from
the Holy Bible, New International Version, © 1978 by
New York International Bible Society.

Library of Congress Cataloging-in-Publication Data
Kniskern, J. Warren, 1951–
Courting disaster : what runaway litigation is costing you and what can
be done to stop the fallout / by J. Warren Kniskern.
    p. cm.
Includes bibliographical references and index.
ISBN 0-8054-6162-0
1. Law—United States. 2. Church and state—United States. 3.
Law—United States—Religious aspects. 4. Dispute resolution
(Law)—United States. 5. Christianity and law. 6. Christians—legal
status, laws, etc.—United States. I. Title.
    KF380.K65   1995
    349.73—dc20
    [347.3]
                        94-46121
                        CIP
99 98 97 96 95 5 4 3 2 1

To the ultimate Peacemaker,
Jesus Christ,
and to all who follow in His path of peace.

This book would not have been possible
without the vision, unselfish service, and
encouragement of these good people:
Dr. Julia Benfield, Elise S. Kniskern,
Ancil Jenkins, Juan D. Milian,
Dr. Kieth A. Mitchell, Trish Morrison,
F. LaGard Smith, Greg Webster,
Janis M. Whipple, and Rusty Wright.
Thanks so much!

Contents

FOREWORD

The temple of justice in America has now been built so high that it is crumbling beneath its own weight. No one dares breathe without a lawyer's advice; lawsuits multiply; and courtrooms are clogged. It's a system run amuck; a noble idea profaned. Lady Justice is not just blind, but crippled as well by rights-obsessed combatants who hold her hostage for their own selfish ends. And the ransom which must be paid by all of society—in legal costs, taxes, and insurance premiums—is breathtaking.

On a broader canvas, civility itself has given way to "Sue me!" and "I'll see you in court!" The spirit of litigation has set neighbor against neighbor, spouse against spouse, brother against brother. We are a house divided, a people engaged in an uncivil civil war in which the rules of engagement are reduced to "take no prisoners" and "win at all costs." Gone from our vocabulary are words like "accommodation," "compromise," and "forbearance."

Gone, too, is the bedrock of any ordered society: personal responsibility. One need only look to "no fault insurance" and "no fault divorce" to appreciate how cleverly we have learned to evade accountability and indemnify against our own failures—all in the name of "streamlining the court." Victimization, with its typical shifting of the blame, has become a national pastime in which law has become the gameboard and lawyers the players. And they all cry "Justice, justice!" but there is no justice.

The halls of justice are crowded not only with the greedy, the malicious, and the self-absorbed, but also with the ungodly who would employ the judicial system as a weapon in a great battle between the secular and the sacred. Under the banner of church-state separation, these advocates for the devil have used the courts to aggressively block the Constitutionally guaranteed expression of one's religious beliefs. They have happily joined forces with disgruntled believers in lashing out against all things biblical, using the threat of lawsuits in an effort to repress the forces of faith.

For a nation conceived in the very womb of religious fervor, born of painful compromise and concession, and dedicated to liberty and justice for all, the insidious spirit of litigation threatens to destroy us community by community, church by church, home by home, one by one.

For the man or woman of God, the challenge is not simply how we might better fulfill the prophetic call to "do justice" amidst the shambles of a collapsing judicial system. Nor in the face of legal persecution is it our task to somehow "beat them at their own game." Rather, it is for the Christian to take seriously Jesus' teaching about going the extra mile and turning the other cheek. More than ever, it is for us to explore His entreaty that we learn forgiveness, forbearance, and even loss for the sake of the kingdom.

For a nation buckling under the weight of a burdensome legal system, alternative means of resolving disputes is rapidly becoming a practical necessity. Every avenue needs to be explored. However, for the Christian, the problem is not simply some human system of justice in need of fixing, but harmful habits of the heart that turn conflict into confrontation, and confrontation into a destructive litigation conflagration.

Fail to fix America's legal system, and we still might limp along as a society. But if we fail to see the true face of justice in reconciliation and individual spiritual renewal, then we are missing the great calling of Christ and truly courting disaster.

F. LaGard Smith
Author
Professor of Law, Pepperdine University

❧

With pleasure I introduce this Christian attorney, who is also my professional colleague in offering the team approach to private mediation. As a Christian, I find it deeply encouraging to work with an attorney who is willing to face and expose some of the societal curses of litigation.

In relational disputes, it is clear that mediation, with the expressed goal of reconciliation, is the only faithful course for the sons of God to pursue.

Blessed are the peacemakers for they shall be called sons of God.

Reconciliation is the core issue of the gospel. The gospel is the story of the Lord who became a man of incredible humility, appearing to take the weaker posture in His obedience to the cross. What a verdict was rendered! He won the case hands down. He made intimate friends out of former enemies by graciously attempting to preserve their dignity while seeking to call both parties to a higher relational accountability than to cold greed or revenge.

The Master Mediator was our Lord Jesus Christ. He personified poverty of spirit, identification with suffering, meekness, mercy, and purity of heart. He was, and is, the Master Peacemaker but was ultimately executed by the carnal forces of litigation. His deepest desire was not to judge *who* was wrong or right, but He so effectively highlighted *what* was wrong and right that millions have chosen to adjust their lives and conflicts to His will.

My commendation of Joseph Warren Kniskern, as an author, is first and foremost that he is passionate in his own desire to be like his Lord, reflecting the divine nature especially in a ministry of reconciliation. Or in cases where full reconciliation is not feasible, the author sees that mediation seeks to serve the best interests of both parties in conflict and do the least harm to the essential needs of either party.

Coming from two professional disciplines, Mr. Kniskern from the legal profession and I from the mental health profession, we arrived at a solid commitment to professional mediation from our mutual commitment to our common Lord. We took our formal training for Family Court Mediation together and committed ourselves to serve together as a mediation team. Warren's being an attorney gives him a keen appreciation for applicable law, and I have an abhorrence for the emotional toll that litigation takes on individuals, especially spouses who once loved each other deeply, and their children.

I commend this book and its author to all who deplore the cold havoc of litigation and who aspire to help move conflict resolution to a new level of professionalism and spirituality.

Dr. Kieth A. Mitchell
Certified Family Court Mediator
Licensed Mental Health Counselor

૱

Preface

THE CHALLENGE

This book is a personal challenge to you. You will read about how the American legal system is self-destructing from the inside out. This book will open your eyes. It will make you mad. It asks this question: If the opportunity presents itself, will *you* lay aside the legal weapons of this world and exercise faith in the wisdom and power of God? This is a call for you to accept personal responsibility for your life and actions. Will you have the courage and perseverance to love those who dispute with you and still be forgiving and generous to those who harm or offend you?

We live in a society where accountability for sin in one's life falls prey to excuses and rationalizations. Communion with others is replaced by a narcissist and selfish isolationism in the guise of individualism. Freedom is balanced precariously above an abyss of decadence and decay that scorns and mocks authority, virtue, and moral absolutes.

In the face of these significant failures, will *you* stand up and speak the truth in love? Will *you* resist the cultural bias against acknowledging and repenting from sin, and be willing to accept righteous judgment? Will *you* work with your neighbor—even if it means personal sacrifice? Can God use *you* to bring a biblical perspective to churches increasingly influenced by worldly philosophies? Will you fulfill the mission of the Church *God's* way, and in obedience to His Word? Instead of hiding behind the many excuses provided by a rapidly changing and increasingly complex society, will *you* reverse the trend toward dispassionate litigation through legal strangers? Will *you* do your part to restore the honor, civility, and simple neighborliness Americans used to treasure in resolving disputes peacefully and face to face?

Can you meet the challenge of Psalm 15?

LORD, who may dwell in your sanctuary?
Who may live on your holy hill? He whose walk is blameless and
who does what is righteous,
who speaks the truth from his heart
and has no slander on his tongue,

who does his neighbor no wrong
and casts no slur on his fellow man,
who despises a vile man
but honors those who fear the LORD,
who keeps his oath even when it hurts,
who lends his money without usury
and does not accept a bribe against the innocent.
He who does these things will never be shaken.

———

In many ways this book embraces a call to integrity, courage, wisdom, and perseverance in relationships. It is grounded in a surpassing reverence for God's way of dealing with problems. This book invites you to make a personal commitment to put your daily life on the line for Him no matter how long it takes, no matter how much it costs, and no matter what the ultimate outcome will be.

As he reflected upon the revolutionary birth of America and its constitutional form of limited and representative self-government, James Madison, one of our founding fathers, said this: "We have staked the whole future of American civilization, not upon the power of government; far from it. We have staked the future of all of our political institutions upon the capacity of each and all of us to govern ourselves, to control ourselves, to sustain ourselves according to the Ten Commandments of God." Remember these concepts— "to govern ourselves," "to control ourselves," "to sustain ourselves" according to God's commands. We will come back to these important words in the following pages.

As a Christian lawyer, my goal in writing this book is to stimulate creative thinking in dealing with difficult disputes and conflicts of all types. This book examines the harsh realities of conflict and proposes individual responsibility for resolving conflict peacefully.

The material in this book is not a substitute for wise legal counsel. If you have any questions at all concerning matters in this book, I urge you to consult immediately with your attorney, minister, or spiritual advisor. Be sure that the specifics of your particular situation are analyzed carefully and professionally before taking any action. Your personal advisors will have the experience and information necessary to provide wise counsel concerning your specific situation.

The people, places, and events mentioned in this book come from named sources the author believes to be reliable. Some of these sources include reported legal case decisions and published news accounts detailing various facts, as cited in the text and chapter notes. However, neither the author nor the publisher has made any independent personal inquiry into the source investigations relied upon for this book. Therefore the information supplied in these pages is only as accurate as the original sources utilized for this project.

No mention of any religious group or denomination in this book should be construed as an endorsement by the author or publisher of that group or denomination, or its teachings and practices. The reader is urged to carefully investigate and personally evaluate any religious group of interest within the context and truth of the Bible.

Introduction

ARE WE COURTING DISASTER IN OUR LEGAL SYSTEM?

They call it the China Syndrome. Normally, uranium fuel pellets rapidly heat water in the core of a nuclear reactor. By design, the reactor process generates steam used to put a turbine into motion, which turns a generator to produce electricity. But when matters go awry in a project with such enormous risks, disaster threatens. If there is not enough water cooling the reactor core, the incredibly hot fuel pellets theoretically could melt the nuclear plant and sink on through the earth to China. In reality, the core eventually would hit the water table under the plant and blast clouds of radioactive material into our atmosphere. The number of people affected, or even killed, and the square miles of property made permanently uninhabitable depend on which way the radioactive wind blows.

The experts reassure us, "Don't worry. This will never happen." They design our nuclear plants to account for every conceivable accident. Quality control focuses on every detail. There are backup systems to backup systems. Teams of technicians test, check, and recheck everything. Huge concrete containment buildings housing each reactor provide a formidable line of defense if any radioactive particles leak from the reactor or the connection lines. But still the Three Mile Island incident in Pennsylvania occurred. More recently, there was the Chernobyl disaster with its reactor now permanently entombed in a concrete sarcophagus. As we wait for the next crisis, we watch potentially dangerous stockpiles of nuclear waste grow. We begin to wonder—are our systems safe? And if an unthinkable horror happens, can we put the genie back in the bottle?

America's founding fathers designed a beautiful system of government and justice. There would be many checks and balances. Everyone would receive fair and impartial trials. In theory, the system works. But in practice, we have major problems. There are not enough funds coming in to our court system to reduce the rapidly rising heat of increasing litigation. Some radioactive fallout in the form of mismanaged cases and overwhelming costs and delays is spilling into our court containment buildings. The

1

alarms and buzzers are sounding loudly. Gauges and indicators are flashing in courthouses across the country. Computers churn out more alarming data year after year. And our normally reassuring judicial experts watch a potential meltdown in our justice system and confess that we have a major problem!

Americans are probably the most litigious people on earth. We litigate almost everything. According to the National Center for State Courts (NCSC), during the eight-year period between 1984 and 1991, civil caseloads rose by 33 percent, while the national population increased by only 7 percent over the same period. In 1990, for the first time since the NCSC began reporting data in 1984, new cases filed in state courts exceeded 100 million. That is the equivalent of about one court case for every three persons in the United States!

Our federal courts are no different. J. Clifford Wallace, chief judge of the 9th Circuit U.S. Court of Appeals, noted recently that the number of cases filed in the federal appellate courts between 1981 and 1991 increased by nearly 60 percent.

When will we learn that we can never dance with the devil and just walk away? When conflicts collide, our lawsuits become white-hot, like those millions of uranium fuel pellets after removal of the fuel control rods. In each case, chain reactions explode in geometric progression, becoming potentially uncontrollable. And unlike a nuclear power plant, we cannot shut down our courts. We must find a cure while the legal turbines keep on spinning.

The time has come to do something to reduce the number of conflicts pouring into our courthouses each year. We have to vent the pressure on our overheated justice system. Each of us must assume the responsibility for finding alternate means of dispute resolution and reconciliation of warring parties before it is too late. In our courts, churches, schools, and homes it is time to ask, *"Where are the peacemakers?"*

Those were the first words spoken by a former minister of my congregation when he returned to mediate a serious disagreement among the church leaders some years ago. Those words cut into me. How could we have ignored the teachings of Jesus as we tore into each other? We were too busy pushing our personal agendas to see the damage and fallout raining down on us.

Where are the peacemakers? As a lawyer, I can recall too many occasions when a client angrily swore, "I've had enough of dealing with Mr. Smith. I want you to sue that [expletive deleted—and, believe me, there are very few expletives I have not heard inserted here]! I don't care how long it takes, or how much it costs. I want him to pay for everything he's done to me!" Usually I ask the client, "But have you sat down and talked with Mr. Smith? Is it possible there is a misunderstanding causing this problem?"

"No!" is the usual quick reply. "I haven't talked to him, and I don't want to waste my time even trying!"

I cannot tell you how many times I have heard fighting words like these in my almost two decades of legal practice. Maybe you have said them yourself. When frustration reaches the breaking point, it is tempting to pick up a legal sword and start cutting an opponent down to size. But it's a trap that could very well ruin you emotionally and financially. The rush to litigate disputes drives a wedge into relationships. It is bringing America down under a mountainous weight of complaints, legal briefs, case decisions, and appeals. It is ruining our country. Societies prosper or falter based upon how well they resolve disputes. Right now, we simply aren't doing a very good job of it all.

Where are the peacemakers? When marriages fail, spouses facing divorce who would do well to seek mediation instead turn to their respective lawyers. In my first book, *When the Vow Breaks: A Survival and Recovery Guide for Christians Facing Divorce*, I urged husbands and wives to seek out concerned and loving Christians to help them through their difficulties. But all too frequently, warring spouses throw uncompromising and aggressive legal advocates into the gap between them. Result? Prolonged litigation, increased heartache and sleepless nights, depletion of the marital estate for legal expenses, and destruction of the family.

Sure, we have read Jesus' teachings about sacrifice and reconciliation in Matthew 5:23–26, 38–42. We know of His admonitions in Matthew 18:15–17 to follow specific steps in dealing with Christians who sin against us. We note how Paul shamed the Christians in Corinth for bringing lawsuits against one another in front of unbelievers in 1 Corinthians 6:1–8. The Bible speaks to the hearts of humankind for all time. But somehow we naively believe these Scriptures do not apply to us and our disputes today. They are old news—not high tech enough for us!

Where are the peacemakers? The truth is we really *like* to fight with each other. We enjoy winning arguments. We don't want to compromise. Reconciliation with an adversary—Christian or not—is repugnant. Forget about love, peace, patience, kindness, self-control, and other fruits of the Holy Spirit. We want to compete and champion our cause of justice. We may not admit it to others, but something inside us wants to beat those who oppose us. Some of us even want others to suffer for trivial offenses! We enjoy facing off with each other in a civil battle that declares someone the winner. Victory brings vindication. When we war with one another in this fashion, we lock horns and play for keeps. We won't give up, and we won't give in—just so we can win.

Former American Bar Association president R. William Ide III astutely observed that our legislative and judicial systems of governance are "a living testament to the uniquely American idea that people can govern themselves peacefully, rationally, through mutual agreement of the many instead of through fear and intimidation by the few." [1]

But others view the courts as an arena for human combat. The basic human emotion of "I won't give up without a fight!" makes the process of warring in court today no less a ritual duel of challenges through pens and procedure than it was by swords and muskets in centuries past. And many thrill in the fight, finding it very affirming and exhilarating.

This win-at-all-costs mind-set leads too many of us into a dark valley of uncertainty. A parade of horribles lurks at every turn. By design, the courts rule one party the winner and the other the loser. But too often the parties to the case, their lawyers, the jurors, and even a few judges are repositories of prejudice, bigotry, envy, and hatred. The verdict often is dissatisfying to everyone concerned. And any delay in resolving a case breeds more contempt from those who must wait for months or years to see their case decided. As both sides in the case assess their losses, bitterness and resentment lead them to blame their attorneys and the court. The meltdown begins when the public views the civil process as the antithesis of justice. This process is already underway.

What is the fruit of our unwillingness to resolve disputes peacefully? Civil courts that can barely cope with the flood of litigation, final decisions delayed for years after the filing of the first complaint, drained resources as plaintiffs spend time and money fighting defendants, and, worst of all, a growing trend toward vigilantism that bypasses the justice system altogether as some prefer to use their own methods to extract a pound of flesh from a neighbor.

Who pays for all the time and administration required to oversee this mess? You and I do! Taxpayers in 1950 could keep about 95 percent of their earnings to provide for their families. Today, even as real incomes of some have increased above inflation over the years, our government bites into our pocketbooks to take almost 38 percent or more of our earnings. And where do our tax dollars go? In large part to fund the courts, lawyers, judges, and juries that are needed to handle the litigation explosion we created. So each of us spends more on legal expense each year than on groceries—even if we never file a lawsuit!

Where are the peacemakers in our country? By involving ourselves emotionally in our cases, we sacrifice the objectivity that is needed to reach a reasonable settlement. Instead of viewing disputes as transactions open for quick resolution, conflicts tempt us to make the most mundane matters a holy crusade. Obviously, for peace to prevail, we need help from other sources.

Many ill-equipped lawyer advocates cannot (and should not) fulfill the role of peacemaker. They blindly dedicate themselves to winning your case, no matter what it takes. There is nothing wrong with receiving the full advantage of your legal rights and remedies, if that is your wish. But a lawyer's litigatory mind-set and actions narrowly focus on these goals only—too often ignoring your needs and interests in the process. So litigation often polarizes and isolates parties. It discourages consensus and peaceful resolution of conflict.

Judges and juries strive to serve in a neutral, peacemaking role. But they focus too much on the legal nature of disputes. They give little or no concern to the personal trauma people experience outside the legal conflicts. Therefore any justice received is incomplete.

Don't get me wrong. I still have faith that the American justice system is the best in the world. But it is not perfect. It is imprecise—much like trying to perform brain surgery with a club instead of a scalpel. Litigation too often generates disputes within disputes as opposing counsel battle over technical, procedural issues more than over the substance of the conflict. Look no further than the infamous O. J. Simpson trial to see some sad examples of this!

God offers us a better way when disagreements and controversies arise. God's answer from the time of Christ (and before) is *mediation* between adversaries—face-to-face, personal, and with a humility that listens before speaking.

As a Christian lawyer, and as one feeling many of the same frustrating emotions you might experience when others wrong you, I believe we rely too much on human courts of law. The better way to resolve conflicts peacefully is through seeking mediation. The judicial system has only recently praised the new forms of mediation and other alternative dispute resolution (ADR) mechanisms. But it was the product of our loving God who, centuries ago, gave His people this powerful entreaty: "Come now, let us reason together."[2]

In these pages we will see how the traditional ways of American justice are not serving the needs and interests of our country, our churches, or our families. God's answer is to follow the simple command to reason together. Face to face. It involves a willingness to listen and compromise on issues in order to save a relationship. If you need help in working matters out with your neighbor, involvement of third-party mediators is God-ordained and commanded.

This book is a call to return to reason and reconciliation. It is a plea to relieve the pressure on our overburdened courts, and reduce the dangers of runaway litigation. Haven't we fought with one another long enough? How much longer will we rely upon expensive and unpredictable civil litigation? Why not use God's prescription for dispute resolution? Why not mediate differences directly among the parties involved, making each person responsible for his or her decisions? Why not encourage people to use their creative resources to forge workable solutions in a private, confidential, informal, and flexible environment rather than destroy each other among strangers? Why not provide an easily accessible forum that fosters the sharing of information and constructive communication? Why not expose the strengths and weaknesses of arguments to find the truth, rather than intimidate and berate the persons involved? Can we focus more on *what* is right, rather than battle over who is legally right or more able to coerce submission from weaker parties?

We must resolve more of our differences privately, as God encourages us to do. Why not look for ways to accommodate the needs and interests of *all* parties as much as is reasonably possible? Let's satisfy our needs and interests more in the context of continued fellowship with each other, and less in dollars and legal combat victories.

It is true that, in our fast-paced, complex society, finding competent advisors to be peacemakers can be like trying to find an oasis in the desert. But they are out there—those committed and loving individuals who are solution-oriented and who balance a keen grasp of the issues with negotiating finesse and a respectful emotional detachment.

You don't have to go to court to receive justice, nor is a lawsuit necessary to grant mercy. With the help of God and His children, you can resolve your disputes peacefully and help our entire nation in the process.

Where are the peacemakers? As we explore our existing judicial system in the chapters to come, the chaos and despair will alarm you. But take heart! We will end on the mountaintop learning from the ultimate Peacemaker, Jesus Christ. There is a way out of the crisis we face in America. My prayer is that you will embrace whatever you find to be good and useful in this book and share it with others around you. May this book speak to your heart, marshal your resolve to become a part of the solution, and inspire you with hope!

Part One:

OUR PROBLEM—
THE LITIGATION EXPLOSION

No one calls for justice; no one pleads his case with integrity. They rely
on empty arguments and speak lies; they conceive trouble and give
birth to evil. They hatch the eggs of vipers and spin a spider's web.
Whoever eats their eggs will die, and when one is broken, an adder is
hatched . . . So justice is driven back, and righteousness stands at a
distance; truth has stumbled in the streets, honesty cannot enter.
Truth is nowhere to be found, and whoever shuns evil becomes a prey.
(Isa. 59:4–5, 14–15)

Settle matters quickly with your adversary who is taking you to court.
Do it while you are still with him on the way, or he may hand you
over to the judge, and the judge may hand you over to the officer, and
you may be thrown into prison. I tell you the truth, you will not get
out until you have paid the last penny. (Matt. 5:25–26)

*T*he prophet Isaiah's lament more than twenty-five hundred years ago in a totally different culture and faraway land is too close to the mark for us today. It makes Jesus' warning to us even more urgent.

These are wise words from those familiar with the justice courts of men. Fallible men and women being what they are, little has changed over the years. Many courtrooms have a sign, "We Who Labor Here Seek Only The Truth." But too often there is distortion of the truth. These days, many people lie under oath (*perjury*). Many judges shrug their shoulders when a lie is exposed, tolerating it instead of enforcing the existing penalties for that crime. The justice system is fair and balanced. People are the problem. Impartial judgment is difficult for anyone.

As an undergraduate at the University of Florida business school some years ago, I took a real estate course from Professor Louis Gaitanis. He was a short, balding man with wire-rimmed glasses who delighted the class with humorous adventures and war stories. But the most striking memory I have of Professor Gaitanis is of how, with a twinkle in his eye, this curious little man would stand on a chair in front of the class, raise his index finger in the air above his head and yell, "Life's too short!"

After nineteen years of practicing law, I see first hand how people can litigate for years and even decades over the most petty of disputes. Now I respect the urgent imperative to resolve conflicts and disputes through biblically-based mediation by saying to you, "Life's too short to litigate!"

In Part One, we will see the critical need for a better way to resolve disputes—for the sake of our faith, our livelihood, and our great country. Despite the best efforts of our founding fathers in giving us our Constitution, our existing justice system cannot help people consistently achieve justice in a peaceful and timely manner. We will review the religious freedoms Americans enjoy, and the inherent conflict that exists in the supposed separation between church and state. Some key court cases involve believers who ignore Jesus' command in Matthew 18:15–17 to resolve disputes peacefully within their own fellowship. This compounds our problems as church lawsuits multiply, forcing legislatures and courts to intervene and try to govern religious beliefs and administration.

The temptation to litigate everything—even conflicts within our families—is leading all of us to the brink of disaster. Our courts absolutely cannot keep up with the growing caseload of all those who want to fight out matters before judges and juries. And if our justice system collapses under the weight of paper, where will that leave all of us?

Today, citizens cannot secure quick and inexpensive justice through the courts. If we do not act at once to take personal responsibility for ourselves by resolving our disputes peacefully and privately, our country faces the worst sort of anarchy and vigilantism.

Chapter 1

One Nation Under God: America's Dream of Justice, Equality, and Individual Responsibility

Seeking new ways of peace and reconciliation involves reminding ourselves of our heritage as Americans. How has God shed His grace on us? What was the dream of our Founding Fathers? How can we fulfill the dream today?

ঌ

By God's providence, America is a place where miracles not only happen, but where they happen all the time.[1] The Declaration of Independence, U.S. Constitution, and Bill of Rights were among the first miracles.

Referring to the adoption of the Constitution, James Madison sent a letter to his good friend Thomas Jefferson (in France at the time) in October 1787, marveling, "It is impossible to consider the degree of concord which ultimately prevailed as less than a miracle." In February 1788 George Washington echoed these words when he wrote to Lafayette: "It appears to me, then, little short of a miracle that the delegates from so many states . . . should unite in forming a system of national government, so little liable to well founded objections."

America truly is a land of miracles. But our nation did not become this way by accident.

A Dream Inspired by God and Born from Mediation

The colonies in America despised British rule and rebelled against an oppressive monarchy. In the summer of 1774, thirty-three-year-old lawyer Thomas Jefferson took five weeks to draft "A Summary View of the Rights of British Americans." Its premise? That Americans should govern themselves as a natural right of humankind. This led to the beautiful words penned by Jefferson as he sat hunched over his folding writing box for seventeen days on the second floor of a rooming house in Philadelphia. The forefathers of our country embraced his ideas as they put their lives at risk in signing the Declaration of Independence on July 4, 1776, stating in part:

> We hold these truths to be self-evident, that all men are created equal, that they are endowed by their Creator with certain inalienable Rights, that among these are Life, Liberty and the pursuit of Happiness. That to secure these rights, Governments are instituted among Men, deriving their just powers from the consent of the governed. . . . We, therefore, the Representatives of the United States of America . . . appealing to the Supreme Judge of the world for the rectitude of our intentions do . . . solemnly publish and declare, That these United Colonies are, and of Right ought to be, Free and Independent States . . . And for the support of this declaration, with a firm reliance on the protection of divine Providence, we mutually pledge to each other our Lives, our Fortunes and our Sacred Honor.

———

Twenty-four lawyers and judges. Eleven merchants. Nine owners of large plantations. Fifty-six men in all who had a lot to lose and did not take this pledge lightly. And many of them paid the price by sacrificing their property, financing the cause of freedom, or losing their lives in battle— frequently after torture from British soldiers. But signing this legal document was more than a rallying cry for public opinion—it established a case for declaring independence and giving birth to a new nation.

These valiant men believed it was necessary to dissolve the political bonds that tied the colonies to Great Britain. They rested their case primarily on the eternal truth that God endowed His creation with inalienable rights of self-governance. This meant people could choose their own government rather than have government imposed upon them through coercion or force. No one, by divine right or otherwise, had the self-appointed authority to rule over any other person because "all men are created equal."

As the American Revolution raged on, the colonists quickly adopted the Articles of Confederation, drafted in 1777 as the nation's first charter, but it really did nothing more than provide a way for the thirteen new states to pay for a national defense. It provided for no chief executive or judiciary. This was not at all surprising, however, since state representatives were suspicious of any new centralized government and jealously guarded the interests and powers of their individual jurisdictions.

Thirteen small sovereign states cautiously banded together for the specific and limited purpose of fighting the Revolutionary War, but they never enjoyed true unity. Immediately after winning the war, they were in complete disagreement about the future. Long-range prospects were poor. England and France stood poised like buzzards, waiting to pick over the carcass of a failed experiment in democracy.

Then, in late spring of 1787, delegates came from each of the states to the Constitutional Convention in the Pennsylvania State House (now Independence Hall) in Philadelphia. Their goal? To amend the Articles of Confederation into a workable alliance of states at odds with each other. It was a time of deep uncertainty, lack of trust, and turmoil. When presiding officer George Washington left his mahogany chair vacant for one moment, Benjamin Franklin noticed a half-sun carved into it. Franklin wondered whether it would prove to be a rising or setting sun. Would order come from the distress and chaos of post-Revolution trauma?

On opening day, May 14, 1787, only representatives from two states were present. Almost two weeks would pass before a quorum of seven states convened the session. Delegates from New Hampshire did not arrive until midsummer. Rhode Island representatives never showed up at all.

Closed windows in the upper floor State House meeting place maintained security and confidentiality for those expressing often radical views. Debate was vigorous and heated. The scene became hotter as those in the room sat for hours in uncushioned Windsor chairs and sweltered while wearing wool suits and scalp-clenching wigs during the hot summer months. The stifling air stirred only when they opened the windows briefly each day at noon. Then black flies and mosquitos stormed in to attack the delegates while the noise from the large cosmopolitan city and curses from prisoners in the nearby Walnut Street prison distracted everyone concerned. Even so, the environment was not nearly as challenging as the task these men set about to complete.

The strong-willed and highly opinionated delegates, fifty-five in number at its highest point, argued and reasoned with each other from May until mid-July. Five hours each day, six days a week. Debate dragged on for weeks. The primary driving force was their mutual desire to reach *some* sort of agreement.

Eventually the delegates saw the futility of trying to fulfill the original purpose of the convention—amending the existing Articles of Confederation. In doing so they sacrificed the sovereignty of each state for a new constitution that would set up a *representative* central government. But this would be a new form of government strong enough to provide order and stability on a national level, while not abridging the God-given rights of individual citizens.

This raised many questions. How could the delegates resolve the natural tension between the individual and government? How could this government secure citizen participation in social and political decision-making that would last for ages to come? What should the respective powers be between any centralized government and the states? Would there be one or two houses of Congress? How would congressional members be chosen? Should there be only one person serving in an executive capacity of government, and what should the term of office be?

Fortunately, the convention provided an excellent chance for delegates to exchange ideas and viewpoints. They listened to each other, reflecting on the substance of the debate while exploring the limits of various proposals. They began working on compromises together.

Benjamin Franklin, who ultimately lost on many of his own proposals, performed an important mediation function. Time after time this eighty-one-year-old elder statesman, his body riddled with gout, would encourage those assembled to continue to focus on the common good of the new nation. He stressed the need for unity and set an example of reflection and compromise. During one session, after a particularly bitter and divisive speech from a delegate, Franklin used the analogy of a table with plank edges that did not fit. To make a good joint, he pointed out, the craftsman must shave a little off the edges of each plank. "In like manner," Franklin concluded, "here both sides must part with some of their demands, in order that they may join in some accommodating proposition."

The result? Reaching the Great Compromise on July 16, 1787, and a major agreement to pass disputes through a representative Congress—just in time to save the convention from dissolution by many frustrated and exasperated delegates. They continued to compromise, test out ideas through trial and error, and work together on many details for two more months. Finally, on September 17, 1787, they adopted the Constitution as we now know it, and George Washington (who did not speak in the debates until the last day) adjourned the convention.

Although he disagreed with some of the convention's decisions, just before adjournment Franklin urged all delegates to support the new Constitution unanimously despite personal interests. "The older I grow," he remarked, "the more apt I am to doubt my own judgment, and to pay more respect to the judgment of others." Wise words born of experience.

This Constitution clearly defined our newly-centralized federal government and its roles: (a) the legislative law-making branch, with taxing power to raise national funds; (b) the executive policy-making branch and president; and (c) the judicial federal court branch. Each branch was carefully counterbalanced against the other. Why? To vest power in the people to govern themselves through a representative government subject only to God, rather than to any oppressive earthly king.

The Preamble to the Constitution says it all: "We, the people of the United States, in Order to form a more perfect Union, establish Justice, insure domestic Tranquility, provide for the common defence, promote the general Welfare, and secure the Blessings of Liberty for ourselves and our posterity do ordain and establish this Constitution of the United States of America."

What were the "Blessings of Liberty"? The Declaration of Independence showcased a few of these godly graces; "all men are created equal," "endowed by their Creator with certain unalienable rights," "Life, Liberty and the pursuit of Happiness." The Constitution binds government officials to share power and authority, given by consent of the people, to preserve the God-given rights of all citizens. But the ultimate power remained with "We, the people."

Once the Constitution had been sent to the states for ratification, it hit a roadblock. Anti-Federalist opponents protested strongly that the Constitution did not fully protect these "unalienable rights." The authors of the Constitution disagreed, but in the spirit of continuing compromise and to accomplish state ratification within ten months (by mid-1788), the delegates agreed to attend an additional convention and add the first ten amendments to the Constitution. These amendments, commonly known as the Bill of Rights, begin with the words, "Congress shall make no law." The Constitution resolved the question of what the national government needed to fulfill its purpose. The Bill of Rights confirmed the restraints on what the federal government could do.

These amendments, adopted by the states in 1791, comforted those who were justifiably afraid of another intrusive centralized government like that of the British monarchy. For example, now Congress could not stifle expression of one's opinion, shut down an unpopular press, force or prohibit religious expression, or jail a citizen without a fair and speedy trial.

OUR GOD-GIVEN LEGACY

Perhaps our greatest legacy from the founding fathers is not so much the words of the Declaration of Independence, Constitution, and Bill of Rights. Instead it is the firm commitment to respect elemental human rights given by God in love to every man and woman—rights which no human authority should restrict or abolish. Though people may seek to justify themselves, arguing that the end justifies the means as occurred during the infamous Iran-Contra hearings, our Constitution abides with us. Through the tragedy of a president risking impeachment to abuse his power, the Constitution abides with us still. It ensures our God-given right to express our beliefs and opinions without fear of reprisal.

America. Land of divine Providence. Envy of the world. What we share as Americans today is more than a mere rendezvous with destiny. We are free because God willed it to be so. A nation of many miracles where people can marvel at "Believe It or Not," while many other nations of the world tell their citizens, "Believe It or Else."

We are heirs of a promise. President John F. Kennedy said it well for all of us living in this century: "Let the word go forth from this time and place, to friend and foe alike, that the torch has been passed to a new generation of Americans." But this bold pronouncement carried a charge of commitment: "Ask not what your country can do for you—ask what you can do for your country."[2]

In his work *Commentaries on the Constitution of the United States*, still quoted by U.S. Supreme Court justices to this day, Justice Joseph Story admonished:

> Let the American youth never forget that they possess a noble inheritance, bought by the toils, and sufferings, and blood of their ancestors; and capable, if wisely improved, and faithfully guarded, of transmitting to their latest posterity all the substantial blessings of life, the peaceful enjoyment of liberty, property, religion and independence. The structure has been erected by architects of consummate skill and fidelity; its foundations are solid; its compartments are beautiful as well as useful; its arrangements are full of wisdom and order; and its defences are impregnable from without. It has been reared for immortality, if the work of man may justly aspire to such a title. It may, nevertheless, perish in an hour by the folly, or corruption, or negligence of its only keepers, THE PEOPLE. Republics are created by the virtue, public spirit, and intelligence of its citizens. They fall, when the wise are banished from the public councils, because they dare to be honest, and the profligate are rewarded, because they flatter the people in order to betray them.[3]

Indeed, in our Declaration of Independence, Constitution, and Bill of Rights, we own a "noble inheritance reared for immortality," as God willed it to happen.

America's famous poet, Carl Sandburg, treasured our country with these words: "I see America, not in the setting sun of a black night of despair ahead of us; I see America in the crimson light of a rising sun fresh from the burning, creative hand of God. I see great days ahead, great days possible to men and women of will and vision . . ."[4] But he also warned, "If she [America] forgets where she came from, if the people lose sight of what brought them along, if she listens to the deniers and mockers, then will begin the rot and dissolution."[5] So now we must ask ourselves the question . . .

IS OUR NATION'S BEAUTIFUL DREAM FADING?

My prayer, along with many other Americans, is that God will continue to bless our great country and breathe life into our dynamic Constitution for another hundred years. But our Constitution, framework of government, laws,[6] and judicial court system[7] are only as dynamic, useful, and practical as are "We, the people." Are we living up to our responsibilities as citizens, as James Madison noted in his remarks, quoted in the preface of this book? Are we acknowledging the good fruits of our forefathers and the Source of our many blessings? Almost two hundred and eight years after adoption of the Constitution and the Bill of Rights, are we, the people, forgetting where we came from and the God who made it all possible?

Over a century ago, President Abraham Lincoln worried about our drifting away from God. This wise man earnestly desired "that this nation, under God, shall have a new birth of freedom—and that the government of the people, by the people, and for the people shall not perish from the Earth."[8] But he saw the seeds of apostasy already plaguing our nation:

> We have been the recipients of the choicest bounties of Heaven. We have been preserved, these many years, in peace and prosperity. We have grown in numbers, wealth and power, as no other nation has ever grown. But we have forgotten God. We have forgotten the gracious hand which preserved us in peace, and multiplied and enriched and strengthened us; and we have vainly imagined, in the deceitfulness of our hearts, that all these blessings were produced by some superior wisdom and virtue of our own. Intoxicated with unbroken success, we have become too self-sufficient to feel the necessity of redeeming and preserving grace, too proud to pray to the God that made us![9]

———

Today many quickly echo this concern. We have become too urban and secular. America was better off when folks opened their meals with prayer rather than with a can opener.

Have we lost sight of who we are and how our nation came into being? Many among us in this country can recite where and when the Pilgrims landed, but have no idea why. How many Americans have taken the time to read the Declaration of Independence, Constitution, and Bill of Rights?

Can we sever ties with our God and succeed by bootstrapping ourselves as "rugged individualists?" Consider Judge Thomas M. Reavley's assessment in 1988 from his vantage point on the bench in the United States Court of Appeals:

How are we today? Have we reached the perfect union? Well, hardly. The separation of powers, with checks and balances, is not working because so few are willing to share and cooperate in the process and so many think that only they have the answers. Congress is unable to produce a budget and the President is unable to conduct foreign relations. The media sets our agenda, and it is constrained by the brief attention span of the general public. Too many people are alienated and consider themselves outside the larger community. The gap between rich and poor grows. All of our prisons and jails are full. The zero sum adversary and the single interest zealot stalk our courtrooms, the pages of our periodicals, and the Washington scene. And our values are askew. [10]

———

Left to our own devices, the fruit of our efforts is chaos, confusion, and gridlock.

Our founding fathers labored for so long in birthing our nation with sacred respect for our God-given inalienable rights. Given this commitment to all Americans, why do so many of us who believe and claim to obey God not follow His commands? More specifically, why are we Christians not resolving our disputes peacefully according to Matthew 18:15–17 and similar passages? Our failures are causing the erosion of our individual freedoms. Unwittingly, we are encouraging our increasingly powerful government to take over responsibilities that are properly ours. And this is where we are all falling into a legal abyss.

THE LITIGATION TRAP

When national problems increase and moral values decline, a nation rises up of "victims" who refuse to take personal responsibility for their actions. No one asks what he or she can do for America. Instead, America caters to individuals who selfishly gorge on personal rights, seeking to blame others for their shortcomings. Result? Neighbors suing, not serving, neighbors. Unceasing litigation. Disunity. Pervasive selfishness and pride.

At the same time, our diverse and complex society creates another dilemma: complex laws. And complex laws, frequently written by lawyers, require more lawyers to interpret them, enforce, or defend against them, and change them into even more complex laws in order to close any loopholes. This legal mumbo jumbo confuses the common American, who could understand the Constitution, but chokes on our bulky statutes and codes today. Result? More lawsuits demanding that judges decipher, interpret, and apply these laws to many of the most ordinary circumstances.

Some blame lawyers for creating their own demand by stirring up these troubles. Many view the legal profession as business that exploits conflict. Many of these observations are true. As a lawyer, I question the premise in the legal world that each individual needs an advocate and protector from fellow Americans who are viewed as adversaries. This sets in motion a centrifugal force spinning all Americans away from each other. It puts us on guard against one another. It raises suspicions, doubt, and uncertainty as to motives and actions.

But I firmly believe the springboard for most of our litigation, and the inherent evils that come with it, begins at the most basic social level. It is not the failing of government, statutory flaws, or lawyers who plague us most. It is you and me no longer talking to each other. We, the people, could stop the evils and maddening frustrations in our legal system if we truly wanted it to happen. But to do it we would have to stand together. And right now, too many of us just don't want to get involved.

What Happened to Neighborliness?

Do you know what made the Ten Commandments (and the New Testament teachings) so remarkable and distinct from all other laws? They underscored that how we treat each other is of profound interest to God. God did not concern Himself solely with how we treat Him; it matters greatly to Him whether we lie, cheat, or steal from one another.

Our Declaration of Independence, Constitution, and Bill of Rights build upon this early foundation from the Lord. Our nation's charter documents confirm the individual's God-given right to make personal choices and decisions, but assume that each person will exercise this freedom responsibly. Our success as a nation depends upon each of us sticking together as Americans and working for the common good.

Yes, there was a time when we knew how much we needed one another. We overlooked minor offenses. We worked together to resolve major disputes because of our common bond and desire for fellowship. In Chuck Swindoll's excellent book, *Dropping Your Guard: The Value of Open Relationships*, I have never forgotten one powerful illustration highlighting the vital importance of our national fellowship:

> The Europeans who came here to settle North America found it vast and unexplored. "Self-reliant" was the watchword, and the scout, the mountain man or the pioneer, with his axe and rifle over his shoulder, became the national hero.
> In those early days the government gave away quarter sections of land to anyone who would homestead, in order to encourage settlement. People flocked west from crowded cities and villages to have their own land at last. Before they could farm the land they had chosen, their first job was to build a sod hut to live in, and we

know that most families built them right smack-dab in the middle of their quarter section. The reason was obvious. People who had never owned land before had a new sense of pride and ownership. They wanted to feel that everything they saw belonged to them.

————

But that custom changed very quickly. This chosen isolation did strange things to people. Occasionally, photographers went out to record life on the frontier and returned with photographs of weird men, wild-eyed women, and haunted-looking children. Before long most of these families learned to move their houses to one corner of their property in order to live in proximity with three other families who also lived on the corners of their property. Four families living together, sharing life and death, joy and sorrow, abundance and want, had a good chance of making it.[11]

But America today is so different. We are the detached, the loners who can be lonely in a crowd. Why did we give up the need to be with each other? How did we lose touch with one another?

We discovered that communion with our neighbors carries a price. It requires tearing down barriers erected to protect ourselves. It means dispelling our fears to move into uncharted territories and mingle with the people there. It means crucifying predetermined, but distorted, expectations and prejudices to see others as they really are and accept them. It requires humility and the confession that maybe we do not have a lock on the only right way to live. The spirit of neighborliness leaves no room for a self-centered need for control and manipulation. It flourishes in an atmosphere of openness, empathy, faith, love, acceptance, and trust that welcomes interdependence among friends. Some have found that these interconnections, care, and concern for one another are just too cozy to endure. And so, in recent decades, the pendulum has swung back toward individual Americans isolating themselves.

Look at the American scene in the 1990s. What do you see? Folks seeking to wall off and barricade themselves into their houses. Community microcosms buttressing themselves with gatehouses, twenty-four-hour roving guards cloistered behind protective lakes, rivers, walls, fences, berms, canals, and whatever else is available to keep others out of our yards and lives. We have gone far beyond installing fences to make good neighbors, to shutting each other out almost completely. We reason that peace in isolation is worthwhile because it raises our property values, although it does so at the price of fellowship with our neighbors.

We are fast becoming a very territorial nation of little islands. We close off public streets and barricade them. We retreat into personal hideouts from the world each day after going to work or to the store. We have divided entire cities into little compartmentalized fiefdoms. The closest many of us come to neighborliness is watching out for whatever the people next door are doing that might annoy us. And we don't want any strangers on our island. After all, self-protection always justifies a lack of concern for other human beings.

A few years ago columnist Bob Greene returned to his hometown in Bexley, Ohio. What did he find there?

> In the nicer sections of town the homes were still lovely, but very few had the names of their owners displayed on address signs in front, the way they used to. Instead, the signs on the lawns bore the names of security agencies, announcing to would-be burglars that the homes were wired and connected to the police station. It's like this everywhere now, all over the United States, in our new age of fear and discretion. Don't let strangers know your name; just tell them you are wary and well-protected. Security on those streets we were walking was once something that was taken for granted—and it was not the kind people had to order from a company and pay for each month. [12]

———

The tragic result of this isolation and lack of neighborliness is that some folks will inevitably fall into the widening gap between us. Consider the late Adele Gaboury of Worcester, Massachusetts. Her neighbors were kind enough to mow her lawn, keep some of her mail, and even call a utility company to fix some broken pipes. All the while, Adele's badly decomposed body lay dead among the trash piled up on her kitchen floor for about four years until the police finally found it in October 1993. Although she lived in the same house for forty years, a stone's throw of her neighbors, she was lost in the shuffle of detached living, as so many others are. "My heart bleeds for her, but you can't blame a soul," confessed a next-door neighbor. "If she saw you out there, she never said hello to you."[13]

With increasing isolation comes incivility. It is easier to cross swords with, and curse, a stranger. And the media relishes and magnifies our personal malice in words and pictures masquerading as entertainment.

Whatever the reasons—declining morality and confusion arising from fuzzy value systems, fears, or insecurities—we simply are not willing to discuss our interests and positions on issues in the way the founding fathers envisioned. The result of this alienation? An exaggerated sense that our rights are more important than those of anyone else, and an increasing dependence on formal litigation where our lawyers square off and argue with our neighbors in our place. As Terence Moran once astutely observed:

> If you can't truly talk with someone, you can't very well trust them, so you might as well sue them when things take a bad turn. And, of course, it's your right to sue them—for just about anything. . . . The problem, . . . observers say, can be traced to the

country's fixation on rights . . . Behind the loss of civility and alienation, the argument goes, lies the constant clamoring for more rights to do unto others and to keep them from doing unto you. If the only way to solve a problem is to hold a competition to determine whose right is stronger, a disputatious and distrustful citizenry will inevitably result. . . . The task consists, in large part, of shoring up the non-political aspects of our lives, in recapturing a sense of charity and duty to one another in the workplace, on the street corner, or at the beach. [14]

Well said. Again the conviction expressed in James Madison's comment in the preface of this book rings true. "We, the people" must assume our God-given responsibilities once again. Where are the Americans who look down on no one, but look straight into the eyes of everyone? We can no longer ignore our duty to watch out for each other, to care for each other, and to love one another genuinely without excessive reliance upon our courts or governments to do it for us. We are our brother's keeper.

When we retreat from the call of Jesus to love each other as He loves us, we pierce ourselves with greater sorrows than the loss of fellowship with our neighbor. The parties to court litigation make administration of true justice an almost impossible task. Substituting our heritage of neighborliness for sterile courtrooms marks us as a defeated people who are easy prey for human error and inconsistent judgments. And as we fail to reconcile with one another privately, our collective public failings diminish us as a society. We set in motion the "rot and dissolution" of our great country that Carl Sandburg warned us about long ago.

The road of modern American court-ordered justice is far from being a highway of holiness, as we shall see in the chapters to follow.

Questions for Personal Reflection

1. Am I willing to be personally accountable to others for my actions and to accept responsibility for my own decisions without making unwarranted excuses for myself?

2. As an American, do I fully appreciate the freedoms God gave me and why the founding fathers sought to protect those freedoms from governmental interference?

3. Do I feel a spirit of neighborliness toward my fellow human beings? Do I even know who my neighbors really are?

4. In what ways do I find myself drifting away from others into a more isolated lifestyle that keeps me from truly knowing other people and appreciating their God-given and unique qualities?

5. Have I fallen into the litigation trap of seeking my own ends though it may hurt other people—even those who offend me?

Chapter 2

WHAT'S HAPPENING TO OUR FAMILIES: THE DIVORCE DILEMMA

Trying to resolve divorce disputes with litigation is like trying to extinguish a fire with gasoline. Result? Depletion of marital assets, displeasure with results, and bitterness and resentment that invite further damage and pain.

ॐ

When we speak of problems in America's justice system, we must look to ourselves. One of the greatest factors in the overwhelming caseload crisis our courts face today is divorce litigation. How does it happen? What can be done?

THE SORROW OF DIVORCE

"I feel so sorry for them, but at least it hasn't happened to me!" How many times have you heard those very words expressed about another couple facing a divorce? Maybe you have said this to yourself.

Bart Giamatti was speaking about baseball, but he could have been talking about an unhappy marriage that ends in divorce: "It is designed to break your heart. The game begins in the spring when everything else begins again. It blossoms in the summer, filling the afternoons and evenings. Then, as soon as the chill rains come, it stops and leaves you to face the fall alone." Divorce never fails to leave a trail of tears. The Chinese proverb that states, "In the broken nest there are no whole eggs" is true.

REAPING THE WHIRLWIND OF DIVORCE

A severe divorce crisis plagues America today. By the mid-1980s, the annual divorce rate was over 1,160,000—nearly 50 percent. That means more than two divorces every minute of every day! A century ago in the U.S., there was only one divorce for every eighteen marriages. This rate increased only gradually (except for a brief surge after World War II) until the 1960s. But now, in just twenty-five years, we have experienced a divorce explosion in which the rate of divorce has more than tripled. In 1993 there were 16.7 million currently divorced persons, up from 4.3 million in 1970.

Today, there is only a fifty-fifty chance that a man and a woman marrying for the first time will keep their vows. These odds increase if it is a second marriage for either spouse. No wonder some note with disdain that today's "nuclear families" are "nuclear *fission* families."

Divorce leads to other breakdowns in society as well. The faltering American economy and the federal deficit are problems that will be with us into the next millennium. Skyrocketing consumer bankruptcies fuel these fires. Bankruptcies rose from 289,979 in 1980 to more than 971,517 in 1992. In Massachusetts and Florida, bankruptcy filings were increasing by more than 500 percent between 1984 and 1992. What is causing the increase? One reason may be that bankruptcy filings roughly approximate the rise in the American divorce rate. As Americans divorce, financial debts of the marriage often fall disproportionately on one party, who is unwilling to pay the debt. One spouse sues the other. When the debt is overwhelming, either or both file for bankruptcy. As this trend continues, businesses and credit providers suffer. Employers suffer business losses as worker productivity plummets. Soon we all feel the pinch and pay the price.[1]

The divorce epidemic also makes many people skeptical of marriage today. Then what happens? "Let's live together instead," they reason. After all, society's taboos on this subject have eased over the years. Why take on the entanglements of a marriage commitment? In 1993 alone, there were 3.5 million unmarried-couple households, compared to 0.5 million in 1970. There were six unmarried couples for every one hundred married couples in 1993, compared to one couple per one hundred in 1970. But this represents faulty logic that breaks down families and ignores God's clear commands against such practices.

Every action we take has a ripple effect on others and on our entire country. Each of us has a personal responsibility to become part of the solution to this tragedy rather than passively becoming another statistic and part of the problem.

DIVORCE—WHAT IS IT GOOD FOR?

Divorce is as close as you can get to death without actually dying. Only those who have experienced it can truly understand its dark power to test emotions and intellect to the ultimate degree. The only social trauma greater than divorce is the physical death of a loved one. Saying that divorce is an ugly nightmare is an understatement. Divorce is full-scale devastation! It rips families apart. It cuts into hearts and souls deeper than almost any other tragedy imaginable. It shatters precious memories as it strips us of family, roles, and identity. It saps our strength and breaks down the core of our spirits until an emotional numbness and fog set in. It reduces one of the most intimately personal relationships we can ever share with another human being to sharp shards of broken dreams. Divorce, quite simply, is the most brutal, bloodless crime of passion known to man. Even that description understates the destruction if physical violence and abuse are also present.

Divorce litigation is war. We may not think our spouses are going to war against us, but plans for divorce, and the completion of them, are often warlike. What once was "You and me against the world," now quickly becomes you against me. The spoils of this conflict are everything we treasure and have worked hard for all our lives. This battlefield is in the most private and intimate recesses of our lives. It is a contest of wills and a battle of hearts and minds on our home turf. When love falls prey to hatred or apathy and the personal stakes are high, there are no dispassionate foot soldiers.

That is the way I described divorce in my first book, *When the Vow Breaks: A Survival and Recovery Guide for Christians Facing Divorce.*[2] But my words were so inadequate to express how deeply wounded divorcees fall prey to greater sorrows as they litigate during this terrible crisis.

THE HEARTBREAK OF DIVORCE

What is it like to pursue divorce in today's civil courts? One good fictional account can be seen in the 1989 black comedy, *The War of the Roses.* Actor/director Danny de Vito, playing a lawyer, narrates the tale of an awful divorce battle. In the movie, a husband and wife fight over who will receive the house in the property settlement. They make a suicide pact of mutually assured destruction and fiendishly carry it out. The moral of the movie is: "Civilized divorce is a contradiction in terms."

Real life isn't far from this fantasy. Consider the case of Los Angeles millionaires Stanley and Dorothy Diller. Their divorce took more than seven years to complete.

The Dillers disputed every issue possible. The case in the trial court required 110 court hearings and a marathon trial lasting forty-nine days. The divorce continued until the case transcript had consumed 5,165 pages in twenty volumes more than six feet high. Attorneys' fees well exceeded $3 million as appeals went all the way to the U.S. Supreme Court.[3]

Trial judge Robert Fainer described Dorothy Diller as "a frightened, bitter woman." She was "obsessed" with the idea that her husband was concealing assets. He described Stanley Diller as "an avaricious, covetous, and stubborn man." Clearly no judge could stop this couple from grinding out the litigation without concern for the time and costs of doing so. In fact, if spouses fail to agree, the court process has the potential for this type of result in almost any divorce case.

Divorces so often destroy family relationships for generations to come. After six years of marriage, Richard and Laurel Schutz divorced in November 1978. The former Mrs. Schutz received sole custody of the couple's two young daughters, while Mr. Schutz had visitation rights. Between 1981 and 1985, the mother moved with the children from state to state without telling Mr. Schutz before each move. When Mr. Schutz finally found his children, he discovered that they "hated, despised, and feared" him.

Mr. Schutz went to court for help. The judge determined that "the cause of the blind, brainwashed, bigoted belligerence of the children toward the father grew from the soil nurtured, watered and tilled by the mother." The court believed "the mother breached every duty she owed as the custodial parent to the noncustodial parent of instilling love, respect, and feeling in the children for their father. . . . She slowly dripped poison into the minds of these children, maybe even beyond the power of this Court to find the antidote." Consequently, the judge ordered the mother "to do everything in her power to create in the minds of [the children] a loving, caring feeling toward the father . . . [and] to convince the children that it is the mother's desire that they see their father and love their father."

The mother was not content with this decision, however. She appealed the ruling to the Florida Supreme Court, arguing that her First Amendment rights guaranteeing free speech protected her from any legal obligation to undo the harm to the children.

The Florida Supreme Court agreed that she had freedom of speech. But the father of her children and the state of Florida had a stronger interest in encouraging a good relationship between father and child. If it were otherwise, the court reasoned, any such encouragement would do no good if the mother could undo it. No one required the mother to express opinions she did not hold (a practice disallowed by the First Amendment). She was, however, required to take the necessary measures to restore and promote the frequent and positive interaction (such as visitation, telephone calls, letters) between father and children, and to refrain from doing or saying anything likely to defeat that end.[4]

In his novel, *Cannery Row*, John Steinbeck poignantly noted: "The things we admire in men, kindness and generosity, openness, honesty, understanding and feeling are the concomitants of failure in our system. And those traits we detest, sharpness, greed, acquisitiveness, meanness, egotism and self-interest, are the traits of success. And while men admire the quality of the first, they love the produce of the second." Are we, as Steinbeck says, agreeing with qualities of mercy and forgiveness, but falling prey to expediency and self-protection at the expense of others? Will we go for the jugular vein in our divorce situations whenever the going gets tough or it becomes easy to do so?

SIGN OF THE TIMES: NO-FAULT DIVORCE

Before 1970, divorce required one spouse to prove the other was at fault for ending the marriage. Judges did not grant a divorce until some proof of misconduct justified it. So, tragic and embarrassing personal problems like alcoholism, cruelty, desertion, adultery, felony convictions, impotency, or insanity shocked the courtroom. In searching for grounds for a divorce, the finger-pointing, exaggeration, and deceit by each spouse had no end.

After decades of divorce between warring spouses with imbalanced bargaining positions, California tried a new approach in January 1970. Then California Governor Ronald Reagan signed the first No-Fault divorce law in the United States.

This No-Fault law promoted several ideals:

- If a marriage fails, no one person is usually at fault, so assigning blame is unnecessary.
- Marriage partnerships have assets requiring liquidation similar to dissolution of any business.
- As equal partners in marriage, husbands and wives deserve equal treatment in divorce.
- Both spouses should move on with their separate lives with a minimum of restrictions (permanent alimony, etc.).

Under No-Fault, courts could grant divorce if the marriage was irretrievably broken by irreconcilable differences or incompatibility between the spouses. This was a reasonable effort at making the divorce process more rational and fair. It reduced the economic and emotional trauma suffered by husband and wife. Presently, forty-one states have adopted modern no-fault factors as the sole basis, or additional ground, for dissolution.[5]

In the years following adoption of these new No-Fault laws, divorces became less scandalous, as expected. But many complained that No-Fault is an oversimplification of divorce. Pointing to the liberalized divorce laws developed over the last two decades, they ask, "Has this trend produced less human suffering or more?" It provided a quick way out of a troublesome marriage, but what is the long-term effect on our society? This legislation does not end the hostility and revenge arising over child custody and visitation, spouse and child support, and equitable division of assets. More often than not, it does not square with biblical divorce teachings such as those found in Matthew 19:1–9 and 1 Corinthians 7.

Is the cure worse than the disease? Divorce on demand encourages more divorce actions, with a divorce explosion further backlogging our courts. According to the National Center for Health Statistics, the number of divorces has increased almost 200 percent in the last three decades. There were 708,000 divorces in 1970 when the first No-Fault law appeared in California. Five years later, the number rose to 1,036,000. The approximate annual average of divorces since 1980 has been 1,180,000. In 1994, single-parent families are as common as two-parent families. The U.S. Census Bureau reports that in 1940 nine out of ten American households were married-couple families. In 1993, this number fell to five out of ten. Meanwhile, according to ABA Family Law Section Chairperson Lynne Z. Gold-Bikin, employers lose billions of dollars in lost productivity stemming from employee marital difficulties.[6] Will having too many broken homes continue to take its toll on our society? Few doubt that it will not.

One major problem with No-Fault laws is in ignoring fault entirely. Is this just? Should the law allow people to cheat on their spouses without it having some legally recognized impact? Why should a faithful spouse suffer loss through divorce simply because a mate decides to break the marriage vows? Shouldn't an adulterous spouse still bear some individual accountability for his or her actions?

Many believe courts should consider marital fault. Why reward an errant spouse who leaves a mate for a homosexual relationship, tries to murder a mate, abandons a marriage while stealing family savings, uses physical abuse, or makes life intolerable through alcohol or drug abuse? Certainly those spouses who destroy a short-term childless marriage should not claim benefits equal to those provided had the marriage remained intact over a long term of years.

At least thirty-eight of fifty-three jurisdictions in the U.S. still consider fault in awarding dissolution, property division, or alimony. Even some states with strict No-Fault requirements, such as Florida, account for fault in property division and alimony.[7] But No-Fault fails to account fully for the damage done to a marriage.

Do No-Fault laws treat women fairly? Current practice says, "No." Since housewives with custody of children are clearly financially unequal to working husbands, No-Fault led to many inequities for women. As spouses sold their homes to divide sale proceeds, they displaced their families. Jobless spouses received little or no financial support after dividing marital assets. Overall, women, especially those unskilled or unable to work, began a slide down the economic ladder, while the standard of living for men with comfortable incomes rose. Many women spent decades devoting themselves to rearing their children. But under No-Fault, they suddenly faced the ultimate disaster: no mate, no marketable skills, no job, and, when sold as part of the divorce settlement, no house.

Legislators around the U.S. review many alternatives for reform each year. Due to the economic imbalance between husband and wife, they seek to include a spouse's business assets and professional benefits among the marital assets for division. They want more penalties to enforce child support debts. They want to protect the disadvantaged spouse through greater post-divorce support awards.

Since many divorce issues are so unique from other court actions, another reform has been to create family court divisions that handle only family law cases. In 1992, for example, Florida began organizing such family court divisions. These divisions coordinate marital disputes with other services like court-ordered mediation, domestic violence support programs, guardians for needs of children, and psychological home assessment programs. One judge monitors all divorce and related legal matters concerning one family. Eventually divisions of this sort will have separate and specialized rules different from other civil law cases.

These family court divisions help judges develop special sensitivity to the emotional side of divorce, as well as become experts in family law issues. It helps them to be more consistent in their rulings from case to case. The division also provides better protection for victims of domestic violence.[8] Family law cases, accounting for almost 50 percent of all court cases filed in many states, move on a fast track in these new divisions. This family courty division should cut the time for completion of typical cases by as much as 50 percent.

It may take many years to complete necessary reforms to existing divorce laws in every state. Meanwhile, those who advocated liberalizing divorce laws during the sexual revolution of the 1960s and 1970s are finding very challenging flaws in the No-Fault system. Before enactment of the new laws, women and children stayed in difficult marriages, many times out of economic need. The number of people adversely affected by divorce was relatively small. Today, as divorce rips through our country like wildfire and bailing out of a marriage is easy, many are discovering that equal treatment between men and women is not as equal as they had hoped—especially in property division.

How the Courts End Marriages and Divide Property

Effect of No-Fault Divorce Laws

As more states have moved toward a No-Fault divorce standard, equitable (in many instances, simply splitting assets fifty-fifty) distribution of all marital property has been a major part of that law. In making divorces easier to secure, the civil law is retreating from the centuries-old legal view that marriage is a union that cannot be broken except in very limited instances. Today, more courts view a marriage as a type of business partnership. As such, marriage vows are similar to a partnership agreement subject to breach like any contract. [9]

Under No-Fault, property division calls for equal treatment of men and women. Since the marriage is similar to a business partnership, both spouses help in acquiring property during the marriage. To keep the property each spouse either generates income or provides the family with homemaking or childrearing services.

Even so, discrimination against women still exists in the judicial system. This is not to suggest that this is fair. But it is reality. Many courts have trouble viewing a homemaker as an equal partner with the breadwinner who earns most of the family income. Result? Husbands often receive court awards of about three-fourths of the property bought or improved during the marriage. Wives receive the remaining fourth of the same assets. In fact, some judges require that a wife prove that she put *more* into the marriage than the husband before receiving an *equal* distribution of assets.

Why are women shortchanged in gender bias like this? First, the wife's one-fourth share is about the same as a dower right under the oldest U.S. laws (originally coming from England, known as the *common law*).[10] Second, it is easier economically to measure a husband's breadwinning abilities than a homemaker's work. Finally, male judges identify with the husband's role in marriage more than the wife's. The legal system offers few safeguards against such gender bias, simply because it defies description and conclusive proof of its existence.

In any event, allowing a court to decide property matters is an uncertain venture for both spouses. Therefore it is better, *much* better, for both spouses to settle property matters privately in mediation outside the courts.

If a judge does review property rights under No-Fault, however, there are certain rules to follow in ordering property distribution.

How the Courts Equitably Distribute Property

Each state has its own property distribution laws.[11] In states using equitable distribution standards for dividing property in divorce, a court usually begins by dividing *marital assets* and *non-marital assets.*[12]

Marital Assets and *Liabilities* are those assets acquired and liabilities incurred during the marriage based upon the following factors:

- Assets acquired, and liabilities incurred, *during* the marriage by either spouse individually, or jointly by both of them
- Increases in value of non-marital assets (described below) resulting from the efforts of either spouse during the marriage, or from use of marital funds or assets, or both
- Gifts between husband and wife during the marriage
- All vested and non-vested benefits and funds gained during the marriage in retirement, pension, profit-sharing, annuity, deferred compensation, and insurance plans

- All real property held by the spouses as joint property for the marriage, whether bought before, or during, the marriage

Non-Marital Assets and Liabilities are those assets that are acquired and liabilities incurred by either the husband or wife based upon the following factors:

- Assets acquired, and liabilities incurred, by either the husband or wife *before* the marriage, and assets acquired, and liabilities incurred, in exchange for such assets and liabilities
- Assets acquired separately during the marriage by either the husband or wife by gift, bequest, devise, or descent (other than between the husband and wife themselves) and any other assets bought in exchange for such assets
- All income earned from non-marital assets during the marriage, unless the spouses treat, use, or rely upon this income as a marital asset
- Assets and liabilities excluded from marital assets by agreement of the spouses, and included among the non-marital assets and liabilities

The courts then put all of the marital assets into one pot. Many judges assume this pot of marital property will be split fifty-fifty between the husband and wife, but real life does not always work this way. Before distributions occur, courts frequently adjust the fifty-fifty split.[13] Ultimately, the parties receive a percentage of the marital assets, and whatever non-marital assets belong to either of them as separate property. Judges have discretion in considering these factors (or others like them).

When judges decide property rights, two results may occur. First, neither spouse can ever be sure of the final award. Court decisions are rarely the same in similar cases. This uncertainty is troublesome. Second, both spouses can be certain that neither person will be completely happy with the court's decision. One divorce expert even recalled one beleaguered man who became so disgusted with a fifty-fifty split of marital property that he took a chainsaw and cut the family car in half before switching to perform the same operation on the house.[14] But, as each party is dissatisfied with the result, appeals of a judge's ruling generate even more litigation.

This is why mediated private settlements between spouses work better. Husbands and wives who irrevocably decide to divorce have more control over how their property is split. The law allows for private settlement, and judges encourage it. Wise spouses take advantage of this opportunity to reduce disastrous infighting during divorce.

SPOUSE SUPPORT CONSIDERATIONS

In determining the amount of any spouse support, judges consider many factors such as the

- standard of living during the marriage;
- duration of the marriage;
- age and physical and emotional condition of each spouse;
- financial resources of each spouse (including the marital and non-marital assets given to each person);
- time necessary to get an education or enough training to find appropriate employment;
- contribution made by each spouse to the marriage (such as home-making, child care, education, and career building of the other spouse); and
- all sources of income available to each spouse.

Additional consideration, apart from the divorce, of marital miscon-duct (adultery, illicit cohabitation, homosexuality, etc.) *may* occur in some states to limit or even deny the amount of spouse support the errant spouse receives.[15]

The most important factors, however, are each spouse's financial resources and duration of the marriage. In No-Fault states, any support awarded after equitable distribution of marital assets is likely to pay only for education or learning job skills (called *rehabilitative alimony*). This probably would not last more than a couple of years at the most. [16]

While each case may vary considerably, those entitled to support (and not everyone is) quite often receive about one-third of the net income of the spouse who is compelled to pay. Also, judges will not award spouse (or child) support that is more than the paying spouse can afford.

The court usually retains power in the divorce decree to enforce payment of spouse or child support. This is done through holding the nonpaying spouse in contempt, levying fines, imprisonment, and income deduction orders that take money out of the spouse's paycheck. If the spouse quits a job to frustrate income deduction, the court can order him or her to seek employment. The judge can enter a judgment for unpaid sums and authorize foreclosure on other assets the spouse may own. But the reality is that judges do not act swiftly enough to use these remedies.

As a result of the unresponsive court system, some enterprising people have set up self-help organizations to collect unpaid spouse and child support. Nevertheless, success rates on these ventures have been mixed. In addition, some organizations use illegal tactics that violate fair debt collection laws due to the pressure to produce results.

Some state reforms for spouse support are also underway. For exam-ple, some states are moving toward encouraging *permanent* support for spouses. This is especially true for those in long-term marriages to help equalize the post-divorce standard of living for both spouses. The cries of many deprived divorcees are moving state legislatures to enact more reforms every year.[17] But there is so much abuse of support payment debts, it is difficult for reformers to keep up with the crush of problems.

FURTHER COMPLICATIONS OF DIVORCE

Lawyer-Client Conflicts

Many of the problems between spouses spill over into their lawyer-client relationships during litigation (reviewed in chaps. 6 and 7). More than in any other area of the law, family disputes arouse volatile emotions in *everyone* concerned. While "friendly" divorces frequently result in a sinking sadness or bitterness, feelings rage in contested divorces. When hostile emotions and economic problems plague ex-spouses, lawyers become easy targets—even if the representation was fair, with advance warnings about the effects of divorce. So the conflicts and disagreements surrounding warring spouses multiply.

Florida Bar Family Law Section Chairperson Nancy S. Palmer understands this problem firsthand. She commented, "It has been my experience when very litigious clients go to the birth of their first grandchild, the wedding of their child, or the college graduation of their child, they cannot look their ex-spouses in the eye, and it is us, the family lawyers, to whom they transfer their anger because they cannot imagine that it was their decision and their very behavior which brought this kind of result within their family." [18]

Divorce Is No Small Claim

A few years ago, Neil and Marie-Helene Katz locked horns in a divorce lawsuit filed in Broward County, Florida. The net worth of their marital estate was about $650,000. But, by the time their litigation ended up on appeal in 1987, legal and accounting fees exceeded $325,000. This put almost $400,000 of equity in their home in danger of foreclosure. In a frequently cited opinion, the Florida appellate court warned: "This type of case must be tried and reviewed quickly, without needless and wasted motion. Without responsible direction, not only will the parties—who are represented—have their assets dissipated without good cause, but also their innocent, unrepresented children will see their opportunity for higher education vanish in a nightmarish plethora of motions, transcripts and time sheets." [19]

More recently, Nancy D. Tomaino hired an Illinois lawyer, who charged $300 per hour, to work with her Florida lawyer, who billed $250 an hour, and with various associates and paralegals in both law offices to sue husband Joseph M. Tomaino for divorce. A Florida appellate court, offended at the cost of having two prominent high-priced lawyers charging top dollar for their duplicative efforts, made this insightful observation:

Getting divorced is a very costly proposition . . . Attorney's fees seem to rise astronomically. If the parties have assets to fight about, attorney's fees of $50,000 to $200,000 are not unusual. We have warned about excesses in this area. . . . This problem of escalating litigation and fees has to be solved. There must be an incentive on *both* parties to economize on legal fees and costs if the cost of divorce is to be controlled. There may be ways of limiting discovery, using court-appointed experts to review financial information rather than having each party hire their own, or allocating the sum total of reasonable fees of both parties between the litigants on some proportional basis so that each shares at least some responsibility for fees in the ultimate award. The Bench, Bar and the legislature need to do some serious thinking about solutions to preserve the validity and integrity of the system. Otherwise, it will fall by its own costly weight.[20]

———

Aside from other gender bias matters they must face, women also come up short in funding and pursuing divorce litigation. Husbands often have more control over family finances and property, while wives frequently are in the dark about this information. So many wives do not have the resources to hire lawyers without a court ordered payment from the husband. Then lack of access to financial records makes it more time-consuming and expensive for the wife's lawyer to uncover the facts about the couple's income and assets.

Divorce Cases Do Not End Quickly

Many, if not a majority, of all civil cases filed in America's state courts are domestic-related disputes (dissolution of marriage, juvenile, and dependency cases), which overload the entire judicial system. Many courts can dispose of enough pending civil cases each year to counterbalance new filings. Not so with divorce cases. They keep coming back through the legal system for more action, further clogging the court dockets. Family members do not go away after entry of a divorce decree. There are spouse and child support disputes and enforcement, child custody and parent relocation issues to resolve, and similar conflicts arising from the original divorce decree. Some court officials view each divorce as an eighteen to twenty-one-year process until all minor children become adults.

Self-Representation by Divorcing Spouses

Another problem arising in many divorce cases is the increasing number of *pro se litigants*—spouses who try to handle their legal problems without using a lawyer. Again, most, if not a majority, of all divorce cases filed in many states involve pro se litigants on both sides. Of course, everyone has the right to self-representation in court. But what happens? Typically, people who are unfamiliar with laws and legal procedures improperly or incompletely fill out forms that require many hours of clerk and court time to correct. To the court staff, this is a constant source of stress. Legal and procedural problems unwittingly caused by divorcing spouses who are not thinking rationally swamp these already overworked court administrators.

Florida Circuit Court administrator Doug Wilkinson (20th Circuit) noted that emotionally drained court personnel struggle by day's end after listening to problems from pro se litigants and helping them deal with a perplexing legal system. Wilkinson explained, "Judicial assistants are spending 65–70 percent of their time explaining to pro se litigants what's going on." [21] This problem compounds in even more frustrating ways if one spouse using self-representation faces an attorney on the other side.

Unreasonably Rejected Settlement Offers

With all the backlog in our judicial system, encouraging litigants to settle their disputes is vital to keeping the courts functioning. But many existing divorce laws and rules of procedure work against that happening.

For example, a husband may submit a written property settlement offer to his wife for a particular amount. Many times the wife may reject the offer because there is no disincentive against doing so. Nevertheless, the final court ruling may be close to the husband's original offer. This means the husband may have spent court time and thousands of dollars in additional legal fees before the parties end up in the same place.

Unreasonable failures to settle by one spouse work against everyone concerned. So some judicial reformers want spouses who reject settlement offers to pay for the other spouse's legal expense incurred after the offer if the final court ruling is not an improvement. Unfortunately, many state laws do not allow for this.

Bankruptcy

If the loser in a divorce is not content to honor an adverse court judgment, he or she simply files for bankruptcy to make collection difficult or impossible. William C. Moog, Jr. was a millionaire inventor whose cousin, R. A. Moog, invented the famous Moog synthesizer (an electronic keyboard that imitated sounds of conventional instruments). Moog's wife filed for divorce in May 1991 after fifty-two years of marriage. By November, the couple agreed to a multi-million dollar settlement that split marital assets evenly between them. Moog was to pay his ex-wife a large sum of money over four years, but he did not meet his payment schedule. In August 1992, he filed for Chapter 11 bankruptcy court protection in Miami, acknowledging that he had no creditors other than his ex-wife.

In an October 1, 1993 ruling, Bankruptcy Court Judge Robert Mark concluded that Moog's move was a calculated dodge born out of greed in a case driven by "arrogance and abuse." The judge issued a harshly worded decision noting, "Simply stated, this Chapter 11 petition was filed in bad faith in an effort to avoid execution on a divorce judgment and to improperly use the bankruptcy court as a forum to renegotiate the divorce. . . . Mr. Moog filed his petition solely to prevent or delay the consequences of his failure to pay the divorce judgment, and more specifically to frustrate Mrs. Moog's legitimate efforts to collect that judgment."[22] Unfortunately, no matter how this matter ends up, Mrs. Moog did not receive any money from her ex-husband. And she never will. She passed away in May 1993.

Inconsistent Judicial Decisions

Among the 1990 findings of the Florida Supreme Court's Gender Bias Commission are the following:

- Post-divorce families headed by women are the fastest growing segment of those living in poverty (the "feminization of poverty").
- Although existing laws require judges to order financially secure spouses to pay the other spouses' justifiable request for ongoing legal fees and support, few judges obey these laws (and in a way that also discriminates against women).
- Most Florida circuit court judges dislike dealing with family law matters and have negative attitudes that could affect the outcome of cases.
- Many litigants (particularly women) cannot appeal an adverse or incorrect trial court decision because of limited finances.
- Many courts have abandoned awards of permanent alimony or substituted unrealistic rehabilitative alimony awards.
- Trial court judges use almost unlimited discretion to distribute marital assets (either as property or alimony) with a lack of certainty and consistency which leads to inappropriate property settlements between parties.
- Many courts order shared parental responsibility custody orders without full consideration of all relevant legal factors, including parental desires and the best interests of the child.
- Visitation allotments disadvantage noncustodial fathers.
- Child support awards are frequently inconsistent in cases with similar facts.
- Judges often reduce or forgive child support debts unjustifiably or fail to incarcerate those who ignore child support orders despite an ability to pay.[23]

IS LITIGATING A DIVORCE A WISE COURSE OF ACTION?

Noted author and lecturer Dr. Charles Swindoll wrote recently, "Whatever else may be said about the home, it is the bottom line of life, the anvil upon which attitudes and convictions are hammered out. It is the place where life's bills come due, the single most influential force in our earthly existence." [24] What is divorce and, even worse, excessively litigating a divorce, doing to our homes and families—God's foundation for our existence as a nation?

Divorce has become so tame, so routine. Because of liberal No-Fault laws, divorce does not carry the social stigma it once did. Talk shows won't give the subject a second look because it has become so commonplace and is not scandalous enough. Even that American cartoon icon, Dick Tracy, received divorce papers from his wife after forty-five years of marriage.

In the "For Sale or Trade" column appearing several years ago in the Scottsbluff, Nebraska, *Business Farmer News*, this ad appeared: "Will trade one white wedding gown size 16—never worn. Will trade for 38 caliber revolver."[25] No doubt this item came from a woman mightily fed up with some fellow who broke his marriage promise! Parties to broken vows often fall into extreme apathy or become warlike in wanting offenders to pay. Either case is a profound trap for the people involved and for our society.

Divorce often results when couples don't try hard enough to make their marriages work. At times it is a by-product of keeping up a lightning-fast pace in life, leaving marital longevity in the dust. But the terrible effects of each marriage fatality create a ripple effect, breaking down social order, burdening our failing court system, and killing our economy.

For spouses whose marriages implode into the emotional void of divorce, the chaos created is anything but tame and routine. The social stigma may dissipate over time, but the sting and pain of separation remains real for years. It is war raging in one's own living room—emotional and economic annihilation in many cases. One wonders whether the tears will ever go away. Divorcees wonder if there will be any end to the all-consuming emptiness and loneliness. They ask, "Where do I go? What are my days going to be like now?" Can divorcees accept that what once was may never be again?

Divorce destroys the most important element of our society—the family. As many divorcees sink into vindictive and revengeful behavior, how is our adversarial justice system affecting their recovery and our country? What is it doing to the caseloads that overwhelm our judges who try to manage these potential time bombs? They cannot provide the attention these divorcing couples need to cope with the tricky and emotionally volatile problems that demand immediate resolution as their families come unglued.

Forcing hurting spouses to carry their personal battles and deep wounds into a public forum is courting disaster. The peaceful road leads to mediation. Mediation—a private place of confidentiality where, with the expertise and support of qualified, neutral third parties, a couple decides what is best based upon intimate knowledge of their situations.

ઠ

Questions for Personal Reflection

1. If I am facing separation or divorce, am I willing to face an uncertain future in court as opposed to doing whatever I can to settle matters with my spouse now?

2. Do I need to protect legitimate rights in court or am I simply making matters difficult for my spouse for power, control, or revenge?

3. Have I prayerfully and lovingly considered the short-term and long-term effects that submitting my case to civil litigation will cause my spouse, my children, my family and in-laws, friends, and the church?

4. Do I have a firm grasp on the issues involved in my case enough to know how a judge's decision of these matters will affect my own life goals and needs?

5. Even if I win my case, am I still willing to show compassion and empathy to make some reasonable adjustments if necessary?

6. How can I best minister to and counsel others facing a separation or divorce?

Chapter 3

CHILDREN CAUGHT IN DIVORCE LITIGATION CROSSFIRE

Adults can decide whether to litigate or not. Not so with children, who are too often the unwilling and bewildered parties to a divorce proceeding or other lawsuits.

꙼

There is an urgency about giving our children our very best. As writer Gabriela Mistral once cautioned us:

> We are guilty
> of many errors and many faults
> but our worst crime
> is abandoning the children,
> neglecting the
> fountain of life.
> Many of the things we need
> can wait. The child cannot.
> Right now is the time
> his bones are being
> formed, his blood is being made,
> and his senses are being developed.
> To him, we cannot answer
> "tomorrow".
> His name is "today".[1]

———

After caring for ourselves, our children and their needs must be our first priority. In this litigation age, watching out for our children is our most critical, and challenging, task. But what legacy are we leaving them?

CHILDREN: THE REAL VICTIMS OF DIVORCE

Our children are our heritage, blessed by God Himself. Our future as a nation. They are the innocents, the humble, the trusting. They are examples of how we should approach God. In Matthew 18:2–6, the disciples came to Jesus with the question, "Who is the greatest in the kingdom of heaven?" How did Jesus respond?

He called a little child and had him stand among them. And He said: "I tell you the truth, unless you change and become like little children, you will never enter the kingdom of heaven. Therefore, whoever humbles himself like this child is the greatest in the kingdom of heaven. And whoever welcomes a little child like this in My name welcomes Me. But if anyone causes one of these little ones who believe in Me to sin, it would be better for him to have a large millstone hung around his neck and to be drowned in the depths of the sea."

_____

Too often we lose children in the busy shuffle of adult life. Even after Jesus praised the childlike attitudes of humility and trust, His disciples failed to understand the high regard God has for children. But Jesus knew the worth of these little ones. See how He brings the point home to His disciples when they have their minds on hectic schedules: "Then little children were brought to Jesus for Him to place His hands on them and pray for them. But the disciples rebuked those who brought them. Jesus said, 'Let the little children come to Me, and do not hinder them, for the kingdom of heaven belongs to such as these.' When He had placed His hands on them, He went on from there" (Matt. 19:13–15).

And yet, so often we neglect our children and trap them in the divorce dilemma. As the powerful forces and emotions of separation and divorce whirl about in their lives, children twist and turn in a world of bewilderment, confusion, and fear. _What will I do when Daddy leaves? Why is Mommy crying all the time? Why can't I have a happy family like other children at school?_

If separation or divorce is like death to parents, we can only begin to imagine the devastating impact it has on our children. They may bravely bear up under the pressure and turmoil, but they pay the price. They are losing a loved one—an irreplaceable parent. But there are also children who have suffered emotional, physical, and even sexual abuse from a parent. This can absolutely suffocate them. In desperation, they must break free to survive.

The pain children feel does not begin with the act of separation or divorce. The genesis of their pain comes with the first hint that Mommy and Daddy may not love each other much anymore. Angry words from shouting matches in the parents' bedroom or the kitchen always work their way through the walls to the child's ear. Fights between adults in the front car seat are always heard by the little ones in the backseat. This often happens long before any separation or divorce occurs.[2] Then, to compound the confusion and trauma a child experiences, parents fight in a frightening courtroom full of strangers to tear their children away from each other.

GOING TO WAR WITH OUR CHILDREN AS BAIT

You may be among the fortunate few who have escaped being a party to any litigation. But woe to the children of America, who are becoming unwilling litigants in record numbers—even from the time of conception as adults argue over embryos!

In the Schutz case (discussed in chap. 2), father and mother grappled in court for years over their children. Sadly, the real victims in the Schutz divorce were the children. Despite the best efforts of the judicial system, will they ever appreciate their father fully after the damage that was done by the mother? Who suffered more from the mother's vindictive behavior? Sowing seeds of resentment and bitterness against a parent in the young, impressionable minds of children reaps a whirlwind (Hos. 8:7; Gal. 6:7–8).

Another example is the case of John and Esther Lock of Chicago, Illinois, as reported in *Newsweek* of May 4, 1992. The Locks had been through more than one hundred court hearings about their divorce and child support matters for over nineteen years. The State of Illinois figured that Mr. Lock owed his former wife more than $160,000 in child support for their four children. This was certainly an intolerable situation for mother and children.

How was the situation handled? In February 1977, Esther Lock was doing all she could to keep the electricity on in her home while eating a diet of rice and cereal. Medical and dental coverage lapsed for nonpayment of premiums. Meanwhile, Mr. Lock, a dentist, lived with his new family in an affluent suburb of Highland Park. This infuriated Esther Lock so much that she gave her two teenage sons overnight packs and deposited them on their father's front porch in subzero weather. Esther Lock knew that Mr. Lock did not want the children. She decided to use them in a scare tactic against their father. Result? John Lock called the Highland Park police with the request that they come remove two young trespassers from his yard. (Mr. Lock later stated that one of the boys was trying to kick his door down.) Revenge this destructive is worse than the original wrong.

What a tragedy when spouses go to war with their children as the ammunition! Instead of putting their differences as ex-husband and ex-wife aside and focusing on their important roles as *parents*, expediency and revenge burn and consume everything in their path.

The children suffer so much at the hands of warring or neglectful parents that, in recent years, some have fought back by divorcing themselves from their parents. Consider Gregory Kingsley, the eleven-year-old Florida boy shuffled back and forth between an abusive father and a neglectful mother from the time he was four. His father was an alcoholic who beat him, and once threw his younger brother through a plateglass door during a drinking spree. His mother left Gregory and his brother at a temporary shelter for almost a year. Two months after picking up the boys, Gregory's mother returned them to the shelter and didn't see them again for another eighteen months. From the time he was eight years old, Gregory had been in and out of foster homes. He once told a social worker that all he ever wanted was a "place to be."

But Gregory had taken enough abuse. In what may be the first case of its kind in American history, Gregory filed suit in 1992 seeking a divorce from his natural parents so his foster parents could adopt him. This lawsuit shocked the legal community.

Traditionally, children had no part in a custody decision. They were property of their parents. Not until 1874 did abused children achieve legal status as individuals—and then only after the American Society for the Prevention of Cruelty to Animals moved in court to protect a little girl under laws barring cruel treatment of animals. But the evolving law in Florida and elsewhere is to more seriously consider a child's interests, as we shall see in this chapter.

Today, judges in most states use personal discretion in making custody decisions in the best interests of the child, but quite often the court's decision is contrary to the child's own wishes. With most custody laws favoring reunion of family, some courts have returned children to abusive and neglectful parents. Although the courts in Gregory's case upheld the termination of his biological parents' rights, a Florida appellate court ruled in August 1993 that children in Florida have no right to sue on their own. Nevertheless, his case shows that children have been pawns in divorce for too long.

Despite the appellate ruling in the Kingsley case, it is probable that this court action will spawn many other children's rights cases in the future. For example, in March 1993, a twelve-year-old Brevard County, Florida, girl filed suit to leave her stepfather and mother and live with her maternal grandmother.[3] On March 26, 1993, over objections of the parents, Circuit Court Judge Charles Holcomb ruled that the girl did have the right to maintain the court action and to intervene in custody determination issues pending between her parents. "I sit here week after week and hear divorce cases where the mother and father go at each other with tooth and claw and with every dirty and nasty thing that they can dredge up and throw at each other," Judge Holcomb remarked in making his ruling. "I see it over and over where the parties don't seem to be so much interested in their children as they are in venting their own anger and getting what they want out of the divorce. I think the child has to have an independent voice to tell the court what the child's perspective is in the whole thing."[4]

Then there was the nationally publicized lawsuit in 1993 of Kimberly Mays, the fourteen-year-old biological daughter of Ernest and Regina Twigg. A rural Wauchula, Florida hospital inadvertently switched Kimberly at birth in 1978 with another baby girl born to Robert and Barbara Mays. The Twiggs learned of the error through genetic testing after the Mays's biological daughter, Arlena Twigg, died during heart surgery in 1988. A nationwide search for their real daughter led the Twiggs to Robert Mays. They sought to gain custody of Kimberly although she had known Robert Mays as her only father for her entire life.

This began a five year tug-of-war between the Twiggs and Mays, with the Twiggs trying to portray Mays as an abusive parent to win custody. There was some suggestion by Regina Twigg that the Mays family may have switched the children on purpose. Finally, Kimberly had had enough. The Twiggs' efforts to secure visitation rights, and then full custody, was ruining her life. She filed suit against the Twiggs to terminate their parental rights.

After a seven-day trial, Judge Stephen Dakan granted Kimberly her wish. He terminated any parental rights of the Twiggs on August 19, 1993. The Judge noted in his opinion that the Twiggs' attacks on Mays "created a chasm between Kimberly Mays and the Twiggs that may never be bridged."[5] "There can be no winners here," Kimberly's attorney David Denkin remarked before the trial began. "There will be survivors."[6]

What a shame it is when children must file a lawsuit and create a public spectacle in court to protect and separate themselves from harmful parents! Are not these cases best decided in private mediation between all the parties involved? When will parents put themselves in the smaller shoes of their children before running to court to resolve family disputes?

THE WORST MISTAKES DIVORCING PARENTS MAKE WITH CHILDREN

We must concede that, regrettably, divorce is inevitable among some couples. And when some spouses cut their marriage bonds to each other, the family unit shatters. But the key consideration then is: Do the parents engage in prolonged litigation or help each other, as best they can, to limit and control the damage? Here are a few stumbling blocks that push too many divorcing parents into court because of what is happening to their children:

Mistake #1—Making Spouses Enemies of Children

Fighting in front of children and blaming a spouse for a divorce is a recipe for disaster. With all the fears, panic, guilt, anger and resentment, and loss of physical and emotional security children experience in a divorce, excessively or unfairly criticizing a parent can destroy everyone concerned.

Focusing on an ex-spouse's behavior diverts attention from the real concern for any parent—the children's welfare. Personal irritations and resentments between parents frequently fall upon the children. They become wounded pawns in the process. Each spouse has rights and needs to interact with his or her children without unreasonable interference. But these rights and needs deserve respect for the sake of the children as well. If an ex-spouse continues being hostile and harmful to the children, mediation is necessary. Use legal action, like that taken by Mr. Schutz, only as a last resort. Ideally, however, each parent will separate the differences of opinion and wounds of the past marriage from parental decisions regarding the best welfare of their children. This calls for compromise, cooperation, and a mutual resolve to avoid using the children as hostages in games of manipulation and blackmail.

Mistake #2—Withholding Visitation Rights or Child Support

The custodial parent needs child support payments from the non-custodial parent. No payments come. The custodial parent then resorts to payback by holding the children hostage from the other parent when he or she comes for a visit. Usually everyone ends up back in court—a double tragedy!

Some parents entitled to receive support believe there could be times when withholding visitation until a spouse fulfills prior commitments is reasonable. But the usual outcome is that the needs and wishes of the children become a secondary concern in a game of manipulation, control, and one-upmanship between parents.

It doesn't end there either. If the non-custodial parent is denied visitation or not allowed to participate in significant events with the children, intimacy fades over time. A vendetta between parents leads to estrangement from the innocent children. Parent and child drift apart. Love dies. Eventually some noncustodial parents quietly believe, "It's not *my* kid." The noncustodial parent rationalizes by thinking that it is better not to pay child support. After all, the custodial parent probably spends payments on personal whims rather than on the children. The real conflict is between the parents, but it cuts up the children in the cross fire.

Mistake #3—Using Visitation Exchanges as a Battleground

For parents who live separately, it is tempting to catch up on hostilities when the non-custodial parent comes to pick up a child for visitation.

Visitation wars often begin in the divorce proceedings. Inattentive parents may fiercely contest custody matters, not because of desire for the child, but solely to oppose the spouse and use it as a bargaining chip for other divorce concessions. When visitation schedules are set up, one parent will intentionally forget scheduled appointments to inconvenience the other. He or she will discourage the children from visiting the noncustodial parent. The kids are bombarded with negative remarks, or competing activities arise to create a conflict with regular visitation. Parents bribe children with better entertainment or by slacking off on discipline to make the other parent appear mean or unreasonable in the child's eyes.

To some extent, use of these tactics is understandable. *Everyone* is struggling with an enormous load of emotional turmoil during visitation. The noncustodial parent may want to visit, but wrestles with the understandable reluctance and anxiety of doing so. Each parent feels at least some unhappiness or nostalgia when picking up the child at the family home. Each parent is reminded of the divorce by the sight of the child's empty room while the child is visiting the other parent. The failed marriage haunts every visitation meeting. Everyone suffers when they have to share responsibilities.

Some visitation problems are inevitable even for the best of parents. Consider the classic case of two sons who left their mother in Virginia for a visit with their father in California. The boys felt frightened and anxious about their first flight out to the West Coast. Weeks later, however, they returned to their mother happy with tales of the beach and staying up late watching cable movies. Obviously mother and father have different lifestyles now. This has created unavoidable friction in parental authority and discipline.

But in games of one-upmanship where the child is spoiled to best the other parent, the child suffers tremendous psychological damage and alienation. It also creates a false impression in the child's mind that good times will never end. This distorts reality. The holiday atmosphere won't last. A "Disneyland Dad" or "Mall Mom" using visitation time to impress children and outdo each other with gifts and parties loses more than he or she gains.[7]

Mistake #4—Forcing a Child to Choose Which Parent Will Have Custody

This is a most unfair position for the child. Even if the child is mature enough to give input into such a decision, it capitalizes on fears that the disfavored parent will see the child as disloyal. What will this parent do? Does the child risk losing that parent's love, affection, and support? Concerned parents who cannot agree on custody matters should seek agreement through mediation. Even asking the court to decide the issue based upon the recommendations of examining counselors and experts is better than putting a child in this trap. But too many parents blindly rush to court and unwittingly put the child on the hook, creating significant guilt within the child.

Mistake #5—*Using a Child as an Informant, Messenger, or Mediator*

The greatest temptation is to pump the child for information for use against the other parent. If a third party lover exists, a parent may want to find out from the child what that person is like. This traps the child in a classic catch-22 situation—having to choose between disloyalty in spying on one parent or alienating the other parent by refusing to become involved. Parents who succumb to this temptation debase themselves in front of their children and lose respect.

How does the child feel who takes this message from a mother to a father: "Tell your father that I don't know how he can look you in the face with the way he hasn't paid your support on time"? One parent will ask a child, "Now I ask you, who's right—me or your mother?" Children caught in this double-bind situation must disengage with the help of one or both parents without delay.

Mistake #6—*Forcing Children to Deal with Divorce Too Quickly*

Chastising a child for not recovering from the shock and trauma of a divided family as quickly as an adult is unfair and insensitive. A related problem is telling the child that he or she must now step into the role of the missing spouse—an unreasonable, and unrealistic, burden for the child. He or she has enough of a challenge in working through personal feelings. It robs a child of joy. Instead of allowing the child to recover and work through grief and loss at his or her own pace, parents push children for premature resolutions of internal conflict. This only causes repression of feelings and emotions—bottled up to spring forth in individual and marital problems when the child reaches adulthood.

WHAT IS IN A CHILD'S BEST INTEREST?

Given these mistakes that take their toll on children of divorce, what should parents do to minister to their kids and reduce potential litigation?

Parents, churches, courts, and legislatures must learn what is truly in a child's best interest. A March 1991 report of the Florida Study Commission on Child Welfare concluded that each child needs protection from harm; a supply of basic food, clothes, and shelter; provision of necessary medical services and a basic education; and opportunities for cognitive, aesthetic, and emotional development. But there is more to it than that.

If you are a parent who is in touch with your child, you already feel the incredible weight of this responsibility. You are particularly susceptible to guilt in this area if your children suffer. Mothers remember worrying about eating the right foods during pregnancy, and taking care not to miss the many midnight feedings with newborns. This maternal instinct for care and protection stays with them as children grow up. Both parents think about many missed opportunities when their weariness caused them to tune out their child's plea for playtime. If children suffer at school, fall into drug usage, or rebel at authority, many parents blame themselves.

When this guilt arises, keep matters in perspective. A possible root of our guilt is that we want to protect our children from the harsh realities of life. If we do not, we believe we have failed. But is this true? Is our desire to keep our children in a situation free from physical and emotional pain really in their best interest? Is it better for them to learn about survival in life?

Despite our greatest overprotective efforts, our children still cut themselves with rusty nails. They will break their arms on the slide. They will be intimidated or beaten up by schoolmates, have dearly loved pets hit by cars, or lose playmates to fatal illnesses. They will have nights with bad dreams and tears. Hardships bear equally upon adults and children to remind us of this truth: facing pain is part of growing up in life. Parents need to face unavoidable situations with grace and dignity, without guilt. Our children watch for this in us, just as they often gauge our reaction first before deciding whether to cry after feeling hurt.

Life is not perfect—nor are any parents. We are weak, flawed, selfish, immature, and sinful people. Children need to learn this truth. But we can turn bad situations into good learning experiences for children as we cope and try to solve problems in ways that lessen the damage. If a divorce is unavoidable, we can still strengthen existing family bonds among those who must depend on each other.

What is the common element through all the suggestions made above in dealing with children? Sensitivity and empathy toward children's feelings, compassion, and a personal, direct approach in parenting. This common allegiance to the children and spirit of cooperation between divorcing parents reduces the likelihood of prolonged litigation. No lawyer or court can provide this type of nurturing and comfort to children. But when parents abandon their children's best interests in an attempt to try and win in litigation, everyone loses. And the greatest temptation to do that is when a court is to decide who keeps the kids.

CUSTODY ARRANGEMENTS AND PAYMENT OF CHILD SUPPORT

Nothing more directly affects a child's best interest than deciding which parents will have custody of the children. And nothing brings out fierce litigation between spouses like custody battles often do.

Custody of Children[8]

State legislatures and courts traditionally have believed it preferable for young children to stay with their mothers under the legal Tender Years Doctrine. In recent years, however, this is no longer a foregone conclusion. With No-Fault divorce laws in most states, in theory courts are to treat husbands and wives equally. This theory of equality carried over into a related Shared Parental Responsibility Doctrine that equally favors fathers and mothers in custody arrangements.[9] The key is in objectively determining who is the "principal nurturing parent," both physically and psychologically.

Who Is the "Principal Nurturing Parent"?

What factors determine which parent qualifies as the "principal nurturing parent"? If a court reviews this matter, it will look for the parent who has primary responsibility for these caring and nurturing duties:

- Preparing and planning of meals
- Housing, bathing, grooming, and dressing
- Purchasing, cleaning, and care of clothes
- Provision of medical care, including nursing and trips to physicians
- Arranging for social interaction among peers after school, such as transportation to church meetings, Cub or Girl Scouts, or houses of friends
- Arranging for temporary care such as day care or babysitting
- Bedding of the child for the night and attending to illness or needs throughout the night, and waking of the child in the morning
- Administration of discipline measures, including public courtesies, manners, and toilet training
- Providing of religious, social, and cultural education
- Teaching of basic learning skills (reading, writing, and math)

The court then rules on a custody arrangement that is in the *best interest of the child.*

Each parent must make an honest self-appraisal as to who would be best to foster the child's growth and development:

- Who derives more pleasure out of spending *quality* time with each child?
- Who is likely to have more time to spend with each child in the future?
- Will a career be given priority over care of the children?
- Given the child's age, who can provide better care for a toddler, preschooler, preadolescent, or teenager? Are there any special parenting bonds with particular children?
- With whom does the child feel more comfortable?
- Who can better provide for the children financially?

- Will a move from the existing home environment be necessary?
- Will disruptions occur in a child's school relationships or recreational activities?
- Which custody alternative provides each child with the most free access to both parents?
- What other people are significant in each child's life other than the parents (i.e. grandparents, step-parents, etc.)?
- Which arrangement provides the most continuity of a parent-child relationship?
- Has there been any physical, sexual, or emotional child abuse?

Tough questions like these need reasonable answers before any custodial arrangements are made. But each of these questions is another potential court battle between warring spouses. Why not allow the best parties to make this decision—the parents, rather than a judge—in mediation?

Important Legal Factors

Both parents should see the wisdom of cooperation and compromise in making a good custody decision. Each parent should read 1Kings 3:16–28 to learn how King Solomon determined who had a child's best interest at heart in a custody dispute. This vivid story from the Old Testament reminds us that pressing custody disputes too far may hurt the children we love. The truly loving parent wants what is best for the child—even if it means losing custody. Settling issues like these privately or through mediation is best. If a judge makes the custody decision, the result may be unpleasant for everyone.

Legal factors considered by the judge in making a custody decision include the following:

- Which parent is likely to be more cooperative in allowing frequent and continuing visitation by the non-custodial parent
- The love, affection, and other emotional ties existing between the children and each parent
- The relative ability of each parent to provide the children with food, clothing, medical care, and other material needs
- The length of time the children have lived in a stable, satisfactory environment and the desirability of continuing that arrangement
- The permanence, as a family unit, of the existing or proposed custodial home
- The moral fitness and mental and physical health of the parents
- The home, school, and community record of the children
- The reasonable preference of each child.[10]

The judge must make legal and very public determinations about each parent. This can prove very embarrassing or provide a severe blow to one's ego beyond the obvious pain of having a stranger decide custody rights for one's children. Even so, instead of trying to work out an acceptable arrangement with each other in advance, spouses fall into the trap of battling everything out in court to the detriment of their children and themselves.

If parents fail to agree on custody matters, what can they realistically expect if a court decides these issues? For children under the age of six who usually stay at home with a non-working mother, custody will generally go to the mother unless there is good reason for the court to deny it. For school-aged children between six and twelve, the judge is still most likely to favor the mother. Custody of children over twelve can vary, with the father having much more leverage—especially if teens express a personal preference.[11]

When loss of custody is a grim reality for a parent, unfortunately many do almost anything out of desperation to keep their child. Tactics include abduction or bad-faith relocation out of state, fabricated sexual abuse charges,[12] and parental alienation and manipulation.[13] Needless to say, these strong-arm measures absolutely destroy families in the most public way. It is too great a price to pay. Those not receiving custody of their children should abide by a court's decision while seeking relief through the mediation or the judicial system. Then try to increase visitation rights, and patiently wait for a future change of custody.

So many issues in divorce are purely a matter of considering what is best under the circumstances for everyone concerned. For example, under many state laws, before an out-of-state relocation occurs with a child who is subject to a custody order, the parent wishing to move usually must prove to the court that he or she has a compelling interest to move and that it is in the best interest of the child. The non-custodial parent may try to show that he or she is a suitable temporary custodial parent and uprooting the child is harmful. Courts will then apply a balancing test to determine if custody arrangements merit any change.

Factors that are considered include the following:

- Whether or not the move is likely to improve the general quality of life for the custodial parent and child
- The motives for seeking to move (and specifically whether the intent is to defeat the non-custodial parent's visitation rights)
- The likelihood that the custodial parent will obey substitute visitation schedules after the relocation
- Whether or not adequate substitute visitation is possible (given travel and other expenses) between the child and noncustodial parent

But why not try to consider these factors and work out the logistics privately in mediation instead of going to court?

Regardless of the custodial arrangement, in most cases the custodial spouse must allow visitation by the non-custodial parent unless the court denies that right. If the non-custodial parent violates visitation rights or kidnaps the child, the custodial parent must act *immediately.* Taking prompt and proper legal action in this instance is essential.[14]

Child Support

Financially, how will each parent care for the children? What is a fair allocation of the expense for this care between each parent? What is the cost of supporting each child? How much will housing, food, clothing, transportation, medical and dental care, education (grade school and college), entertainment, allowances, counseling, and unusual or extraordinary expenses arising from special physical or emotional needs cost? Despite a divorce, both parents must shoulder the responsibility of providing for their children regardless of their financial circumstances. Children should not suffer economic deprivation while struggling to cope with the separation or divorce of their parents. Nor should they have their emotional and economic well-being threatened by seeing parents argue about support matters.

This child support commitment usually continues until the child legally becomes an adult.[15] In making child support awards, courts usually consider the *net* income of *both* spouses. Some states add both parents' net income together for a combined net income. Then the court determines each parent's percentage share of child support by dividing each parent's net income by the combined net income to arrive at a percentage. The court then multiplies the minimum amount of support needed for each child by each parent's percentage to arrive at a monthly amount.

After this is done, the court then has the flexibility to adjust either or both parent's share of the minimum child support award by considering factors such as

- extraordinary medical, psychological, educational, or dental expenses;
- independent income of the child;
- payment of spouse support and child support to the same spouse (to account for a custodial parent who uses child support payments for needs otherwise covered by spouse support);
- seasonal variations in one, or both, parent's income and expenses;
- the age of each child, taking into account the greater needs of older children;
- special needs traditionally met with the family budget (such as advanced football training programs or gifted pianist lessons);
- the custodial arrangement, such as where the non-custodial parent spends a lot of time with the children and reduces the financial

expenses of the custodial parent or, alternatively, to account for the greater expense incurred by the custodial parent where the noncustodial parent fails, neglects, or refuses to become involved in the lives of the children;
- the total assets available to each parent and each child; and
- any other factors the court believes reasonable, necessary, or fair, such as payment of an existing expense or debt to help the children.

One particularly controversial and expensive item of child support is whether or not children must receive a college education. If one or both parents can afford to pay for this education, the courts may order support. However, this is a matter of discretion, rather than an absolute right of each child.[16]

Finally, what can parents do if there isn't enough money to go around? The children, who cannot provide for themselves, must come first. This may mean postponing the purchase of a new home, canceling vacations, or getting a second job. It may mean exhaustion of a nest egg savings account or even an emergency fund account. Loans from family or friends and borrowing money from a bank or on a line of credit may be necessary. Whatever it takes to provide for the children, it must be done.[17]

But why allow a court to consider these factors and sometimes make arbitrary support decisions when the parents usually are the best judges of these items? Aren't these additional matters that can, and should, be the subject of private mediation?

Failure to Pay Child Support

A major divorce litigation problem arises when parents ignore child support responsibilities. In August 1992, the U.S. Commission on Interstate Child Support issued its report on this problem after a two-year study authorized under the 1988 Family Support Act.[18] The commission concluded that America's state-based system of collecting child support was a "cumbersome, slow-moving dinosaur fed by paper." Each year, the report said, the judicial system failed to collect about one-third of the approximate $15 *billion* of child support ordered or promised for about eleven million children. The commission further noted that too many parents escaped child support responsibilities by moving to other states.

To address this serious problem, the Commission considered, but rejected, federalizing child support payment enforcement. Instead, the panel recommended the following measures, among others, to the U.S. Congress:
- Expanding the information available to states by broadening the information that all employees must furnish on the IRS W-4 form when they take a job[19]
- Creating a national computer network to improve state access to data on the location of a parent who is ordered to pay support

- Enhancing existing support collection efforts across state lines by mandating that employers in one state honor orders to withhold income for support issued by another state
- Making greater use of liens against property and withholding of driver's and occupational licenses from parents who don't pay

It is always tempting for the non-custodial parent to become apathetic about paying child support. He or she moves on with a new life and does not see the children as much. Unfortunately for the children, out of sight quite often means out of mind.

The court cannot force a parent to meet with a child—it may actually be a disaster if this could be done. But until Congress enacts stricter national enforcement laws, parents must enforce child support payments through existing state, legal, and administrative measures with varying degrees of success. Judges usually have the authority to withhold money from a parent's salary or to sell assets to satisfy this debt. If a parent has moved to another state, local state attorneys can use the Revised Uniform Reciprocal Enforcement Support Act to enforce child support orders in that other state. But this is often expensive and time-consuming.[20]

PROLONGED LITIGATION IS A TESTIMONY AGAINST HONORING PRIORITIES

When we aggressively litigate our divorces at the expense of preserving the well-being of individual family members, and especially our children, we lose before we begin. People are worth more than power and money. Is there any greater resource on this earth than our children? Why not look for alternative ways to protect their welfare and our interests rather than fall into the litigation trap?

Questions for Personal Reflection

1. If I am facing separation or divorce, am I willing to put my children at risk before a dispassionate court as opposed to doing whatever I can now to settle child custody and support issues with my spouse?

2. What effect will continuing litigation have on my children now and in the future?

3. If I see harm coming to my children by asserting my legal rights, am I willing to sacrifice these rights to spare the children further injury?

4. What are some specific ways for my ex-spouse and me to cooperate in parenting our children in ways that are in their best interest?

5. What have I done to explore mediation options available for resolving disputes that could generate more litigation?

6. How can I best minister to children of other couples who are experiencing a separation or divorce?

Chapter 4

What's Happening in Our Churches and Schools?

We have strayed far away from biblical guidelines for justice and discipline in our churches and schools. Our love for offensive litigation, and our defensive fear of personal liability, make our institutions introspective agencies with a "live and let live" mentality of permissiveness and tolerance of sin. If we don't correct the problem, the courts may march in!

&.

Christian sisters Euodia and Syntyche in the Anytown, USA, congregation have a major disagreement. Euodia asked Syntyche to start a Christian tape ministry. Over time, however, Euodia discovered that her business partner was donating tapes and material to the local homeless shelter without her prior approval. This resulted in a substantial loss of revenues. Syntyche believes she has done nothing wrong since, she reasons, a Christian tape ministry involves giving to those less fortunate.

Euodia demands that the church elders force Syntyche to pay back the money lost. When they do not act quickly on her request, Euodia becomes exasperated. Storming out of an elder's meeting, she yells over her shoulder, "I've had it with all of you elders. I'll see you in court!" She checks in with a local lawyer and files a lawsuit against Syntyche and the elders. The charge is breach of fiduciary duty and failure to oversee Syntyche's activities. Considering Matthew 18:15–17 and 1 Corinthians 6:1–8, was Euodia following biblical guidelines? How far can a civil court go in sorting out a religious conflict like this?

This hypothetical example is not too different from what often happens when Christians squabble with each other. Someone is not happy with the pace of church justice and wants to take matters into his or her own hands. When someone wrongs you, why not act like so many others in the world do? See a lawyer and file suit! But in this chapter we are going to see how church lawsuits create havoc for our courts and our religious freedoms. Our overburdened courts cannot handle these disputes, and litigation is certainly not what God wants!

TURMOIL IN THE CHURCH

There was a time when our nation respected and revered her churches, and those devoting their lives to serving others in the congregations. It was a sacred fellowship, set apart from the worldly trappings of society, where God dwelt among His people. People sacrificed to the point of poverty for one another if necessary. They believed in turning the other cheek. The thought of suing a church or its leaders was almost unthinkable. Even lenders balked at making church loans for fear that any default enforcement would cripple public goodwill by appearing to be an attempt to foreclose on God.[1]

But our society has changed. We are a warring, litigious people now. When we want someone to pay for our troubles or losses, we spare no one—not even the church—from our furies. The lure to litigate anything and everything is just too great, too overpowering to resist.

As we shall see in the next chapter, the U.S. Constitution does not really allow for courts and legislatures to become involved in the establishment of religion or exercise of our individual religious beliefs. Traditionally, the courts have refused to become involved in church disputes. But that is changing rapidly. In recent years, more and more the courts are poking into church matters and disputes and we are encouraging them to do it! This isn't healthy for our churches and religious schools, or for our country.

Let's look at a few examples:

THE COLLINSVILLE CHURCH OF CHRIST CASE

On Sunday, October 4, 1981, the preacher of the one hundred and twenty-member Collinsville Church of Christ in Tulsa, Oklahoma yielded the pulpit to the elders of the congregation. They read a prepared statement to everyone assembled for worship that morning. The statement spoke of Marian Guinn, a thirty-six-year-old divorced registered nurse with four children, and a member of the Collinsville congregation for the previous seven years.

On the authority of Matthew 18:15–17, and in Guinn's absence, the elders read aloud several Scriptures dealing with fornication, adultery, or immorality that, they claimed, Guinn violated. The elders advised the congregation that it was time to withdraw fellowship from Guinn. The elders also alerted congregations in other Tulsa suburbs as to their decision.

For seven months before this incident Guinn had missed many Sunday worship services due to her work at the Oklahoma Osteopathic

Hospital. She was, admittedly, also sexually involved with the former Collinsville mayor. When the Collinsville elders learned of her impropriety, they counseled with her over a period of many months. They urged her to break off her relationship with the person involved. The elders further warned her in writing on September 21 to publicly repent by September 27. If not, they would have no alternative but to advise the congregation of the matter according to Matthew 18. They wrote:

> Dear Sister Marian:
> It is with tremendous concern for your soul and the welfare of the Lord's church that we exhort you to consider the impact of the results of the course you have elected to pursue. We have and will continue to follow the instructions set forth in the Scriptures in dealing with matters of church discipline. The Lord set forth the procedure in Matthew 18:15–17. We have confronted you personally . . . , however to date you have not responded, so you leave us no alternative but to "tell it to the church." . . . If by the close of the worship services Sunday morning, September 27, 1981, you have not indicated a penitent heart by a public acknowledgement of your sin of fornication, a statement will be read aloud to the congregation, with an exhortation for each to make contact with you for the purpose of encouragement, that you might "hear them" and repent. If you so choose not to heed these exhortations, by the close of the worship services Sunday morning, October 4, 1981, a statement will be read by the elders, to exclude you from the fellowship of the Body of Christ, (V–17) and notify sister congregations, which means (1) Not to associate with you, 1 Cor. 5:9, (2) Not to eat a meal or open our homes to you, 1 Cor. 5:11, (3) Not to bid you "God Speed," 2 John 11, (4) To hold ourselves aloof from you, 2 Thess. 3, and (5) Have no company with you, 2 Thess. 3:6 and 14. . . . It is the prayerful desire of the entire body of Christ that you correct this serious matter and avert the "withdrawing of fellowship" of the saints.

————

Guinn refused the counsel of the elders. Instead, she had a handwritten letter delivered to Elder Ron Witten on September 25 stating: "I do not want my name mentioned before the Church except to tell them that I withdraw my membership immediately! . . . You have no right to get up and say anything against me in church. . . . I have no choice but to attend another church, another denomination! Where men do not set themselves up as judges for God. He does His own judging."

The elders advised Guinn that a member of the family of God cannot withdraw membership. Therefore, the church's responsibility for her spiritual welfare continued. In essence, Guinn could not withdraw from the church, but the church must withdraw from her.

Before sending her letter to the elders, Guinn also contacted an attorney. In a letter sent to the elders on September 24, the attorney threatened legal action against the church if the elders proceeded with the public reprimand against Guinn. The elders nevertheless addressed the Collinsville congregation on the matter on October 4 as they promised, about nine days after receiving Guinn's letter.

After the October 4 service, Guinn filed a $1.35 million lawsuit against the Collinsville congregation and its elders for invasion of privacy and intentional infliction of mental anguish (after amending her initial petition for libel and slander).

Legal counsel for the church argued that Guinn's moral life was never just her own business. Upon becoming a Christian and joining with the Collinsville congregation, she gave authority to the elders to care for her spiritual growth. Guinn's attorney countered by arguing that even if the church could exercise discipline over its members, it lost that right if a member voluntarily withdrew.

After a long period of litigation, on March 15, 1984, a twelve-member jury serving in the Tulsa County District Court awarded Ms. Guinn a verdict of $205,000 in actual damages and $185,000 in punitive damages after five hours of deliberation. The $390,000 award amounted to more than six years worth of contributions for the Collinsville congregation.

In winning the trial, Guinn's attorney likened the church's action to the public branding of the adulteress Hester Prynne in Nathaniel Hawthorne's *The Scarlet Letter*. While still encouraging Ms. Guinn to repent, the congregation appealed the decision.

CAUSE OF ACTION

The Collinsville elders relied upon the authority of Matthew 18:15–17 in disciplining Guinn. This passage of Scripture calls for a personal meeting with a sinning Christian, followed by rebuke and, eventually, disfellowship if there is no repentance and restoration. It commands face-to-face confrontation—initially in private and then publicly. The purpose is to make the offender fully aware of the bad fruit of continued sin while, hopefully, restoring the individual through repentance. Ultimately, if these private warnings are continually disregarded, the offender loses the privilege of privacy and confidentiality and a public report of the sin is made to the congregation. Internal church discipline is, above all, a serious family matter among Christians (Gal. 6:10; Eph. 2:19; 1 Cor. 5:12–13).

For her part, Marian Guinn did not pursue a lawsuit for defamation. (*Defamation* is a legal action based on a written or verbal communication that holds someone up to hatred, contempt, or ridicule or causes others to shun or avoid that person, resulting in injury to that person's reputation.) Guinn admitted the truth of the elders' statements about her sexual involvement, which would be a defense to any legal action for defamation (coupled with the elders' qualified privilege to make such remarks). Instead, the basis of her legal action involved an alleged invasion of her privacy.[2] She argued that she voluntarily withdrew from the jurisdiction of the Collinsville eldership. Therefore, the elders should guard her privacy as a former member of the Collinsville congregation in particular and the larger church community in general.

Issues on Appeal

There was no question that the Collinsville Church elders did, in fact, reveal offensive and embarrassing facts about Guinn's sexual relationship to the public. Under American civil law, this was an invasion of her privacy. The court transcripts showed that Guinn made every effort to withhold her consent by voluntarily withdrawing from the Collinsville congregation and the church at large, and in advance, she advised the elders of this fact in writing. She even threatened the Collinsville elders with legal action to stop public disclosure. To defend the lawsuit, the elders had to prove that Guinn initially consented to the right of the elders' publishing facts about her private life in becoming a member of the Collinsville congregation. Furthermore, the elders must show that Guinn's withdrawal from the Collinsville congregation just before application of public discipline did not revoke her consent.

The primary issue on appeal, therefore, was whether an individual who exercises a First Amendment right of freedom of association by voluntarily joining a Church of Christ congregation may unilaterally withdraw, despite pending disciplinary proceedings according to Matthew 18:15–17. Did this withdrawal remove Guinn from the jurisdiction of the church? Did her unilateral revocation of membership cause her initial consent (to be bound by Scripture governing her personal conduct in the church) to terminate immediately?

Guinn's counsel argued that Matthew 18 applied only to individuals who voluntarily continue to associate with other Christians in the same church and who claim or expect recognition as members. It would not apply, nor is it practically necessary, to the offending individual who voluntarily withdraws and no longer associates with other members. He also argued that permanent lifetime membership in a church (or any other organization) is contrary to the basic freedom of voluntary association in the United States.

Attorneys for the Collinsville elders countered that scriptural discipline protects not only the church's reputation and purity of its members, but also ministers to the spiritual and moral well–being of the person being disciplined. Church members are to be submissive to their leaders. Elders must watch out for the souls of those in their charge (Heb. 13:17).

Scripture, the lawyers argued, does not allow for avoiding or evading this responsibility by withdrawal from a congregation. It is a commitment springing from being a part of the body of Christ—not solely from membership in a local congregation. If withdrawal is possible, anyone could ignore church discipline, and the command of the Holy Spirit to withdraw from those who are disobedient would be made meaningless (2 Thess. 3:6).

THE APPELLATE DECISION

After more than eight years of costly litigation the Supreme Court of Oklahoma made a difficult decision. The Free Exercise Clause of the First Amendment shielded all the elders' disciplinary actions against Guinn from judicial scrutiny *before* her withdrawal from the church. However, the elders had no such legal protection when they continued to denounce Guinn *after* she had withdrawn. The elders enjoyed neither an absolute or a qualified privilege to continue to speak against Guinn after she voluntarily disassociated herself from their congregation.[3]

Dissenting Oklahoma Supreme Court justices disagreed with the majority's decision. They believed the First Amendment protected the elders in disciplining Guinn both during her church membership and after her unilateral withdrawal from the church. They saw the post-withdrawal actions as consistent with Matthew 18, serving the purpose of: (1) causing a disobedient member to miss the fellowship and to desire to repent; and (2) purifying the church and preventing other members from committing the same sin. Therefore, the court's review of the church's moral discipline according to Scripture was precisely the kind of action the U.S. Constitution forbids. "Whether the Church of Christ's doctrine of withdrawal of fellowship may be viewed as unwise or improvident from an individual preference, is no concern of the courts. Our personal beliefs are not the constitutional standard; but rather, separation of church and state. Furthermore, the courts may not delve into whether the discipline imposed by the Elders was arbitrary or contrary to the Church's own doctrine law and procedures."[4]

THE WATCHTOWER BIBLE AND TRACT SOCIETY CASE

Not long before the Oklahoma Supreme Court's decision in the *Collinsville* case, the Federal Ninth Circuit Court of Appeals considered an unrelated lawsuit also involving disfellowship of a church member. There, too, the court found church disciplinary action to be a form of religious expression protected by the First Amendment.[5]

Mrs. Paul, a Jehovah's Witness member, became disenchanted with the faith and beliefs of the church, withdrew her membership and moved to another state. When she returned to her old neighborhood a few years later, however, her former church members refused to speak to her. The church elders instructed all members to shun her.

Mrs. Paul sued the church. She claimed that, by shunning her, the church had defamed her, caused her severe emotional distress, and invaded her privacy. The court determined that shunning was a form of religious expression protected by the Free Exercise Clause. This action did not present a threat to the peace, safety, or morality of the community. The church elders admonished members of the church not to speak to Mrs. Paul; by obeying this directive the members exercised their own religious freedom by not associating with her.

To impose liability for the shunning practice would have the same effect as prohibiting the practice. It would compel the church to abandon part of its religious teachings and directly restrict the free exercise of the Jehovah's Witnesses' religious faith. Therefore, courts usually give churches great latitude in exercising discipline on members or former members—even in cases like the next one.

THE ANDREW BAPTIST CHURCH CASE

A few members of the Andrew Baptist Church in Tulsa, Oklahoma, held some grievances against their pastor, the deacons, and the trustees of their church. Specifically, these members complained that the leaders of the congregation listed the church property for sale without consent or approval of the members; that church staff received salary increases without membership approval; that unauthorized persons used telephone and gasoline credit cards provided by the church to the pastor; that members had to pay for use of church facilities for weddings and funerals; and similar complaints.

When the church leaders did not resolve these grievances, the church members sued them in Oklahoma state court for access to the church's financial records and an accounting of all church funds. This suit inquired into the use, abuse, or misuse of church property.

The church bylaws provided that a legal proceeding against the church was grounds for expulsion. It was no surprise then that, shortly after bringing the civil lawsuit, the church leaders acted to discipline and expel all parties to the lawsuit from church membership. The affected members then asked the court to stop the church leaders from disfellowshipping them for executing their legal rights.

The trial court threw out the lawsuit on the First Amendment principle that courts will not interfere with the internal affairs of a religious organization. The only exception arises when civil or property rights require protection. (The court determined that this suit did not involve any such property rights.)[6]

The disfellowshipped members appealed this decision to the Oklahoma Supreme Court (the same court that decided the 1989 *Collinsville* appeal). In a December 1992 decision, that court also refused to grant any relief to the church members, stating:

> We now accept as fundamental the position that a church's decision as to the status of a person's church membership must be considered as binding and beyond the reviewing power of courts such as ours. . . . Church membership, by itself, is not a civil or property right subject to civil judicial regulation, and we will not compel a church to reinstate a member. . . . We therefore find a compelling reason *not* to apply legal principles governing incorporated voluntary associations to church discipline proceedings that expel members of a congregation. . . . Thus, in a church discipline proceeding a church may irregularly, i.e., contrary even to church procedure, discipline or expel a member and still be free of review for correctness by a civil court in this jurisdiction.[7]

When they were expelled from their congregation, the disfellowshipped members lost their right to claim any diversion of church funds or property to nonchurch uses.

But will the courts truly never intervene in church-related matters not involving property disputes? Whenever church members have a conflict over matters of ministry, a significant risk always exists that the courts will intervene and second-guess decisions made by church leaders—especially if anyone suffers personal loss in the crisis. Consider the next case against a popular, nationally known pastor.

THE GRACE COMMUNITY CHURCH CASE

In what was widely publicized as the first clergy malpractice case, a distraught couple filed a $1 million wrongful death lawsuit in 1980 against popular pastor-teacher and radio host John MacArthur and other ministry colleagues at the thousand-plus member Grace Community Church in suburban Los Angeles. They claimed that MacArthur and his co-defendants caused the wrongful death of their son, a member of MacArthur's church, arising out of intentional infliction of emotional distress.

Kenneth Nally was a healthy, intelligent young man with a promising future. He was a star baseball player who had finished college and was contemplating law school. But, in his late teen years, he developed a mental illness that made him depressed and suicidal.

As Nally was a member of the Grace Church for several years, MacArthur and several other church counselor-leaders tried to comfort and counsel Nally using biblical principles. He also received some independent psychiatric care for his condition. After one suicide attempt in

March 1979, MacArthur personally took Nally into his home and tried to minister to his needs. Despite these efforts, however, Nally's illness worsened. Eventually, he killed himself with a shotgun on April 2, 1979, at age twenty-four.

It was a profound human tragedy. Grace Community Church, with 10,000 people attending services on a given Sunday, conducted a very active counseling program as part of its ministry. There were as many as thirty counselors on staff in 1979. They tried to provide biblical counseling to others in need. But it was not enough to help young Kenneth.

On March 31, 1980, Kenneth's parents, Walter and Maria Nally, filed suit in Los Angeles Superior Court. They alleged clergyman malpractice, wrongful death, negligence, and outrageous conduct against Grace Community Church, MacArthur, and several other church leaders. In their complaint, the Nallys stated that, after their son's first suicide attempt, MacArthur counseled him to consult with counselors of the Grace Church. MacArthur told Nally to engage in prayer, read Scriptures, and listen to tape recordings of MacArthur's sermons rather than actively encourage him to seek professional secular counseling. Although their son came from a background of Catholic religious training, the Nallys charged that the defendants "ridiculed, disparaged, and denigrated the Catholic religion and faith." The Nallys claimed that the Grace Church members' efforts to salvage their fellow church member resulted in increasing despair and anguish. Ultimately, this led to Kenneth Nally's suicide.

MacArthur and his co-defendants defended themselves based upon the religious liberties of the First Amendment and the separation of church and state. They countered that secular courts cannot hold religious counselors to any professional duty applicable to secular psychiatrists, for example. To do so would pose a dangerous threat to their religious freedoms. It could seriously inhibit ministers, priests, and rabbis from seeking to help people overcome suicidal tendencies through spiritual guidance.

The Los Angeles Superior Court threw out the lawsuit. The Nallys appealed the decision to the California Second District Court of Appeals. In a highly controversial split decision entered in September 1987, that court reversed the lower court's decision. While the First Amendment absolutely protects the defendants' religious beliefs, the Court held that the Free Exercise Clause does not license intentional infliction of emotional distress in the name of religion. Nor does it shield the defendants from liability for wrongful death for a suicide allegedly caused by such conduct.

In a strong dissent, however, one of the appellate judges protested that the Nallys failed to prove that the Grace Church members acted intentionally or in a reckless manner to bring about Kenneth's suicide. Without such proof, he argued, the decision of the other judges would "have the deleterious effect of opening a virtual Pandora's box of litigation by subjecting all . . . religious faiths and their clergy . . . to wrongful death actions and expensive full-blown trials simply because they were unsuccessful in their sincere efforts through spiritual counseling to help or dissuade emotionally disturbed members of their congregations."[8]

When the case returned to the Los Angeles Superior Court, the trial judge threw the suit out again. In his court opinion, the judge noted, "There is no compelling state interest to climb the wall of separation of church [and state] and plunge into the pit on the other side that certainly has no bottom."

The Nallys appealed a second time to the California Court of Appeals. Once again this appellate court reversed the lower court's decision. This time the court held that a nontherapist counselor who holds himself out as competent to treat serious emotional problems and voluntarily sets up a counseling relationship with an emotionally disturbed person has a duty to take appropriate precautions should that person exhibit suicidal tendencies.

The court did distinguish between professional counseling, on the one hand, and other perhaps less sophisticated remedies such as advice and counsel given by friends, teen hotlines which offer Band Aid counseling, or church members who seek a pastor's casual advice after morning services. But it determined that counseling a suicidal person carries serious legal burdens. The court determined that California has a compelling state interest in preventing suicides, even if any court action adversely affects one's constitutional rights to freedom of religion. This includes suicides by mentally disordered people who choose to seek emotional counseling from pastoral counselors. *All* such counselors must abide by a certain standard of reasonable care.[9]

After nearly a decade of expensive and time-consuming litigation, the parties appealed the dispute to the California Supreme Court. In a November 1988 decision that court agreed with the judge in the Los Angeles Superior Court, holding that pastoral, nontherapist counselors had no duty to refer potentially suicidal persons to a professional secular therapist.[10] "Because of the differing theological views espoused by the myriad of religions in [California] and practiced by church members, it would certainly be impractical, and quite possibly unconstitutional, to impose a duty of care on pastoral counselors. Such a duty would necessarily be intertwined with the religious philosophy of the particular denomination or ecclesiastical teachings of the religious entity."[11]

But the case did not end there. It was still going strong until April 1989 when the U.S. Supreme Court refused to accept review of the California Supreme Court decision.[12]

The *Grace Community Church* case raises a number of questions. Where does one draw the line between psychological and spiritual concerns? Given our First Amendment religious freedoms, how far can the civil courts go in regulating biblical counseling? How should Christians handle disputes of this sort? Will other pastors like MacArthur run the risk of defending against expensive litigation simply because someone claims negligence?

Clergy Malpractice: The Attack on the Church That Won't Go Away

The *Grace Community Church* case spawned many new lawsuits by various church members against their leaders. Most courts have refused to become involved in cases claiming clergy malpractice.[13] Why? In the 1991 case of *Schmidt v. Bishop*, a Federal Court in New York gave us a few reasons and a rather prophetic warning:

> Any effort by this Court to instruct the trial jury as to the duty of care which a clergyman should exercise, would of necessity require the Court or jury to define and express the standard of care to be followed by other reasonable . . . clergy of the community. This in turn would require the Court and the jury to consider the fundamental perspective and approach to counseling inherent in the beliefs and practices of that denomination. This is as unconstitutional as it is impossible. It fosters excessive entanglement with religion.

> It may be argued that it requires no excessive entanglement with religion to decide that reasonably prudent clergy of any sect do not molest children. The difficulty is that this Court . . . must consider not only this case, but the next case to follow, and the ones after that, before we embrace the newly invented [lawsuit] of clergy malpractice. This places us clearly on the slippery slope . . . Where could we stop? Assume a severely depressed person consults a storefront preacher . . . The cleric consults with our hypothetical citizen, reminds him of his slothful life and that he is a miserable sinner; recommends prayer and fasting and warns of the Day of Judgment. Our depressed person becomes more so, and kills himself and few more people. These deaths are followed by lawsuits. As to a licensed psychiatrist or social worker, our lay courts should have no trouble adjudicating a claim of professional

malpractice on these facts. As to a clergyman, it would be both impossible and unconstitutional to attempt to do so.[14]

As this New York court implies, clergy malpractice claims carry two problems: (1) they may impose nonchurch standards on religious leaders in ways that may violate the First Amendment; and (2) they may cause many pastors and other religious leaders to stop religious counseling for fear of not conforming to standards applicable to licensed secular counselors. Many, but far from all, judges today recognize the numerous constitutional difficulties involved in trying to define a standard of care for religious counselors. But how long will this initial reluctance by the American courts to consider clergy malpractice claims last? In this era of antagonism toward Christianity, will an unbelieving world continue to tolerate what it surely perceives to be a double standard of care between religious and secular counselors? And will the courts stand idly by if desperate secular counselors try to shield themselves from liability by claiming a religious exemption in a counseling lawsuit? Dilemmas like these almost force the courts to intrude and analyze religious counseling practices. And the crisis escalates with each suit filed by a disgruntled church member against his or her church leaders.

The pressure on the courts to regulate pastors and ministers is mounting rapidly. The courts already have intervened when church leaders take sexual advantage of individuals in their congregation. In *DeStefano v. Grabrian*, the Colorado Supreme Court allowed a woman to sue her pastor after alleging that he breached his position and duty of trust by having sexual intercourse with her while also providing her with marriage counseling.[15] In 1979, St. Mary's Catholic Church members Robert and Edna DeStefano sought marriage counseling from their priest, Dennis Grabrian. During the counseling relationship, Grabrian developed an adulterous relationship with Mrs. DeStefano despite the risk that this could (and did) jeopardize her marriage with Mr. DeStefano.

The trial court backed off of this matter, dismissing the case. The judge noted that the issues raised were "inextricably linked to questions of doctrine, theology, the usage and customs of the [Catholic] Church, written laws, and the fundamental organization of the Church." This is a problem for the church to handle—not the courts. A divided Colorado Court of Appeals narrowly agreed with the trial court judge.

But the Colorado Supreme Court said the lower court's decision was wrong. Clergy cannot hide behind the First Amendment for conduct like this.

If the alleged conduct of Grabrian was dictated by his sincerely held religious beliefs or was consistent with the practice of his religion, we would have to resolve a difficult first amendment issue. This, however, is not the case. It has not been asserted that Grabrian's conduct falls within the practices or beliefs of the Catholic Church. . . . A priest's violation of his vow of celibacy is contrary to the instructions and doctrines of the Catholic church. When a priest has sexual intercourse with a parishioner it is not part of the priest's duties nor customary within the business of the church. Such conduct is contrary to the principles of Catholicism and is not incidental to the tasks assigned a priest by the diocese.[16]

This allowed the Court to skirt around the sticky First Amendment issues and rule that Grabrian could be liable for breach of fiduciary duty and outrageous conduct. (The diocese could be liable as well for negligent supervision of Grabrian.)

Although the Colorado Supreme Court dismissed Mrs. DeStefano's claim against Grabrian for clergy malpractice, it did cite a 1984 Washington Supreme Court case that appeared to leave open the possibility of "an action against a counselor, pastoral or otherwise, in which a counselor is negligent in treating either a husband or wife." The Washington court noted it was "conceivable that a malpractice action would be appropriate where a counselor fails to conform to an appropriate standard of care."[17]

In a similar case, Richard and Suzanne Strock experienced marital problems in 1985. They went to see James Pressnell, the then minister of the Shepherd of the Ridge Lutheran Church in Ohio, for marriage counseling. In the final weeks of counseling, Pressnell engaged in consensual sexual relations with Mrs. Strock. Mr. Strock, later divorced from his wife, filed suit against Pressnell and the church alleging, among other charges, clergy malpractice. The trial court dismissed the claim. A divided Court of Appeals agreed with the lower court's decision.

The Ohio Supreme Court tentatively concurred that "the tort of clergy malpractice cannot be applied to the facts found in this case." But the court added an ominous footnote: "This opinion should not be read as precluding an action against a counselor, pastoral or otherwise, in which a counselor is negligent in treating a patient. This opinion is limited to the narrow holding that clergy malpractice is not a viable action under the facts of this case."[18] Two dissenting Supreme Court justices went further. They would "hold that a marriage counselor who engages in sexual relations with the spouse of a client seeking professional guidance may be answerable in damages for malpractice. Clergy malpractice . . . is a misnomer. The standard of behavior below which such actions fall does not vary between religious and secular counselors."[19]

Certainly no one condones the sexual misconduct of pastors in counseling church members. But danger waits for all Christians when the courts, rather than the churches themselves, become the enforcer in unfortunate situations like this. Cases like these open the door for more court encroachment into church matters. It is inevitable that courts reviewing any lawsuit against pastors and church leaders also must review religious teachings and beliefs. This brings us back to the New York Federal Court's warning in the *Schmidt* case. What will happen to us if the courts begin a slide down this slippery slope? In the meantime, no minister in America will feel safe in expressing religious beliefs for fear someone will sue him or her for causing a personal problem and make the situation another legal test case.

Think further court encroachment into church matters won't happen in America? In the past, courts have intervened and held pastors and churches liable for other negligent (or intentional) acts. These include slip and fall cases,[20] obtaining gifts and donations of money by fraud (such as the infamous Jim Bakker/PTL Ministries case),[21] exercising undue influence over another person in making property transfers,[22] sexual harassment, child molestations, homosexual assault,[23] and similar failings. One Louisiana church was even held responsible for its pastor's negligence in not clearing the aisles to make way for "running in the spirit," a common form of religious expression at that church.[24] Cases like these prompt one to ask, "Is the line between these church lawsuits clear and distinct enough to keep the courts out of religious counseling negligence cases in the future?" I think not.

In this chapter, we are exploring the legal boundaries between church-related disputes and ministry decisions that church leaders and members can (and should) resolve exclusively within their church organizations, and those which open the door for court intervention. The next case, directly involving Matthew 18:15–17 and other Scripture, shows that the Constitution may not keep the courts and governmental agencies out of all disputes among Christians—even if churches and religious schools rely upon Scripture for their actions!

THE DAYTON CHRISTIAN SCHOOL CASE

Dayton Christian Schools is an Ohio religious grade school academy claiming it provides education "in a positive Christian atmosphere and Christ-centered environment." It teaches all subjects with an awareness of God's supreme authority over all creation. It purportedly presents the Bible as the only reliable and true revelation of God's nature and His redeeming purpose and will for humankind.

The school's mission and goal is to help young people become like Jesus Christ, to think and act like Him, and focus on Him in every way possible. Every teacher of the school must agree to a statement of faith each school year. Included is an endorsement of the school's commitment to follow 1 Corinthians 6:1–8 and Matthew 18:15–17 by internally resolving school-related disputes without going to court outside the school community.

In January 1979, teacher Linda Hoskinson informed Principal James Rakestraw that she was pregnant. A month later, Rakestraw wrote her a letter stating that the school believes mothers should stay home with preschool children. Accordingly, the school did not plan to renew her contract for the upcoming school year.

The school's superintendent, Claude Schindler, explained in his legal testimony: "We believe the Bible teaches that even though we are equal in the sight of God, our role is different, the role of female is different from that of the male. The Scripture teaches that in 1 Peter, chapter 3; 1 Timothy chapter 2; Titus, chapter 2; just to mention a few passages of the Scripture. And in those passages it spells out the role of a woman. We felt they directly related to a woman being home with her pre-school age children."[25]

After learning of the school's decision, Hoskinson consulted with an attorney who wrote to the school threatening legal action for violation of state and federal statutes that outlaw employment discrimination. In March 1979, the school terminated Hoskinson because she had consulted with an attorney and did not follow scriptural guidelines outlined in Matthew 18:15–17 and Galatians 6:1 by resolving a conflict inside the church community.

Hoskinson immediately filed a sex discrimination complaint with the Ohio Civil Rights Commission alleging that the reason for her termination was the school's belief that, during the early years of a child's growth, a mother's place is in the home. The Commission then notified the school that it was conducting a full investigation.

As part of its investigation, the Commission requested employment data on Hoskinson for two years, blank employment application forms, employee handbooks and rules for two years, written policy manuals, job descriptions, model contracts, a list of all school employees who were pregnant during the past two years or more and personal information about each person, a list of all employees suspended or discharged for the past two years, minutes of school director meetings, personnel files, and other information. The Commission demanded reinstatement of Hoskinson, back pay, and a public apology.

On October 1, 1980, the school filed suit against the Commission in Ohio Federal District Court. It asked for a court-ordered injunction to stop the Commission from setting up its investigation and hearings based upon Hoskinson's charges of sex discrimination and retaliatory employer practices. Lawyers for the school argued that the Commission's actions violated its First Amendment rights if the Commission intended to tell the school what it could, or could not, do despite scriptural commands to the contrary.

Could the Commission interject itself into the private dispute resolution process at the school? In January 1984, the District Court finally said yes, and dismissed the school's complaint asking the court to stop the investigation. The court reasoned that the Commission's investigation and hearings on the charges would only be a brief imposition on the school's belief in internal dispute resolution. The investigation "only incidentally or minimally infringed upon the school's religious freedoms, overridden in any event by Ohio's compelling state interest in eliminating sex discrimination in employment."

If you were on this school's board, would you trust the District Court's analysis? The Dayton officials didn't and appealed the case to the U.S. Sixth Circuit Court of Appeals. That court reversed the District Court's decision in June 1985. The court ruled that allowing the Commission to investigate and conduct hearings against the school for declining to rehire Hoskinson due to her failure to follow Matthew 18 and other biblical guidelines, violated the First Amendment.[26] Governmental inquiry into a religious school's decision on the religious qualifications of a religious instructor raised serious questions, the court found. It was an impermissible entanglement of the government in religious affairs in violation of the First Amendment. This is especially true when a governmental agency seeks to monitor or second-guess decisions or activities of a school that is founded upon religious doctrine.

Think the case ended there? Not so! The Civil Rights Commission appealed the Federal Appeals Court decision to the U.S. Supreme Court. In June 1986, seven and one-half years after the dispute first arose at the school, the Supreme Court reversed the prior court decision.[27] The court held that the Federal District Court never should have considered the school's complaint in the first instance since, in doing so, it impermissibly interfered with an ongoing state administrative investigation by the Commission.[28]

In his opinion for the Court, Justice Rehnquist wrote:

We have no doubt that the elimination of prohibited sex discrimination is a sufficiently important state interest . . . . We also have no reason to doubt that Dayton will receive an adequate opportunity to raise its constitutional claims. Dayton contends that the mere exercise of jurisdiction over it by the [Ohio Civil Rights Commission] violates its First Amendment rights. But we have repeatedly rejected the argument that a constitutional attack on state procedures "automatically vitiates the adequacy of those procedures . . . ." Even religious schools cannot claim to be wholly free from some state regulation. . . . We therefore think that however Dayton's constitutional claim should be decided on the merits, the Commission violates no constitutional rights by merely investigating the circumstances of Hoskinson's discharge in this case, if only to ascertain whether the ascribed religious-based reason was in fact the reason for the discharge.[29]

____

The Supreme Court's decision allows the Commission to come into the school, audit all its records and procedures, and disrupt the school's operation simply because a teacher refused to obey the rules and Scriptural principles she knew about in advance. Is there any reason the same sort of interference couldn't happen in *your* church or religious school? This decision is a wake-up call for all Christians to be on guard!

WHERE WILL IT ALL END?

These are only a few of the *many* cases courts accept for review each year involving religious practices and beliefs. A growing number of judges, and especially those with limited or no understanding of religious matters, disagree on how far courts may (and should) intrude into church and religious school matters. Some courts will encroach more than others. It is already obvious from the cases discussed above that judges at different levels of our judicial system arrive at totally opposite decisions on the same facts. This trend is tearing down the long-standing constitutional separation of church and state (reviewed in the next chapter).

Even more disturbing is that unwitting believers are feeding the fire by avoiding biblical guidelines for dispute resolution *within the Christian community. This hurts all believers.* Enlightened Christians everywhere must become increasingly concerned about the encroachments civil judges and juries are making into religious disputes. If we do nothing to reverse this trend, it is reasonable to fear that our governmental agencies and our courts will soon be dictating how we worship and obey God under the guise of "state investigations."

Where did we go wrong? Why are our churches on the defense against governmental interference? To answer these questions, we need to briefly review what our founding fathers had in mind in protecting our religious freedoms. It will help to look at a few examples of how our civil courts have struggled in applying our Constitution to cases that have impacted religion over the years.

The information in the next chapter is vitally important to all religious believers. As Christians, we know the eternal value of the freedoms God gives each of us, as confirmed in the Bible. For us, as Americans, the second most important document protecting these God-given freedoms from governmental interference is the U.S. Constitution (including the Bill of Rights). As responsible believers, we must familiarize ourselves with the laws of our great country and understand how they work to protect our religious freedoms against governmental intrusion or even forfeiture.

Questions for Personal Reflection

1. What do I know about my church's procedures of resolution of conflict between members? Are there any procedures in place? Do they work fairly? Are they effective? Are they designed to resolve conflicts swiftly and promote reconciliation between disputing parties?

2. Am I willing to place my personal disputes in the hands of other Christians for resolution to avoid or reduce litigation?

3. Do I know my constitutional rights and religious freedoms? Have I taken any of them for granted?

4. What disputes have arisen in my church over the past five years? How was each case resolved?

5. In what ways can I see religious freedoms in jeopardy over the next few years?

Chapter 5

RELIGIOUS RIGHTS GOING WRONG

We have strayed far away from biblical guidelines in using justice and discipline in our nation. Our love for offensive litigation, and our defensive fear of personal liability, has turned our churches and schools into introspective institutions captive to a live and let live mentality of permissiveness and tolerance of sin. It is eroding the constitutional shield protecting our religious freedoms as Americans.

The president of Argentina once asked a prominent American visitor to his country, "Why has South America gotten on so poorly and North America so well? What do you think is the reason?" The visitor replied, "I think the reason is found in the fact that the Spaniards came to South America seeking gold, while the Pilgrim Fathers came to North America seeking God."[1] But how times have changed!

God truly shed His grace on our bountiful nation. Our Constitution and Bill of Rights are shining commemorations of this fact. Once these precious documents were the centerpiece for America's independence and individual religious freedoms. Today, however, these national charters are the core of major discontent and legal battles unparalleled in our nation's history.

We have trapped ourselves into irreconcilable conflicts between church and state. How can government co-exist with religious faiths without generating more and more court disputes each year? Are you aware of what is happening around you? Do you know how unbelievers are deciding how you can live out your faith? Have you seen how many of your fellow believers face court action for the mere mention of God's name?

In a *Christian Legal Society* newsletter, Executive Director Samuel B. Casey noted:

Once again, the government is trying to force people to separate their religious beliefs from how they live the rest of their lives. When brothers Paul and Ronald Desilets refused to rent one of their apartments to an unmarried couple, they knew there could be trouble. In many areas, the law requires landlords to rent their property to anyone who applies. Unmarried couples. Homosexual couples. Anyone. But as Christians, Paul and Ronald felt they could not take part in promoting a sinful lifestyle. And as they feared, one day an unmarried couple they had turned away complained to a state antidiscrimination commission. Soon the Desilets brothers found themselves up against the Massachusetts State Attorney General . . .

In Alaska, another landlord was faced with the same kind of decision as the Desilets brothers. And because of similar Christian convictions, Tom Swanner also refused to rent his properties to unmarried couples. . . . [T]he Alaska Supreme Court found that landlords must rent to *all* couples, whatever their marital status or sexual orientation—*even though condoning such relationships violated Mr. Swanner's religious beliefs.* Being a landlord has nothing to do with being a Christian, the court told him—and *you have no right to apply your morals to your business.*[2]

Students in these "enlightened" times must sue for the right to meet on school campuses for Bible study and prayer. They must fight for the right to wear clothing or jewelry with religious messages or express personal religious views in homework assignments. The attacks on one's faith have become outrageous. "In Arkansas, a fifth grader was ordered by a teacher to turn his T-shirt inside-out to hide the Bible verse on it. A boy in Spokane, Wash., was told by his school principal that he violated the separation of church and state when he prayed silently before eating in the school lunchroom. Another student in Florida had her Bible confiscated by a teacher who saw her reading it during recess."[3] Brave souls who are bold enough to pray at student-led graduation exercises or other public events risk the legal wrath of unbelievers.

Teachers fare no better. They must litigate before securing the legal right to meet and pray with other teachers. They dare not express their Christian beliefs freely as their New Age counterparts do without running the risk of reprimand or dismissal.

In the workplace, publication of religious articles in a company newsletter is religious harassment, according to one Pennsylvania court. In the fall of 1993, the Equal Employment Opportunity Commission (EEOC) felt that working Americans expressing religious views created an intoler-

able condition. It proposed guidelines on religious harassment. This proposal easily could have created religion-free workplaces had Congress,
after receiving more than 100,000 protests from concerned citizens, not
blocked funding for implementing the rules in June 1994.

Situations like these should concern you—even outrage you. Looking
over the American scene, one commentator observed:

> As the [Young Rascals] asked in that song of theirs: "How can
> I be sure in a world that is constantly changing?" Answer: You
> can't be, friends, ever, about anything. No way. One absurd
> example: The most important right in the Bill of Rights, the First
> Amendment, which supposedly separates church and state and
> guarantees freedom of religion. The original purpose of this
> amendment was to prevent the establishment of a national relig-
> ion. But now this amendment has been perverted and used to try
> to separate God from government—something our mostly Chris-
> tian founders never, ever intended.

> But, who cares what those who actually wrote the First Amend-
> ment meant, say the civil religion fanatics. So, in North Carolina,
> you have a judge being taken to court because he opens his session
> with (gasp!) a prayer mentioning the dreaded G-word: God. And,
> in Colorado, a public-school teacher has been dragged into court
> because he sat at his desk silently reading his Bible! Such activities,
> we are told by straight-faced, God-hating, civil-religion ayatol-
> lahs, are a violation of the First Amendment. But they aren't. They
> are, clearly, "free exercise" of one's religion, which is guaranteed
> by, and not a violation of, the First Amendment. . . . [Today] the
> only "meaning" is no meaning, up is down, left is right and right
> is wrong. Today, free speech is naked dancing, free choice is the
> right to kill your unborn baby, and criminals have all the rights
> and their victims have none.

> So, celebrate the Bill of Rights, if you must. But you're only putting
> lipstick on a corpse. The document is a dead letter.[4]

More recently, the December 1994 issue of *Reader's Digest* featured an
article entitled "The Supreme Court Is Wrong About Religion," in which
the author notes:

> The [U.S. Supreme] Court has prohibited prayer in state-
> sponsored schools, yet Congress itself has engaged in officially
> sponsored, tax-supported prayer, complete with paid official

chaplains, from the very outset. The day after the House approved the First Amendment's establishment clause, September 25, 1789, it called for a day of national prayer and thanksgiving—the precursor to our present national holiday. . . . We have come to a day when a child's mention of God in a graduation address or the presence of a Nativity scene in a public place triggers threats of legal action. This is a gross distortion of our Constitutional history and a dishonor to our Founders.[5]

———

What is happening in America? How did the beautiful dream of our founding fathers, and the religious freedoms they sought to protect from an oppressive government become such a nightmare of upside-down priorities and militant minorities?

And why are there so many perplexing Supreme Court decisions? For instance, in the famous 1972 U.S. Supreme Court decision of *Wisconsin v. Yoder*,[6] an Amish community sought protection from a state mandatory school attendance law. The Amish did not want to expose their children to values and beliefs contrary to their strict way of life, as would occur if the state forced their children into formal education outside the Amish community. They feared this would create a barrier to the child's integration into the Amish community, with a potentially devastating effect on the continuation of their community. Instead, their practice was to educate their children at home after the eighth grade. The Supreme Court ruled that the state cannot compel Amish children to continue in school beyond the eighth grade.

Contrast that decision with another made by the Court in 1982 when the Amish sought an exemption from U.S. social security laws. The Court denied their request. The justices viewed these laws as "essential to accomplish an overriding governmental interest." It did not matter that the Amish provided for their own elderly. (*United States v. Lee*.[7]) Cases like these highlight the constant friction existing between church and state. Where is the line drawn on issues impacting spiritual and legal areas?

Religious Freedoms in America

One of America's blessings is the freedom to worship and associate with others as we freely choose. This right is given to us by God, and guaranteed by the U.S. Constitution. "We, the people" hold to the principle that church and government should remain separate as much as possible. Why? To avoid any interference with our religion freedoms.

Unfortunately, as society grows more complex and more apathetic toward God, the line of separation between church and government is blurred. Because we fail to exercise our religious rights and freedoms diligently, federal and state legislatures and civil courts are pushed into resolving church-related disputes in ways that deny God, reject biblical teachings, and violate original constitutional principles.

Many of our forefathers left Great Britain to escape the religious intolerance they faced through the governmentally established Church of England. They risked everything to come to America in pursuit of religious freedom.[8] These early settlers in our motherland knew it was foolish for any government to force all citizens to believe and worship in exactly the same way. People will never fully agree with each other on religious issues and doctrine. As the late Chief Justice Walter P. Stacy of the North Carolina Supreme Court once noted, "Men have gone to war and cut each other's throats because they could not agree as to what was to become of them after their throats were cut."[9]

The founding fathers deeply desired something entirely different. They dreamed of a nation that respected the truth that all persons have a natural and inalienable right to worship God according to the dictates of their own consciences, without interference or control of any human authority. So, in the first congressional session, visionary and wise individuals wrote these words in the First Amendment, adopted and ratified in 1791 as part of our Bill of Rights:

> *Congress shall make no law respecting an establishment of religion, or prohibiting the free exercise thereof;* or abridging the freedom of speech, or of the press, or the right of people peaceably to assemble, and to petition the Government for a redress of grievances" [emphasis added].

———

Just those sixteen words, italicized above, were intended to guarantee our religious freedoms.

There are two very different rights: (1) the Establishment Clause (which is actually an *anti*-establishment clause) guarantees that our government will not use its resources to impose religion upon us; and (2) the Free Exercise Clause, which guarantees that our government will not prevent us from pursuing any religion we choose.

These are sweeping prohibitions made by the framers of the Constitution with the purpose of stating general *goals*—not precise laws to govern every case that could arise. The concept was to provide American citizens and the civil courts with flexibility in their interpretations, rather than legal formulas and lengthy checklists. But the inclusion of both restraints in the First Amendment confirms that its authors were not content to protect religious liberty solely on one clause, without the other.[10] (Also, both clauses intermesh with the First Amendment freedom of speech, which has become a major element in deciding religious freedom cases in recent years.)

WHAT DOES THE ESTABLISHMENT CLAUSE MEAN?

The Establishment Clause requires that our government remain neutral on matters of religious theory, doctrine, and practice. Our executive leaders, legislatures, and courts cannot aid, foster, or promote one religion or religious theory over another. They cannot officially prefer one religious denomination or group over another.

This clause further restrains our government from forcing or influencing a person to go, or remain away from, church against that person's will. No one in political power can force that individual to profess a belief or disbelief in any religion.

As the U.S. Supreme Court has stated, the prospect of church and state litigating in court about what does or does not have religious meaning touches the very core of constitutional guarantees against establishment of religion. Government policy violates this constitutional protection when it has the effect of promoting religion in a particular way, such as by requiring specific nationally acceptable prayers in public schools, acting in a way that benefits some (but not all) religious groups by financing certain religious schools, or becoming too deeply involved in the management or administration of a church or religious institution.

But the Establishment Clause does not require government to be *hostile* to religion. The founding fathers did not intend for government to be an adversary of religious believers. The Constitution's protection of religious freedom does not limit religious groups with *fewer* rights than those enjoyed by all other Americans.

The Supreme Court says this about the constitutional role of government: "Government in our democracy, state and national, must be neutral in matters of religious theory, doctrine, and practice. It may not be hostile to any religion or to the advocacy of no-religion; and it may not aid, foster, or promote one religion or religious theory against another or even against the militant opposite. The First Amendment mandates governmental neutrality between religion and religion, and between religion and nonreligion."[11]

Within limited bounds, government may tolerate, and even accommodate, religious beliefs.[12] As Supreme Court Justice and former Harvard Law School Professor Joseph Story wrote in his monumental treatise on the Constitution during the 1800s: "Probably at the time of the adoption of the Constitution, and of the amendments to it, now under consideration [First Amendment], the general if not the universal sentiment in America was, that Christianity ought to receive encouragement from the State so far as was not incompatible with the private rights of conscience and the freedom of religious worship. An attempt to level all religions, and to make it a matter of state policy to hold all in utter indifference, would have created universal disapprobation, if not universal indignation."[13]

Our founding fathers did not intend to strip America of religion, or force it to retreat whenever and wherever government sets its foot in society.

WHAT DOES THE FREE EXERCISE CLAUSE MEAN?

The Free Exercise Clause means we are free to think for ourselves and believe as we wish. And we are free also to act reasonably upon those beliefs (provided there is no threat or danger to public safety, peace, or order).

Religion must have a broad sphere in which to operate since the nature of religious belief requires spiritual, rather than legal, interpretation. The government could breach this clause by coercion, such as having its courts or regulatory agencies decide whether a particular religious doctrine is true or false and force believers to accept its interpretation.

When government conditions the receipt of an important benefit, or withholding of a benefit, upon conduct that runs counter to an individual's religious beliefs, this exerts real pressure on that person to change his or her behavior and violate those beliefs. Coercive governmental burdens upon our religious freedoms nullify those freedoms—even if the pressure is indirect. In the past our courts have required the government to prove that it has a compelling interest—a reason of the highest order—to justify such restrictions on our free exercise of religion. But this is another very gray area where judicial opinions differ greatly.

For our part, the freedom to believe and live out our faith is our absolute right. The courts acknowledge each American's decision to participate in or abstain from activities such as assembling with others for a worship service, participating in the sacramental use of bread and wine, practicing evangelism, and abstaining from certain foods or certain modes of transportation. The government cannot hinder any *belief*—no matter how outlandish or dangerous.

But the freedom to *act* on religious beliefs obviously must be conditional upon who, what, where, how, and when one chooses to express it. There are instances where this freedom of religious expression can go too far in jeopardizing the rights of other citizens.

For example, if the life of a citizen or overthrow of our country is at issue, the government has a compelling interest in protecting itself and its citizens. A person may believe that murder or suicide is not wrong, or that human sacrifices are necessary as part of one's worship, but this does not mean that individual is free to murder, commit suicide, or engage in human sacrifice. Parents have the right to apply religiously motivated discipline to their children, but not when the health or safety of the child is in jeopardy. Religious freedom does not allow a person to refuse vaccination as part of one's beliefs if this liberty exposes society to a communicable disease. Our nation would not last if citizens refused to pay taxes because various government spendings violated particular beliefs of a religious minority.[14]

In short, the First Amendment does *not* give us the right to fulfill our beliefs by committing intentional or reckless acts if those acts could harm other members of society.[15] Otherwise, people's religious beliefs and practices would allow them to become laws unto themselves, superior to the law of the land.

THE WALL OF SEPARATION BETWEEN CHURCH AND STATE

Another principle protecting our religious freedoms is the separation of church and state. Our Constitution fails to mention it specifically, but the Religion Clauses imply it.

This separation concept arose rather curiously. In 1801 the Danbury Baptist Association heard a rumor that the federal government was going to endorse a certain Christian sect (not theirs) as the official church of America. In January 1802, Thomas Jefferson assured the worried religious group that a "wall of separation" prohibited any such endorsement. Commenting on the thought behind the First Amendment, he wrote:

> Believing with you that religion is a matter which lies solely between man and his God; that he owes account to none other for his faith or his worship . . . I contemplate with sovereign reverence that act of the whole American people which declared that their Legislature should "make no law respecting an establishment of religion or prohibiting the free exercise thereof," thus building a wall of separation between Church and State.[16] (Jefferson also may have borrowed the "wall of separation" metaphor from Roger Williams, who later became governor of Rhode Island. Williams spoke eloquently of a "hedge of separation between the wilderness of the world and the garden of the church.")

> ———

Jefferson's controversial quote first gave us the term, "wall of separation between church and state." The principle that government remain neutral in its relations with religious believers and non-believers is crucial to this concept. It complements the modern proverb that "good fences make good neighbors."

In the famous 1962 school prayer decision *Engel v. Vitale*, the U.S. Supreme Court explained some of the reasoning at work in the separation principle:

> [A] union of government and religion tends to destroy government and to degrade religion. The history of governmentally

established religion, both in England and in this country, showed that whenever government had allied itself with one particular form of religion, the inevitable result had been that it had incurred the hatred, disrespect and even contempt of those who held contrary beliefs. That same history showed that many people had lost their respect for any religion that had relied upon the support of government to spread its faith. The Establishment Clause thus stands as an expression of principle on the part of the Founders of our Constitution that religion is too personal, too sacred, too holy, to permit its "unhallowed perversion" by a civil magistrate.[17]

But how can you truly keep church and state separate when so many Americans so intimately involve themselves in both activities? If church and state conflict, which influence deserves greater protection? Should our government submit to religion, or vice versa?

From the very beginning our government acknowledged religious influences—and specifically Christian influences. Consider these remarks made by Benjamin Franklin to the Constitutional Convention in Philadelphia on June 28, 1787:

> In the beginning of the contest with Britain, when we were sensible of danger, we had daily prayers in this room for the divine protection. Our prayers, Sir, were heard—and they were graciously answered . . . I have lived, Sir, a long time; and the longer I live, the more convincing proofs I see of this truth, that God governs in the affairs of men. And if a sparrow cannot fall to the ground without his notice, is it probable that an empire can rise without His aid? We have been assured, Sir, in the sacred writings that "except the Lord build the house, they labor in vain that build it." I firmly believe this; and I also believe that, without His concurring aid, we shall succeed in this political building no better than the builders of Babel . . . I therefore beg leave to move that, henceforth, prayers imploring the assistance of heaven and its blessings on our deliberations be held in this assembly every morning before we proceed to business, and that one or more of the clergy of this city be requested to officiate in that service.

The authors of our Constitution agreed with Franklin's proposal, resulting in opening invocations in Congress and state legislative sessions throughout our nation's history to this very day. In 1983 the U.S. Supreme Court upheld the Nebraska legislature's practice of opening each day's session with a prayer by a chaplain paid by that state, stating that it did not violate the Establishment Clause, based upon historical acceptance of the practice that had become "part of the fabric of our society."[18] (And yet, in the *Engel v. Vitale* decision just mentioned, our modern Supreme Court determined that this voluntary, simple prayer violated the Establishment Clause: "Almighty God, we acknowledge our dependence upon thee, and we beg thy blessings upon us, our teachers and our country.")

Are we a religious nation? Consider our national motto "In God We Trust", and our Pledge of Allegiance (amended by Congress in 1954 to add the words, "under God").[19] The opening of each day's Supreme Court session, inside the Court's Washington, D.C., building with "In God We Trust" permanently inscribed on its walls, begins with the cry: "God save the United States and this honorable Court." There are government-supported art galleries displaying Christian paintings, executive and congressional announcements proclaiming Christmas and Thanksgiving as national holidays in religious terms, and many similar religious national customs. In fact, as late as 1892 Supreme Court Justice Brewer could openly announce that "this is a Christian nation."[20] Even in recent years, a more restrained and "enlightened" Court has noted, "We are a religious people whose institutions presuppose a Supreme Being."[21] Given our strong religious heritage, how can we truly separate church and state? How can we remove the tint from the water once the dye is cast?

Christians can relate to the problems that are posed by this separation dilemma by remembering the apostle Paul's admonition: "I have written you in my letter not to associate with sexually immoral people—not at all meaning the people of this world who are immoral, or the greedy and swindlers, or idolaters. In that case you would have to leave this world" (1 Cor. 5:9–10). It is impossible for Christians to separate themselves from everyone in the world who is immoral since such influences are everywhere one goes. The same is true in trying to keep church and state separate. To make it happen, we would have to put each into its own separate world.

So the wall of separation is, at best, blurred, indistinct, and variable, depending on the circumstances of a particular relationship or circumstance. It is a very tricky tightrope for courts to walk! As U.S. Supreme Court Justice O'Connor stated in a 1985 opinion:

> In this country, church and state must necessarily operate within the same community. Because of this co-existence, it is inevitable that the secular interests of Government and the religious interests of various sects and their adherents will frequently intersect, conflict, and combine. A statute that ostensibly promotes a secular interest often has an incidental or even a primary effect of helping or hindering a sectarian belief. . . . For example,

the State could not criminalize murder for fear that it would thereby promote the Biblical command against killing.[22]

———

Because of the existing separation of church and state, a major question arises:

How Does the Government Remain Neutral on Religious Matters?

How does government truly remain neutral when so many secular matters frequently intersect, conflict, and combine with one's religious beliefs and practices? Is it even possible?

The authors of the First Amendment tried to state it simply: Government may neither advance nor inhibit the exercise of religion. It must remain neutral. But there is nothing simple about defining what neutrality means in complicated cases. Does it mean that if a law happens to benefit society at large, but also one religion in particular in a limited situation, courts must declare the law unconstitutional? Must the law change to benefit all religions equally? Are we to have an ultra-strict neutrality where no law can in any way benefit or hinder any religion? (This could harm many churches since they need some of the same benefits that secular corporations and businesses enjoy.) Should we instead have a more fluid neutrality that allows for indirect accommodations to religious groups as part of the making of our civil laws?

Neutral laws also have *effects* that are decidedly non-neutral. As our government provides for the needs of citizens, the neutrality of the Establishment Clause can conflict with the neutrality of the Free Exercise Clause. For example, if government subsidizes education for all Americans, does the Free Exercise Clause require it to neutrally include or deny aid to religious citizens wanting to go to religious schools? How do we handle these situations?

Over the years, many Christians have become very disturbed as the Supreme Court has tried to put this neutrality principle into practice in sensitive religious areas. For example, to protect school children from various violations of the Establishment Clause, the Court invalidated:

- Use of clergy-led, nondenominational prayer at middle school and high school graduations;[23]
- A statute authorizing a daily moment of silence for prayer in school classrooms;[24]
- A statute requiring that a copy of the Ten Commandments be posted in every classroom;[25]
- A statute prohibiting the teaching of evolution in state-funded schools;[26]

- A statute requiring Bible reading and recitation of the Lord's Prayer before class in public schools;[27]
- A requirement that willing students recite a voluntary, nondenominational prayer drafted by the state and used in public schools each day;[28] and
- A school's practice of allowing religious instruction on school property during the school day.[29]

State courts are following suit. In 1993, the Michigan Federal District court held that a framed print of artist Walter Sallman's *Head of Christ*, displayed for thirty years in the hallway of Bloomingdale Secondary School, violated the Establishment Clause. The court ordered it removed despite argument that Jesus was a notable historical figure who had an enormous influence on American culture, law, and history and deserved such non-religious commemoration.[30] Commenting on this decision, one lawyer complained: "No other person in human history has influenced the West and the United States more deeply than the simple carpenter from Nazareth. No other person has had more influence on American culture, history and philosophy than this itinerant preacher. . . . It is standard practice to honor those who have made valuable contributions to our history and culture by placing plaques, statues, photographs or pictures in a prominent place for all to see and remember. If Jesus Christ does not fit that definition of secular influence, no one does."[31]

There are few Christians reading cases like these who do not inwardly cringe and worry that our courts are going too far. Too many of today's judges are almost trying to sanitize public schools from any religious influence—which conceivably promotes atheism.

Added to these concerned citizens are a growing number of dismayed parents who object to their children's participation in sex education classes that endorse the use of condoms without mention of or sufficient emphasis on abstinence, thereby implicitly approving of premarital sex.

Court critics correctly point out that freedom *of* religion does not mean freedom *from* religion. Many judges would agree in principle with this statement, but somehow it has taken a little twist in our courts. In striving to maintain neutrality, are our judges embracing a standard with perpetual, internal conflict? They want to ensure freedom *of* religion for those who want to participate, *and* freedom *from* religion for those who do not. But this is a virtually impossible task! Trying to please all the people with vastly different value systems usually results in pleasing none—all of the time!

How Do Courts Draw the Line on Religious Freedoms?

Many argue that religious freedom means equal treatment of religion and non-religion. This leaves voluntary choices about religion for each American to make as he or she sees fit. Sounds good, right? But over the years, the issues of what separation, equality, and choice really mean in a variety of different situations have been extremely difficult to sort out. This is especially true as governmental regulation has become so complex and pervasive. As governmental influence increases in a nation that separates affairs of church and state, is America unwittingly squeezing religion into a corner in public life? And are our courts speeding up this process? Are they moving from respecting a long-standing separation of church and state, to separating church from public life?

THE LEMON TEST

Over many decades American civil courts developed some legal rules and guidelines to help apply constitutional principles to the divisive problems and thorny conflicts that arise between governmental regulation and religious freedoms.

For example, in trying to determine what violates the Establishment Clause, the U.S. Supreme Court devised a three-part constitutional review of civil laws called the "Lemon Test."[32] To be constitutional, the law must:

A. Have a secular, rather than religious, purpose

B. As its principal or primary effect, neither advance, nor inhibit, religion (with any benefit to religion, according to later court decisions, being merely indirect, remote and incidental)

C. Not involve any excessive governmental entanglement with religion.

But, in applying this test to many cases, the courts reach inconsistent results.

Many legislatures are clever enough to satisfy the requirement of part A, even if a law does have a religious goal. Politicians can always find some secular reason to disguise and justify a law impacting on religion in a positive or negative manner.

The greatest problem arises with compliance in parts B and C above. Controversy frequently arises over whether any advancement of religion is a direct, or merely an incidental, effect of any government action. But this brings up a catch-22 dilemma. As government involves itself more deeply in making inquiries about the effect of a law that impacts in any way on religion, excessive entanglements between government and religion occur. That violates part C. How can the government intrude into any religious operation *without* becoming *excessively* entangled in some way? For example, consider again how the Ohio Civil Rights Commission made numerous requests for documents and information as part of its investigation of the Dayton Christian School (discussed in chap. 4).

This Lemon Test is now under severe criticism among some of the Supreme Court Justices.[33] It delves into the facts of a case and tries to determine the specific effects of a challenged law or action. Some justices say this goes too far and leads to inconsistent court decisions. Instead, they argue, the test of constitutionality should be whether the law or action actively embraces or *coerces* one to become involved in a particular religion. The only question considered under this *coercion* test is whether a law targets a particular religious group or practice. If it does, it is probably unconstitutional. If it does not, the law may stand. Again, there is no agreement even among the justices in our highest Court on where the line should be drawn.

THE TEST OF PERMISSIBLE GOVERNMENT RESTRAINTS

But what about a law that clearly does burden one's religious beliefs? In those instances the courts require the government to prove:

- The extent of the law's impact upon the exercise of a religious belief;
- That it has a compelling public interest in enforcing the law (since not enforcing it would endanger or adversely affect many more people in society);
- The type and level of burden imposed is the minimum restriction required to achieve the law's purpose; and
- Application and enforcement of the law applies to everyone in a manner that does not discriminate against religion.

These factors interrelate with each other. If the government enacts a law that hinders anyone's religious freedom, the more important the "compelling public interest" must be to keep the law in place. Predictably, many courts disagree on how to apply these factors consistently.

MAJOR RECENT U.S. SUPREME COURT DECISIONS

During the past fifteen years, the U.S. Supreme Court reviewed religious freedom cases more frequently than any other appeals. In fact, in the span of just two weeks in 1993, the sharply divided Court decided three cases of major significance involving religious freedoms.

First, in *Zobrest v. California Foothills School District*,[34] the sharply divided Court voted 5-4 to approve use of federal funds (distributed to states for the educational needs of handicapped children) to pay for a sign-language interpreter accompanying a deaf student to classes at a Salpointe Catholic High School in Tucson, Arizona. By using public funds to provide an interpreter for a religious school student, was the government supporting religion?

Attorneys for the Zobrest family argued that a professional interpreter is nothing more objectionable than providing a student with a hearing aid. The interpreter is not a teacher or authority figure promoting religious beliefs. Justice Scalia asked counsel for the school district if employment of an interpreter was any different from employment of a school bus driver. The school's lawyer insisted there was a large difference: The bus driver would not be saying, "Jesus Christ was the son of God and that He died for our sins."

The Court found that using federal funds to pay for this interpreter did not create any special incentive to attend the religious school. There was no governmental decision-making involved in sending the interpreter to the school. The student involved made the decision to attend—not the interpreter. The student directly received financial aid—not the school (which the Supreme Court consistently rejected as unconstitutional during the 1980s). This successfully promoted equality between religion and non-religion, and respected the value of individual religious choice.

Since the Court's decision, legal scholars have pointed out some inconsistencies presented by the *Zobrest* case and earlier decisions by the Supreme Court. The Court allowed government-employed speech and hearing therapists to go to religious schools, but it also held that secular remedial teachers and counselors may not work in such schools. In other rulings, the Court prohibited public school buses from transporting children to and from religious schools but allowed their use for field trips by such schools. Religious schools may use public funds to purchase secular textbooks, but not slide projectors, tape recorders, and record players. Can you see why many believe the justices of our Supreme Court are trying to dance on the head of a pin in making some of these First Amendment decisions?

In the second case, *Lamb's Chapel v. Center Moriches Union Free School District*,[35] the Court unanimously ruled that there is no First Amendment barrier to after-hours use of a Long Island public school by the Lamb's Chapel evangelical church to show the public (without charge) a film series by Dr. James Dobson entitled *Turn Your Heart Toward Home*, which focuses on Christian family values. The Court used the Lemon Test to find that the film had a secular purpose of addressing common family problems. It did not have a principal or primary effect of advancing or inhibiting religion. It did not foster an excessive entanglement with religion. (The Court's ultimate decision rested on the church's First Amendment right to freedom of speech rather than on the Religion Clauses, however.)

New York law permitted use of school facilities for social, civic, and recreational meetings, and other uses pertaining to the welfare of the community. But the school district believed this could not include any church-sponsored functions. Using this logic, the school could permit atheists to use a classroom to denounce religion, but not permit programs that praise religion. Even if ten atheists were to debate one minister, one Supreme Court justice suggested, the school might exclude the debate. The mere addition of a minister to the debate would cause the school board to forbid it.

Counsel for the church successfully argued that the school board was simply discriminating on the basis of religious points of view. It was an open forum except for any religious viewpoint. The equal right of expressive opportunity under the First Amendment's free speech clause did not allow public officials to choose the messages they would, or would not, tolerate. Since the school made its property available after hours for a wide range of social and recreational uses, it could not bar a group from using the property for religious ends.

In the third major case, *Church of the Lukumi Babalu Aye v. City of Hialeah (Florida)*,[36] the Court justices divided into four separate groups, unable to agree on the reasons for deciding that four Hialeah city ordinances that prohibit animal sacrifices were unconstitutional. These laws singled out and prevented members of a Santeria church from conducting such sacrifices in their religious activities.[37] If the intent of these ordinances legitimately addressed animal cruelty issues, the restrictions did not prevent other animal slaughters such as for kosher sacrifice, extermination for humanitarian reasons, automobile roadkills, or activities of sport hunters. On the contrary, when the Church of Lukumi Babalu Aye announced plans to build a house of worship in Hialeah, the city responded by enacting the animal sacrifice laws with that particular religious group in mind.

The Court held that if Hialeah's true concern was cruelty to animals or unsanitary conditions, it had to regulate *all* conduct creating such risks. Therefore, although the justices had different reasons for doing so, they agreed in invalidating the ordinances as unconstitutional and violating the Free Exercise Clause of the First Amendment.

STOPPING THE COURT: THE RELIGIOUS FREEDOM RESTORATION ACT

Despite the *Hialeah* case, the Supreme Court has been reluctant to shield religious citizens from laws that apply to everyone. In a 1990 decision, *Employment Division, Department of Human Resources of Oregon v. Smith*,[38] the Court ruled that a state may deny unemployment benefits to American Indians who have been discharged from work for using a hallucinogenic herb (peyote) as part of their religious ceremonies. The Court held that a drug-related law of neutral and general application may be acceptable even if it incidentally restricts a religious practice. The government did *not* have to show a compelling public interest to justify the law in that instance.

Why is this case dangerous for Christians? The Court seemed to ignore its own legal tests of constitutionality by not requiring the government to show a *compelling* public interest to overcome a law's burden on religion. Don't let the drug-related nature of the case fool you. The next case could involve a law making one of your church's activities illegal.

The *Smith* decision created confusion and turmoil. To counteract it, and after a three-year campaign by a coalition of many religious and civil rights groups, Congress passed the Religious Freedom Restoration Act (RFRA)[39] (signed into law by President Clinton on November 16, 1993). This act, in effect, reversed the *Smith* decision. It *requires* courts in the future to hold a law that affects religion to be unconstitutional unless a compelling public interest exists *and* the law uses the least restrictive means of achieving its purpose.[40]

THE COURT'S SEARCH FOR ANSWERS

Now if you were a judge, would these legal guidelines be enough for you to fairly and *consistently* decide thousands of complicated religious freedom cases and determine what is constitutional and what is not? Justice O'Connor does not think so:

> It is always appealing to look for a single test, a Grand Unified Theory that would resolve all the cases that may arise under a particular clause. There is, after all, only one Establishment Clause, one Free Speech Clause, one Fourth Amendment, one Equal Protection Clause.... But the same constitutional principle may operate differently in different contexts.... And setting forth a unitary test for a broad set of cases may sometimes do more harm than good. Any test that must deal with widely disparate situations risks being so vague as to be useless.... Moreover, shoehorning new problems into a test that does not reflect the special concerns raised by those problems tends to deform the language of the test. Relatively simple phrases like [those used in the Lemon Test] acquire more and more complicated definitions which stray ever further from their literal meaning.[41]

———

Courts will always struggle in reconciling constitutional issues that involve religion. The First Amendment protections do conflict if extended to their logical conclusions. If the Establishment Clause prohibits posting the Ten Commandments on a wall in a public school, for example, would the Free Exercise Clause also prohibit posting of secular commandments directly hostile to one's religion? Is it any wonder that church and state are destined to battle more and more in the future? This is especially true as America drifts into moral and spiritual apathy and loses touch with its religious roots.

A WINDOW IN THE WALL OF SEPARATION BETWEEN CHURCH AND STATE

Confusion exists in our courts. How can they interpret and apply the First Amendment? Coupled with this dilemma is increasing public pressure on legislatures and courts to restrain churches from perceived discrimination against homosexuals or women, counseling against abortions, and similar controversies. Legislators and judges feel pressure to find ways around constitutional safeguards and to impose secular laws on religious groups.

One way church-related groups feel the pinch involves a loss of tax exemptions. If the government cannot run American churches that have religious practices contrary to certain civil laws, some believe it does not have to extend benefits to those churches. If the government does not like the way your church conducts its business, it could revoke your group's tax exemption. Consider how it affected the religious groups in the next two cases:

The Bob Jones University Case

Bob Jones University, a religious school, had a rule against interracial dating among students. The IRS revoked its tax exemption in 1976 because of racially discriminatory practices and then sued the school for $490,000 in unpaid taxes. In upholding the exemption termination, the U.S. Supreme Court ruled that, notwithstanding any alleged religious tenets underlying racial discrimination, the government had an overriding and compelling interest in ending race discrimination in schools.[42]

The Pierce Creek Church Case

To secure and maintain tax-exempt status with the Internal Revenue Service, an exempt organization must not participate in any prohibited activities such as political activity.[43] Pastor Daniel J. Little of The Pierce Creek Church, a small congregation in Binghamton, New York, found this out the hard way.

Pastor Little's congregation spent nearly $50,000 to take out full-page advertisements in *USA Today* and the *Washington Times* before the 1992 presidential election. The ad, with many biblical citations, had a heading entitled, "Christian Beware" and posed the question whether readers knew that then-Governor Clinton supported abortion on demand (Exod. 20:13; Lev. 20:1–5), homosexual rights (Exod. 20:14; Lev. 20:13; Rom. 1:26–27), and distribution of condoms to teenagers in public schools (Exod. 20:12; Col. 3:5; Rom. 1:28–32). The ad then asked, "How can we expect God to bless our economy if we plunge down a path of immorality? (Deut. 28)." The statement closed with the notation that the Bible warns not to follow man in his sin, nor help him promote sin or God will chasten us

(Deut. 13; Jer. 23; Prov. 4:14; 11:21; 16:5; 1 Tim. 5:22). It concluded with the question, "How then can we vote for Bill Clinton?"

After the advertisement ran, Pastor Little's church received a notice from the IRS. The notice warned that the church's tax exempt status was in jeopardy. The pastor responded to the IRS with some choice words:

> If a church is recognized as being tax exempt, does this mean that the church can no longer use its funds to warn other Christians of perceived dangers if those dangers are in some way connected to anything political? . . . Because the IRS recognizes us as being tax exempt, can the IRS now say to our church, "You cannot communicate warnings to the church at large about the dangers of abandoning the established moral law of the Holy Bible?" Are you saying that because the abandonment of these biblically established moral laws is now political policy that these moral issues have been lifted out of the church's domain?[44]

———

Withholding government benefits, such as tax exemptions, from churches and religious schools that involve themselves in current social and political activities is a very troublesome problem. It chills one's religious beliefs and practices. On the other hand, as the late Senator Sam Ervin once said, churches and religious schools should not expect "to use the taxes of Caesar to finance the things of God."[45] (Tax exemptions allow church organizations to use funds in their ministries at the government's expense in lost tax revenues.) Furthermore, some see the tax exemption as a trade-off. It prevents excessive government intrusion into church matters by avoiding any need to examine church income sources and records,[46] while also keeping churches from engaging in partisan politics without accountability. But termination of religious tax exemptions will remain a political threat to church-related groups as we move into the twenty-first century.

WHY THE CLASH BETWEEN CHURCH AND STATE SHOULD CONCERN YOU

Like it or not, America is drifting away from its religious roots and Christian heritage. And like it or not, agnostic or atheistic men and women who are insensitive to the moral beliefs of many Americans rule our government and enact and enforce our laws.

People in our judicial system change. Laws change. Our elected officials change. The only constant we have as Americans is our ageless Constitution and Bill of Rights. The principles in these precious documents, and in Scripture, have *not* changed (although many use strained interpretations to change the words and meaning). Our constitutional rights as Americans are the only protection (recognized by the non-religious world) that we have against tyranny and oppression against our faith and religious practices.

We cannot trust the courts in an unbelieving world to protect our religious freedoms. Our courts may understand *why* the founding fathers adopted the First Amendment, but they cannot agree on *how it applies.* The nine justices who form our nation's highest Court cannot agree on how to consistently mete out First Amendment justice to hundreds of millions of Americans. In describing the Supreme Court's process of review in one case, one justice noted that the mountains have labored and brought forth a mouse.[47]

The courts are splitting hairs on religious issues as well. If you claim protection under the Religion Clauses, some courts may investigate whether you really are religious enough to qualify for this protection. Although the Supreme Court has warned that courts must not presume to determine the plausibility of a religious belief,[48] many federal and state courts continue to do just that.[49] If your religion fails the court's test, or if you do not sincerely believe in the tenets of your faith and practice it, some courts may deny you your First Amendment freedoms!

Other courts will read the First Amendment and construe it to mean the exact opposite of what it says. For example, before an appeal reversed the decision, a Federal District Court reviewed an Alabama school prayer law in *Jaffree v. Board of School Commissioners of Mobile County* and determined, after reviewing at length some "newly discovered historical evidence," that "the Establishment Clause of the First Amendment to the United States Constitution does not prohibit the state from establishing a religion."[50] Some courts are not above ruling that constitutional provisions do not mean precisely what they say!

As Lynn Buzzard and Thomas S. Brandon Jr. pointed out in their excellent and very scholarly book, *Church Discipline and the Courts*:

> The level of court intrusion into the church's life is clear and multiple. It touches basic doctrinal issues including the nature and meaning of membership, the duties imposed by biblical passages such as Matthew 18 in regard to the discipline of members, the sort of conduct that properly results in the discipline of members whether or not they choose to quit before the process is complete, the moral weight given different types of conduct, and the right of a church to develop its own administrative rules and internal organizational structures—that is, its own constitution and by-laws.[51]

90

Any case involving religious freedoms these days swings on its own merits and the religious, political, or philosophical background of the judges reviewing the case.

Will our legislatures bail us out of this dilemma? Don't bet on it! As Federal Court of Appeals Judge Edith H. Jones warns: "[A]s weak believers mistakenly seek solutions from a secular government, they turn over our freedom to it, and they discover that the government has not grown more just, or society more humane, but quite the opposite. The secular state consumes the power it is allotted, hungers for more, and begins to crush believers who stand in its way."[52]

Given the religious bias and confusion in our courts and legislatures, what happens when members of religious organizations sue their leaders in court? It reinforces this bias and confusion. It also encourages more suppression of our religious freedoms. Claims for defamation, invasion of privacy, and infliction of emotional distress against churches continue to arise despite the admonitions of 1 Corinthians 6:1–8. This not only shows a lack of faith but a crass selfishness and greed rooted in revenge. It ignores Christian principles of turning the other cheek, blessing those who persecute us, and leaving vengeance to God.

WHAT'S ON THE HORIZON?

Believe it. The wall of separation between church and state, in place over the past two hundred years, is crumbling away. Trouble is on the horizon for religious organizations. Why? Too many church leaders are derelict in their duties and responsibilities in handling church problems fairly, diligently, and decisively. As our leaders fail, neglect, or refuse to follow the basic principles of their faith, believers get fed up with the inertia and apathy. We are unwittingly forcing church members out into the world of civil litigation for relief. So more church leaders and religious organizations must make themselves vulnerable to expensive and time-consuming lawsuits. Even if a defense succeeds, the expense and upset of defending a lawsuit destroys too many ministries.

On the state's side of the wall of separation, courts are confused about where to draw the line between noninterference and judicial involvement. There will be more pressure for our courts to retreat from finding a compelling public interest whenever laws burden our free exercise of religion once again. There will be more pressure on the courts to review religious beliefs and make determinations as to whether the beliefs are legitimate enough to qualify for constitutional protection.

Nonreligious citizens already clamor in our legislatures for laws forbidding various religious practices under the cloak of civil rights antidiscrimination legislation. Expect even more of this to happen in the future. There will be more calls for administrative reviews and involvement by state and federal agencies whenever anyone alleges discrimination (as in the *Dayton Christian School* case discussed in chap. 4).

Legislators will grow weary of having to draft laws around an increasing number of widely diverse religions that they do not understand and perhaps even personally abhor. There will be more pressure to revoke tax exemptions of religious organizations (as in the *Bob Jones University* case, and the *Pierce Creek Church* dispute with the IRS) due to a failing economy and an astronomical federal deficit.

Instead of holding to a position of neutrality (with some accommodations for religion), our government may become more hostile to religion. Many government officials will bow to vocal and powerful anti-Christianity lobbyists. As governmental influence affects many more aspects of our private lives, there will be a concerted effort by some to sanitize our schools and all other public places of any religious influences. This will drive many believers deeper into a religious underground and a bunker mentality.

From both sides of the wall of separation, people already are taking pickaxes and chipping away. If the wall comes down, it will, as the Supreme Court has already noted, "destroy government and . . . degrade religion" with the inevitable hatred, disrespect, and even contempt for religion *and* government. We are already seeing the birth pains of this event in America.

Many concerned believers are fighting hard on the civil law side of the wall to defend the religious liberties that are guaranteed by our Constitution. But on the church side, we need to become more active in peacefully resolving our disputes within our church circles. Christian leaders need to put admonitions such as Matthew 18:15–17 and 1 Corinthians 6:1–8 into regular practice. This means relying, from start to finish, on an active love, grace, mercy, and forgiveness to reconcile believers and purify our churches from sinful influences. Quickly casting sensitive church-related disputes before judges and juries who may not understand the nature of religious conflict threatens the religious freedoms of everyone in America.

We must begin resolving conflicts according to Scripture with the help of spiritual men and women, as guaranteed by our Constitution, rather than seek imperfect and inconsistent justice from courts of unbelievers.

Questions for Personal Reflection

1. How much do I know about the Supreme Court's influence on my life?

2. Am I concerned about the erosion of religious freedoms in America?

3. Will I stand up and resist any law that jeopardizes my beliefs?

4. Am I praying for America and God's protection of our religious liberties?

5. With the influence of unbelievers in government, what can I do to counteract the resulting bias and discrimination?

Chapter 6

Shall We Kill All the Lawyers?

Choose any national problem area that makes your blood boil—politicians, IRS, liberal civil rights advocates, news media—but you will not rival America's love/hate relationship with lawyers. In this chapter, we lift the hood of our justice system and see how the engine runs with lawyers doing various tasks—not all of them well.

ౢ

For some, being a lawyer in America today is like being a fire hydrant at a dog show. Even Jesus had his complaints:

> You experts in the law, woe to you, because you load people down with burdens they can hardly carry, and you yourselves will not lift one finger to help them. . . . Woe to you experts in the law, because you have taken away the key to knowledge. You yourselves have not entered, and you have hindered those who were entering. (Luke 11:46, 52)

_____

No wonder that the lawyers, from this point on, opposed Jesus fiercely. They besieged Him with questions, waiting to catch Him in something He might say (Luke 11:53–54).

America is very skeptical of lawyers. Lexington, N.C., attorney Charles H. Harp II was lunching in the Bible Belt hamlet of Denton some years ago when a fellow diner said chidingly, "Woe be unto doctors and lawyers!" Harp asked the man if he knew that Joseph of Arimathea, a lawyer, was the one who took Jesus' body away from the cross, prepared it for burial, and provided Him with a grave when no one else would. "No," the man quickly replied. "But he probably did that hoping he would get to handle the estate!"[1]

Respect for lawyers is waning. Franklin County, Ohio, Judge Tommy Thompson once entered his courtroom to find a defendant standing with his lawyer. The judge inquired about a tattoo on the man's arm. "It's a seven-edged dagger," the defendant explained. "It represents the seven laws of God." Judge Thompson then asked what the number 13 tattooed below the dagger represented. "This courtroom," the man replied. "There are twelve members of the jury, the judge, and my half-witted attorney," said the defendant.[2]

Whom do most people blame for the litigation overload? Lawyers. The December 1994 issue of *Omni* magazine included a cartoon entitled "The Hallelawyer Chorus." It features a variety of lawyers joyously singing in a group between two Christmas trees, "And we shall sue forever and ever."[3]

"LET'S KILL ALL THE LAWYERS"

You've seen that on T-shirts, coffee cups, and bumper stickers, right? Maybe you thought to yourself that it was a pretty good idea. Surprisingly, the remark about killing all the lawyers comes from William Shakespeare's pen in *Henry VI*. The line is not spoken by a character who has been fleeced or treated badly by a lawyer, however. Conspirators in Cade's Rebellion spoke these words as they planned to overthrow the English government, revoke the freedoms of the people, and set up a dictatorship. Shakespeare used this threat by the rebels to remind his audience that lawyers are defenders of liberty against forces of rebellion. Thus, oppression of the people would require oppressors to kill the lawyers who oppose them.

But many believe America has too many lawyers. Too many lawyers, the public reasons, will stir up trouble in order to create their own demand "as if doctors went around injecting diseases for other doctors to cure," as one commentator observed.[4] In the movie *Adam's Rib*, the neighbor of a husband-and-wife legal team played by Spencer Tracy and Katharine Hepburn expressed the sentiment of many: "Lawyers should never marry other lawyers," he declared. "This is called inbreeding, from which comes idiot children and more lawyers."

Movies and television portray lawyers as mouthpieces for criminals that are freed on mysterious "legal technicalities" while police wring their hands in frustration. Matthew Hodel once noted, "Hollywood, of course, finds lawyers to be endlessly and perversely fascinating. See the cynical lawyer transform the devil incarnate into the victim of wrongful eviction and create a landlord's nightmare (*Pacific Heights*). Next, his weakness leads to infidelity and brings terror upon his family (*Fatal Attraction*). Over the years, this cad mentally tortures his spouse (*Diary of a Mad Housewife*). His only hope of ever being normal is to first suffer total amnesia (*Regarding Henry*)."[5]

Many people have a love/hate relationship with lawyers. They love an opportunity to bash lawyers. And they hate missing a second chance to do it again. You've heard the lawyer jokes: "What's the difference between a dead skunk and a dead lawyer in the middle of the road? There are skid marks in front of the skunk." Poet Carl Sandburg once remarked that no tears are shed as a lawyer's body is borne to the grave. Others joke that lawyers should be buried twelve feet in the ground instead of the usual six feet. Why? Because deeper down some lawyers are good people.

Regrettably, there is a crisis of confidence in my profession. Lawyers have a negative public image. It is no secret that lawyers are no longer held in high regard. In a 1993 survey of 815 people across the country conducted by the *National Law Journal*, by a wide margin respondents believed that more lawyers will go to hell than to heaven. When asked to name the top five lawyers they admired most, 52 percent of the respondents said they could not think of anyone, did not admire any lawyers at all, or did not know. Among those stating a preference, one lawyer was fictional and two were dead. Abraham Lincoln and U.S. Attorney General Janet Reno lost to Perry Mason, but did manage to squeeze out a close win over TV's folksy lawyer Matlock (portrayed by Andy Griffith).[6]

Why do people hate lawyers? One commentator offered up these reasons:

> What's at the root of America's animosity toward the Bar? Confusion and anger, for one thing. Many Americans accuse the legal system of betraying our most dearly held convictions about fairness, justice and truth—undermining the belief that what is legal and what is right should be one and the same. Other complaints: There are too many lawyers; their fees are too high; cases take too long to resolve; some never go to court in the first place. Distasteful ads have contributed to the slide in image. . . . Moviegoers who once applauded lawyers immortalized by [Gregory] Peck, James Stewart and Spencer Tracy, now cheer when the *Tyrannosaurus Rex* consumes a cowering lawyer in an early scene in *Jurassic Park*.[7]

Despite these concerns, there are times when you need a trustworthy lawyer to help you. How do you feel about this situation? If you are like many others in a legal dispute, you may dread the personal risk of giving up some control over your affairs to a lawyer. You may feel vulnerable, exposed, and threatened by revealing unflattering secrets about your private life to your legal counselor. You may feel insecure in hiring a particular lawyer without being fully confident that you can trust him or her. Will your lawyer needlessly run up your bill? Will he or she be difficult to contact, fail to explain what is done for you, or confuse you with legal jargon? These concerns create anxiety.

What kind of lawyers do we need to reinspire the dream of our founding fathers and protect our freedom as Americans?

Vital Personal Qualities of Legal Counselors

Finding the right lawyer is important to resolving a legal dispute. You must feel comfortable with and trust whoever is going to represent you. But finding a lawyer whose temperament matches your own is critical.

From a legal standpoint, it is reasonable to expect lawyers to

- provide high quality legal work;
- consistently give a reasonably prompt reaction time in handling cases and responding to questions and concerns of clients;
- offer advice in simple English;
- counsel clients on options and alternatives and relative risks involved in reaching their goals within the law; and, above all,
- offer solutions to problems that keep litigation and legal expense to an absolute minimum.

Some lawyers are reluctant to share power with clients. They want almost exclusive control. They expect clients to follow their directions with a minimum of questioning. Other lawyers listen patiently to clients and answer endless questions. They try to fulfill their stated desires for the case, share decision-making responsibilities, and encourage client participation in preparing the case. But this type of patience often comes with a price—it can mean increased legal fees for the client.

Find out what type of lawyer your candidate is *before* you commit to any representation. If someone does not inspire confidence, keep looking. But seeking a qualified and competent lawyer is not enough.[8] It is as important to consider a lawyer's *personal* qualities. After all, an attorney's character, habits, and prejudices color his or her actions to, and for, the client. On a personal level, lawyers should have the following qualities:

Scrupulous Honesty and Integrity

All lawyers struggle with a basic conflict of interest. There is a delicate balance between the interests of clients and the advancement of a lawyer's career. Therefore it is very tempting, in tough economic times, with cutthroat competition for business, to put the client's best interests aside.

A partner in a now-defunct national law firm once said, "Praise your adversary; he is your friend. Curse your client; he is your enemy." This person is selfishly thinking more about generating legal work for that firm than professionally serving the needs of the client.

Those who fall prey to these pressures cultivate various deceits. They exaggerate legal qualifications, dodge responsibilities, pad bills, unnecessarily run up legal time, and tell "white lies." Lawyers who work in this manner believe that "lies are necessary in order to live," to paraphrase

Nietzsche. But in his 1847 address to the Charleston, South Carolina Bar Association, Daniel Webster rebuked this attitude: "Tell me a man is dishonest, and I will answer he is no lawyer. He cannot be, because he is careless and reckless of justice; the law is not in his heart, and is not the standard and rule of his conduct."[9]

Traditionally, lawyers are officers of the court in a judicial system pledged to a continuing search for truth. This responsibility goes back to Medieval England, when lawyers were "servants at law of our lord, the King." Since some lawyers today do not cherish honesty and integrity to the same degree as their predecessors, the legal profession has lost public confidence. Most lawyers, however, are honorable men and women. But you can only judge the character of a man by how he treats others who can do nothing for him or to him.

Honesty and integrity will keep your attorney from routinely assuring you that everything is fine when issues and problems warrant caution. Honesty requires frank discussions and accurate appraisals of your case rather than unfounded promises. Without honesty and integrity, you, your lawyer, your case, and your credibility with the court will suffer. A good lawyer will give you the respect and loyalty that is vital to your relationship.

Sensitive and Perceptive Communication

If your attorney is unable to write clearly or speak persuasively, the best legal arguments will be to no avail. Lawyers who speak with clarity and precision and who use focused, persuasive, succinct arguments are desperately needed in our court system today. America needs enlightened individuals who strive to help people understand issues rather than give prepared speeches.

Vain, arrogant lawyers are not genuine in dealing with others. They fail to listen with empathy. Instead of communicating, they argue every point and protect their turf regardless of the cost to their client. They are rigid gladiators who consider compromise a personal defeat. They fail to respect their fellow lawyers. Personal baggage destroys their effectiveness, preventing them from helping others.

Good Judgment and Common Sense

Those who are knowledgeable about hiring lawyers often rank good judgment about human nature above technical knowledge of the law. A brilliant lawyer who gives impeccable legal opinions may alienate others and destroy a client's case. There is no substitute for life experiences and the maturity that comes from understanding how and why people think and act in a particular way. We need lawyers who have empathy for others. We need those who understand issues and motivations of people in conflict while also appreciating the needs and desires of adversary parties, opposing counsel, witnesses, and the judge and jury. We need attorneys who keep their egos in check and zealously hold on to a rational perspective of a case rather than becoming emotionally overwhelmed with the action and competition in court. The best lawyer will be a person who exercises mature judgment, who reflects on decisions before actions are taken, and who relies heavily on moral as well as legal reasoning.

Disciplined Toughness

While good lawyers must be objective, perceptive, communicative, and rational, they also should be tough, but fair, and feel comfortable negotiating settlement agreements or addressing the court. When circumstances require aggressive action, they must rise promptly and reasonably to the challenge. Lawyers who are wishy-washy or fear tough negotiations do not inspire confidence. Suspicious and fearful lawyers do not give direct answers and question why they have been asked particular questions. They make themselves vulnerable to others who may see this weakness and exploit it.

Disciplined toughness does not require an arrogant or belligerent attitude. Some say a lawyer should be like a velvet-covered brick. There should be a sensitivity and keen awareness of the conflict between adversaries facing litigation coupled with a firm and uncompromising stand against dishonest exploitation, duplicity, or cruelty in the legal process on anyone's part.

Creativity in Finding Constructive Solutions

Any competent lawyer can take the existing facts and mold them into an argument that will win at all costs. A *good* lawyer will always be solution-oriented whenever problems arise with the goal of reducing litigation time and expense. He or she always will explore reasonable compromises—especially in volatile, but easily defused, situations. The wise lawyer continually reviews options and alternatives. He or she resolves petty issues quickly through concessions and compromise, while focusing on the truly important matters in dispute rather than on minor issues.

A lawyer with the personal qualities listed above is rare, but not impossible to find. He or she does not have to be a Christian, but it certainly helps. This is especially true if you are a Christian. Your lawyer can understand your motivations better if he or she is a Christian.

Bradley P. Jacob, executive director of the Christian Legal Society, eloquently noted the advantage of having a Christian lawyer: "Christianity is not a Sunday-morning religion that leaves our daily professional lives unchanged. Accepting Christ as Savior and Lord means serving Him in all aspects of our lives. For lawyers, this means that questions of ethics, priorities, lifestyle, interpersonal relationships, money management, career choices and even substantive legal issues are analyzed from a different perspective than that of non-Christian attorneys."[10]

THE ROLE OF LEGAL COUNSELORS AS COMFORTERS AND HEALERS

We desperately need more lawyers who are *comforters.* We need legal counselors who help people who are in turmoil and distress move beyond their disputes and conflicts with a minimum of expense and emotional trauma. A gifted lawyer gently consoles stressed-out clients who are angry, broke and broken, hurt and confused as they face unwanted legal expense, unproductive delays in securing resolution of a dispute, and possible loss or destruction of their livelihoods. He or she shields these clients from opposing counsel, unnecessary case complications, and people who will foment strife and derail settlement.

We need more legal counselors who are *healers*—men and women who treat their clients *and* their opponents with kindness, courtesy, respect, and humanity. This means using the law with logic, fairness, reason, and empathy to restore, remedy, and reconcile social and personal wounds as fairly and peacefully as possible. Those who begin working on a case with belligerence close the door to reason.

In 2 Samuel 12, Nathan gives us an excellent example of what a lawyer's demeanor should be as he confronts King David. Read verses 1–14 and note the ways in which Nathan met confidentially with David to deal with an intolerable situation. He marshalled the facts and was aware of the problem, but he listened to understand David's mind-set. He was creative in helping David face his responsibility in a very firm, yet loving, manner. Notice Nathan's character and integrity as he courageously challenged the king! As a result, Nathan's approach did not distract David, who experienced a personal catharsis and repented.

There are individuals in the legal profession who are conflict-resolvers, healers and peacemakers. These comforters sweetly oil our social systems and keep everything from coming to a grinding halt.

Lawyers with these qualities are the true professionals who hold to this creed:

> I revere the law, the judicial system, and the legal profession and will, at all times in my professional and private life, uphold the dignity and esteem of each. I will further my profession's devotion to public service and to the public good. I will strictly

adhere to the spirit as well as the letter of my profession's code of ethics, to the extent that the law permits, and will at all times be guided by a fundamental sense of honor, integrity and fair play. I will not knowingly misstate, distort, or improperly exaggerate any fact or opinion and will not improperly permit my silence or inaction to mislead anyone. I will conduct myself to assure the just, speedy and inexpensive determination of every action and resolution of every controversy. I will abstain from all rude, disruptive, disrespectful, and abusive behavior, and will at all times act with dignity, decency, and courtesy. I will respect the time and commitments of others. I will be diligent and punctual in communicating with others and in fulfilling commitments. I will exercise independent judgment and will not be governed by a client's ill will or deceit. My word is my bond.[11]

———

When litigation is inevitable, clients need to search out and hire more of these men and women whose word is their bond. Unfortunately, many disputing parties ignore these ideals. They hurt themselves, their cases, and the entire justice system by looking for lawyers of the lowest common denominator. There is a strange attraction to those lawyers who seek to delay or deny justice by distorting the true nature of advocacy in pursuit of the personal pleasure of winning at all costs.

AN ADVOCATE OR A LIAR?

Although I have handled court litigation in the past, I do so no longer. There are many personal reasons for my decision to practice business law.

I see most litigation as a destructive process that brings defeat for all parties concerned. One party sues another with the goal of getting something from that other person. Usually the parties butt heads with each other at enormous expense over months or years, involving hundreds, and even thousands, of other people who feed off this destruction.

Contrast this situation with a real estate transaction, for example. The seller transfers a title to a buyer. A pleased seller receives the purchase price. The buyer is happy about receiving the property. Brokers bring the parties together and receive a commission for doing so with pleasure. Legal counsel for the seller and buyer receive fair fees (usually) for their work. The buyer usually improves the property in ways that make our communities better for years to come. Not so with litigation. There is a winner and a loser, but everyone loses in court in emotional and financial costs that often cannot be measured.

But the most disturbing aspect of litigation to me as a Christian lawyer is the very thin line between being an advocate and being a liar. A trial is a search for truth, but too often it is nothing more than a battle of wits between adversaries who try to best each other in court. Our justice system, which pits adversaries against each other, fails miserably in actively encouraging everyone to tell "the truth, the whole truth, and nothing but the truth" beyond merely mouthing these words when taking an oath in court. The "truth" established in a court of law may be totally unrecognizable when compared to objective truth in the larger sense of the word.[12]

Advocacy argues a client's position by defending or pleading the cause of that person before a court. Lawyer-advocates are not to tell an untruth deliberately, speak or act upon what is false to deceive others, or make intentional misstatements in representing others. In fact, as officers of the court we are bound by oath to obey stringent ethical standards that govern our professional conduct. We are guardians of the judicial process. Part of this solemn responsibility includes not bringing or defending a lawsuit if it is frivolous or intended to harass or intimidate anyone. It means not using delay tactics that frustrate or deny justifiable results for an opposing party or that bring our justice system into disrepute. It certainly bars offering any testimony or other evidence that a lawyer knows to be false.

True advocacy also requires that lawyers disclose to the court material facts in order to avoid aiding a criminal or fraudulent act by their clients. It also means showing the court any law known by the lawyer to be directly *adverse* to a client's position—even if opposing legal counsel fails to do so! Many lawyers protest, "Why should I do research and give my opponents good arguments to use against me? That's their job. My duty is to my client!" But this ignores a basic premise for a fair and impartial verdict.

A lawyer who falsely represents the law is being dishonest toward the court. Instead, lawyers should present to the court all the law that applies to a particular case in order to ensure a fair and legal decision. Yet how many lawyers practice this regularly?

An advocate must present a client's case with persuasive force. But performing this duty while maintaining client confidences, is secondary to the advocate's higher duty of truth and candor to the court. The foundation of our justice system is that legal argument is a *discussion* seeking to determine the relevant facts, apply the proper law, and achieve a just and reasonable decision. But many courts and lawyers have strayed far away from these foundational principles. Instead, they focus on the minutiae of individual cases and sell out to pragmatic solutions to problems in particular circumstances. Our failure to follow the principles and rules of justice our founding fathers handed down to us is creating havoc in our courts.

There is another problem with advocacy. Our justice system assumes that each litigating party has a reasonable, competent, and honest lawyer who will work with judges and juries in testing the accuracy and relevance of facts and documents and in making decisions based upon proper evidence. But quite often this isn't true. One party often has inadequate representation, resulting in an imbalance of advocacy. If counsel allows exclusions of important facts or fails to object to evidence that should be excluded, that party is denied justice. Imbalanced arguments distort the truth, keeping opposing forces from finding the middle ground of justice.

In an eighteen-month study polling more than 3,800 jurors who participated in trials at twelve Los Angeles Superior Court locations, Dr. Franklin Strier confirmed that mismatched attorneys had a profound effect on jurors. Dr. Strier found that 56 percent of the survey respondents believed that unequal attorney skills could affect the outcome of a case, and 35 percent believed the difference in skills probably affected the verdict in the actual case they deliberated.[13]

Wealthy clients often capitalize on mismatching attorneys. Consider the example of O. J. Simpson using his fortune to hire a team of the best lawyers and jury experts in America to battle with local Los Angeles prosecutors. To end the imbalance, the prosecutors must also team up and hire high-priced experts. Does stacking the deck like this promote justice? Does it limit the cost of litigation in our country or increase it? Situations like this lead to inconsistent judicial decisions and an inordinate amount of appeals to higher courts. Even then the justice system fails to root out the imbalance at times.

How does all this affect society? The premise of our existing adversary system is that active, partisan advocacy on all sides of a controversy brings out the truth and creates the best possible verdict for everyone concerned. When this does not happen, as often occurs for any number of reasons in a particular case, true justice fails. Improper advocacy leads to unjust results based upon distortion, and even suppression, of the truth. So many people today are asking, "Is our justice system reliable?"

But, aside from the inherent problems of potential imbalance in our adversarial court system, justice breaks down even faster at the hands of aggressive lawyer-advocates using questionable tactics to score a win in a case rather than to achieve a just verdict.

GAMES LAWYERS LOVE TO PLAY

Attorney M. Craig Massey expressed the regrets of many good lawyers by observing: "We have allowed the law and the use of the courts to become a game. It is not a means to the end of justice for everyone or for the parties in any singular case. It has become one of gamesmanship to see who can reach the best bottom line, notwithstanding the effect on one's client, much less the opponent's client. . . . This bottom line is money. The legal business, formerly a profession, has become one of seeking the best dollar return for the attorney, notwithstanding, again, its impact on whoever may be involved."[14] If you have a case you want shuffled quickly through the courts, think again. Here are only a few of the legal dodges working against you to create a crisis in our legal system:

Don't Expect Me to be Civil

Harvard Law School Professor Arthur Miller once said, "Lawyers owe complete allegiance to their client, very little to the system, and none at all to the adversary." Some clients praise lawyers who intimidate, threaten, and browbeat their opponents as good, tough, hardnosed litigators. Their goal is to crush their adversary financially and otherwise. But what happens? When the case is over, the lawyer gets paid and goes home to rest for another day. Meanwhile, clients may find a permanent wedge of hostility and distrust between them, their adversaries, and any common family members, friends, or business colleagues. This poisons relationships for years to come.

Sometimes lawyers love to play up to their clients by reflecting their ill will toward the adversary. When the client wants his or her attorney to abuse others or engage in offensive conduct directed to other counsel, parties or witnesses, the attorney gladly obliges since the client is the one paying the fee—not anyone else.

In a 1992 poll of California lawyers, 81 percent agreed that "hardball tactics and uncivil behavior" are on the rise in America.[15] But this eye-for-an-eye approach by upset and bitter clients pits hard-nosed lawyers against each other. This is like putting four cats in a bag—you'll have a fight that just won't quit! The better approach, I believe, is to hire a reasonable and fair attorney *regardless* of who your adversary chooses for a lawyer.

I Never Said That

In the Nixon Watergate years, the joke was, "Did you tape it? If not, then I never said it!" It has become commonplace, and even acceptable, to deny verbal agreements and to break promises. There are some lawyers who never keep their verbal, or even written, promises and agreements made with opposing counsel. If the lawyers reach a verbal understanding and put it in writing, the written account frequently differs from the oral understanding. Or someone makes changes by cleverly burying them into legitimate agreements without alerting other parties to the revisions.

I'm Going to Sue for Everything

A case dispute may be clear, and the truly relevant allegations easily stated in a summons and complaint, but some attorneys will not stop there. They fill their pleadings with every known legal theory of action known to humankind and then sue everyone in sight. Then, to escape such harassment, the opposing counsel tries to make the first attorney look like an idiot for bringing up all these legal issues. This causes attorneys to declare war on each other, creating even more conflict in a case.

Maybe the Case Will Settle; Maybe It Won't

To delay exchange of documents and information (called discovery) or a trial in a case, some lawyers will falsely hold out a chance of settlement to lure the opposing party into relaxing prosecution of their case.

Before I Agree to Anything, Prove It

Instead of stipulating to relevant and legally undisputed matters, some lawyers hold out on any such agreements with the other attorney solely to delay prosecution of the case.

I'll Flood You with Court Papers

This is a very popular harassment tactic of vindictive lawyers—using legal discovery measures to inundate and intimidate an opponent with requests for all kinds of documents and information irrelevant to the case.

Here Are My Court Papers and the Hearing's Tomorrow Morning

To make life difficult, some lawyers will time the filing or service of court papers on opposing counsel without allowing a reasonable opportunity to review the papers and respond.

I Need an Extension of Time to Respond

Some extensions are necessary, but some attorneys request delays solely to keep from having to deal with the issues in the case or to gain a tactical advantage. Delays tend to make a search for the truth much more difficult, and witnesses less accessible.

You Better Show Up or Else

Instead of working with opposing counsel in rescheduling court dates around good faith calendar conflicts such as other hearings, meetings, seminars, or vacations, some lawyers refuse to give any slack. They make life difficult by wearing down their adversaries personally.

I Had the Judge Cancel the Hearing

Some attorneys secretly cancel hearings at the last minute so opposing counsel spends time and expense in adjusting schedules. Their adversaries then go to court only to find it was a wasted trip.

I'm Taking Statements from Everyone Your Client Knows

Instead of taking depositions (questions and answers made under oath) only when necessary to discover relevant facts or preserve legitimate testimony, some abuse the legal process to harass or wear an opponent down through increased litigation time and expense.

My Client Won't Answer Your Questions

Sometimes a lawyer has every right to object to a question from opposing counsel to protect a client. But, on other occasions, it is another harassment tactic to make matters unnecessarily difficult for the opposing attorney. The failure to answer a reasonable deposition question means another trip to the courthouse for a hearing before an overworked judge and more delays and costs.

You Weren't Specific Enough

When opposing counsel submits a reasonable request for documents as part of discovery, some lawyers look for ways to hide evidence. They strain to interpret the request in an unreasonably artificial and restrictive manner to avoid disclosure.

In one recent case, lawyers for a doctor requested production of any documents from a drug manufacturer "concerning", "regarding" or "covering" a particular drug. In fact, the manufacturer had a "smoking gun" document about the drug in its files but chose not to produce it. Why not? The drug company did not view the document as "concerning" the drug in question, even though it spoke specifically of the drug.

The failure to produce the document after a clear and reasonable discovery request was clearly a subterfuge for hiding the critical truth that the drug company knew of certain dangers concerning use of the drug in question. If the doctor's discovery request was not clear enough, the Washington Supreme Court noted, "no conceivable discovery request . . . would have uncovered the relevant documents." By the way the drug company responded to the doctor's discovery requests, no one would have suspected that anything was being held back. So the court found the drug company's actions "misleading" and "non-responsive," and ordered penalties against the company.[16]

I'll Prepare the Order, Judge

Many times after a judge enters a ruling at a hearing, he or she will ask one of the attorneys to prepare an order for the judge's signature. Some lawyers cleverly try to change the judge's intent by writing the order in a different way. Then, instead of sending the proposed order to opposing counsel for prior approval, they quietly ship it directly to the judge. This is done intentionally with the hope that the judge will sign the altered order without reading it, while forgetting what the order really should have said.

That's the Law, Judge

To force a favorable court decision, some lawyers will knowingly misrepresent, misquote, or mischaracterize facts or the law. Or a lawyer may use very strained interpretations to make black really look white.

Frustrated Florida judges said this about lawyers who misconstrue the Florida Constitution:

> It should not be assumed that the constitution was intentionally written so as to obscure its meaning from all but those specially trained to read, construe, interpret and explain it. It was written to be read and understood by all literate citizens. Neither should the reader of the constitution assume that the reader understands the meaning and effect of the writing better than the writer was able to write and express its true meaning and effect. The constitution should be read with the sense that appears on its surface, not that one thing is stated but another meant, but that the very thing is meant which is stated and that the sense is literal, not figurative nor hidden. With good reason much of the public believes that the legal profession is so accustomed to "construing" vague, difficult and obtuse language that, in the habitual attempt to fathom or deduct some subtle intent, meaning or purpose, the profession seems to have lost the ability to understand or believe that a plainly written statement may have been intended to, and does, mean exactly what it states—no more and no less.[17]

Some lawyers simply cannot allow laws and legal documents to state exactly what they say!

MONEY GAMES

Did you hear the story of a man who asked a lawyer what his least expensive fee was? The lawyer replied, "A hundred dollars for three questions." Shocked, the man demanded, "Isn't that a lot of money for three questions?" "Yes," the lawyer replied with a grin. "What's your final question?"

Clever legal maneuverings of some lawyers can hit clients hard. Frequently this arises through "padding" of time charged on legal bills. Many attorneys amuse themselves with the inside joke about the lawyer who protested to St. Peter that fifty-one was far too young to be dead. St. Peter's response? "That's strange. According to your time sheets you're one hundred and two!"

One Boston law firm buried a $140,000 charge for heating its offices in a $2.9 million bill for a two-year trial. A New Orleans law firm charged $500 for one-sentence letters at least fifty different times. On three occasions, a Los Angeles lawyer turned in billings showing he had worked fifty-hour days. Another legal beagle claimed he worked on five thousand cases in a single day. It is not uncommon to find a few lawyers today who bill more than 3,600 hours per year—equal to fifty-two sixty-nine-hour weeks! This outrageous behavior and greed hurts our entire nation.

Clients should not have to pay for lawyer games like these:

- Overusing intra-office conferences among lawyers in the same office about the same client's case
- Repeatedly passing a file on to new lawyers who will bill the client for reviewing the case
- Overstaffing a case by having more than one person attend hearings and depositions
- Over-researching issues and padding legal research hours
- Charging a high hourly rate for existing computerized form documents easy to use in many cases
- Charging improper rates by billing secretaries as paralegals, paralegals as lawyers, and lawyers not yet admitted to the bar as admitted lawyers
- Marking up fixed costs such as computerized legal research, photocopying and facsimile charges, meals and airline tickets
- Summarizing depositions to an unwarranted degree.

These are only a few of many abuses that even the brightest and most honorable lawyers must guard against every day. Unfortunately, there are still too many lawyers who do not try to avoid these practices. Some even pride themselves on their skills at cheating clients and their non-compliance with the rules and ethics of law! So clients need to be knowledgeable and wary of these abuses before engaging in any litigation.

Attorneys in every state take oaths promising respect for our courts and judicial officers. This means putting aside any defense except that which the attorney reasonably believes to be honestly debatable under the law of the land. It is a solemn pledge never to mislead the judge or jury by any trick or false statement of fact or law. It is a promise to exercise civil conduct and advance no fact prejudicing the honor or reputation of a party or witness, unless required by justice of the cause. But many attorneys are no longer even aware of these oath provisions.

From his view on the bench, Federal Judge Thomas M. Reavley said this about lawyers:

> [T]he lawyers of America . . . [should] go back to . . . the lessons taught by our forefathers 200 years ago. Greed and self-seeking threaten us. In our routines and conflicts we forget and disserve the best interests of our clients as well as the cause of the administration of justice. We try to justify our excesses and misconduct under the banner of the adversary system. We all know

that there is no time and no place for the forfeiture of integrity or betrayal of justice for all. For the sake of the bench and bar, and the client, lawyers should limit discovery, frame the issues and value their cases fairly, and compromise when it is justified by all of the consequences. When we can, we must try expeditious and inexpensive alternative methods of dispute resolution.[18]

PRACTICING LAW TODAY: MORE OF A BUSINESS THAN A PROFESSION

Lawyering today is much different from years past. Professionalism and public service have eroded away with the pressures of operating a law office and being competitive in a complex society with clients who demand immediate service.

Attorney Arnold H. Rutkin's editorial of a lawyer stereotype will amuse you:

> Many lawyers today view the practice of law as an exercise in survival. The stresses are incredible. This was not true 50 years ago, or even 25. Back then, the law was a wonderful, genteel profession for all who aspired to it. As a young man, my image of a lawyer was Atticus Finch, the lead character played by Gregory Peck in *To Kill a Mockingbird* or Paul Biegler played by Jimmy Stewart in *The Anatomy of a Murder*. These characters were typical of lawyers in the movies . . . easygoing, stress-free, vested or shirt-sleeved solo practitioners who practiced law in small, rural, southern towns. They were able to spend time with their wives and weekends and evenings with their children. Sometimes they even went fishing in the afternoons. . . . They always had a loyal secretary, about their own age, who worked late and made no demands about raises, bonuses, or overtime. They were blessed with a friend or colleague—usually an alcoholic—who was interested in their cases and willing to act as a private investigator or do research or paralegal work for nothing. The courtrooms in which these lawyers practiced were congestion-free islands of tranquility in courthouses where nothing else seemed to be happening. Except for a lack of air-conditioning, the courtrooms they tried their cases in were what courtrooms are supposed to be: spacious and elegant. Like the lawyers, judges were pensive, congenial types who smoked pipes and went fishing on weekday afternoons. They could concentrate on the case at hand because their dockets were uncluttered.[19]

But you and I know this is far from reality. Today, you can reverse each of these stereotypical descriptions and still not capture the dilemma many legal professionals are in today.

Abraham Lincoln once said, "A lawyer's time is his stock in trade." Time is the service a lawyer offers for sale to the public—time to focus on a client's problems, to apply his or her expertise and experience in giving advice, and to complete a case. But the legal tradition of professional public service is yielding, almost by force, to the economies of the workplace.

The former days of the gentleman lawyer and general practitioner are over. As society has fast-tracked itself in making so many complex changes, it is virtually impossible to keep up with new laws and regulations without specializing in only a few limited areas. The drive to respond quickly to client demands keeps lawyers on the high technology roller coaster—a major capital cost—as computers and software evolve.

In 1994, there were about 850,000 lawyers in America, or one for about every 260 people in the U.S.[20] With the number of lawyers in the U.S. increasing from about 220,000 in 1950 to almost a million by the end of this decade, competition for clients and work is *very* intense. To survive, a lawyer must commit more time and expense for marketing, and even advertising (which was unheard of until the U.S. Supreme Court allowed it in 1977), to stand out from the crowd. Naturally, as a lawyer dedicates more time to these functions, plus work for existing clients, he or she wants more compensation. This increases fees, and on it goes.

Since time is what lawyers sell, compensation often comes from billable hours that are chargeable to clients. Law firms today routinely expect attorneys to bill clients for 2,000 to 2,500 hours or more a year (in addition to many non-billable hours required for administrative tasks). This is more hours than lawyers in any other world country produce.[21] But unrealistic time and billing targets in such a competitive atmosphere encourages cheating by inflating hours, and overvaluing billing rates for the services received by the client.[22]

Certainly clients lose by having to pay for all those lawyer hours. But what about the individual attorneys? Do they pay a personal price in performing all this work? Former Florida Bar President James Fox Miller stated the problem well:

> What is abundantly clear to me is that even taking 2,000 hours a year, if the time is legitimate, . . . [a] young person has no quality of life. Where is time for a meaningful marriage or for participation in the rearing of children or for simply enjoying what the world has to offer? Lawyers all over the country are chained to clocks. This means they are not working in their communities, churches, synagogues, civic organizations and so forth. There is no time for them to make the contributions to society other than

to "grind it out" for the almighty dollar. The profession is self-destructing.[23]

———

Miller put his finger right on the problem. As Americans, we are already aware that we are losing our common touch—our neighborliness—with others. This is a good example of how it is also happening among lawyers and their families.

The tragedy is that too many lawyers are too busy to care. In 1993, John Leslie and Eunice Morgan stopped work on a California Bar exam to give CPR and help a fellow law student who suffered a seizure and collapsed. Six hundred other students kept busy with their exams. The California Bar examiner then denied Leslie and Morgan's request for an additional forty minutes to complete their exams and replace the time spent with their fallen comrade.[24]

Or consider twenty-seven-year-old Charles McKenzie, a second-year associate at a well-known Wall Street law firm. In a wrongful death suit filed against the firm, McKenzie's father claimed the firm gave his son too much work, set unrealistic deadlines, and assigned him tasks beyond his capabilities. The firm's pressure to produce got the best of young McKenzie. Despite some time off with his family, he could not cope with the demands of returning to work. In 1992, he ended his life by jumping off the roof of a nineteen-story downtown hotel.[25]

In his book, *The Lost Lawyer: Failing Ideals of the Legal Profession*, Yale Law School professor Anthony Kronman laments that the American legal profession "now stands in danger of losing its soul." This would not only be "a catastrophe for lawyers, [but] a disaster for the country as well."

None of the forces at work in the lives of lawyers today—losing the true meaning of advocacy, dealing with the increasing skills and deviancies of the number of dirty trickster lawyers, and the pressures to produce and bill higher fees to survive in the business world—are working in favor of better times for clients and courts in our country. Regrettably, as moral values decline and our nation retreats from its religious heritage, matters in our courts will deteriorate and become worse before it becomes better unless we use our country's lawyers in more productive dispute-resolution capacities.

Questions for Personal Reflection:

1. Do I enjoy ridiculing lawyers? Is it helping, or hurting, America?
2. In what ways have I contributed to the crisis lawyers face today?
3. Am I quick in wanting lawyers to litigate my disputes with others?
4. What responsibility do I have in searching out and hiring lawyers of integrity?
5. Do I fully appreciate how the lawyer crisis affects America's future?

Chapter 7

A Lethal Mix: Clients, Judges, and Juries

The time has come for us to admit that we have failed to provide equal justice for all—fairly, decisively, diligently, and inexpensively. We have become less a nation of conflict-resolvers, and more a people who love litigation for the pleasure of beating up opponents and stripping them down financially. Civil justice is no longer a means to an end. Too often it is a sport of lawyers: the wealthy who love to intimidate opponents, and the poor who hope to win big on a verdict.

§&

The unprecedented media coverage of former football and media star O.J. Simpson's trial in 1994 and 1995 opened the lid on how courtrooms in America operate. People saw firsthand a legal system at work that frequently confuses them. But this learning experience also carried a curse— it increased skepticism toward lawyers, courts, the police, and the media.

What first brought all the court action and media hype to bear on the Simpson case? It began with a local Los Angeles dispute rooted in an unhappy marriage. It was the murder of Nicole Brown Simpson and friend Ronald Goldman that started the big wheel of justice turning. One person's decision to murder another human tied up hundreds of people in processing the case over many months, costing Simpson and taxpayers millions of dollars. All of this happened just because one person made a very poor decision one summer night in June 1994—one neighbor taking private vengeance on other neighbors.

And so it is with most every case that ends up in court. Before the lawyers, before the judges and juries, there is the client. Abraham Lincoln reportedly counseled a younger lawyer saying, "It's more important to know what cases not to take than it is to know the law." Why? Because some cases are not good risks. Because the law makes some claims unworthy of legal action. Because some clients are trouble.

Many in society blame lawyers for the problems in our courts. But they forget that lawyers merely try to fulfill the will of their clients. If lawyers are bandleaders, clients are the band members who play along and actually make the music.

Clients certainly have the right to receive high quality, cost-efficient, representation from their lawyers. This means receiving

- written work easily understood by the client, that reflects a thorough treatment of options and risks in a case;
- advice that is responsive to a client's goal of settling the case or completing any litigation quickly; and
- bills for fees that are reasonable and competitive with those charged by other lawyers for similar services.

But clients have a responsibility to their attorneys. Lawyers expect prompt payment for services rendered. Clients should not deny them a reasonable fee. Clients are their lawyer's eyes and ears. They need to be cooperative and accessible for consultation whenever necessary. To make the relationship work, a client must not be a pest to the lawyer who is handling the case. Lawyers expect clients to avoid any unreasonable interference with the legal work.

Clients also owe allegiance to our justice system and society at large. They have a responsibility not to seek a lottery win in court for personal trespasses of others. The old French proverb is true: "Money is a good servant, but a bad master." Seeking compensation can distort our view of the more important matters in life. We think of our assets as everything we own—cash, property, and investments. The term comes from the old French word, *asetz* meaning "enough." It means having enough wealth left to settle any debts of a deceased person. Even if others take advantage of you, will you have enough assets left to move on with your life? If so, be willing to compromise. Be flexible and avoid resentment.

Clients should strive to keep the economics of their case in proper perspective. The apostle Paul told Timothy (and us): "But godliness with contentment is great gain. For we brought nothing into the world, and we can take nothing out of it. But if we have food and clothing, we will be content with that. People who want to get rich fall into temptation and a trap and into many foolish and harmful desires that plunge men into ruin and destruction. For the love of money is a root of all kinds of evil. Some people, eager for money, have wandered from the faith and pierced themselves with many griefs" (1 Tim. 6:6–10). That's good advice for anyone. Measure your wealth not by what you have, but by what you have for which you would not take money. Peace of mind is worth more than possessions. Further destruction of relationships and resentment is too great a price to pay for winning a few dollars in court.

CLIENTS: OUT FOR JUSTICE OR REVENGE?

Like lawyers, many clients fail to understand and respect the reasons we have a justice system in place. Our founding fathers reserved it for reasonable resolution of disputes—not as a personal playground where we can harass and intimidate others.

How do clients escalate the breakdown in our courts today? Here are a few examples:

Many Clients Fail to Restrain Their Lawyers

Clients really drive the legal system. Too many want their lawyers to be pit bulls. They push their lawyers to take everything their adversaries own in a lawsuit and, in the process, try to strip them of their dignity. They lock themselves into a "never give an inch, take no prisoners" approach in suing their business partners. Too many do not want the honorable lawyers of integrity, reason, and patience who truly are peacemakers. They want a hired gun to do their bidding and win at all costs.

Matthew Hodel noticed that clients create a double-bind situation for attorneys: "When they need a lawyer, they seek out one who is unfettered by ethics and conscience, precisely because he or she strikes them as most likely to get the job done. Later, they blame all of us when their 'advocate' produces nothing but scorched earth, never conceding they victimized themselves by choosing the wrong lawyer."[1]

Patricia A. Seitz, then President of the Florida Bar, wrote these words about combative lawyers, but she could have just as easily addressed equally combative clients:

> Too often . . . some of us act as if we are knights of the realm, dueling to the death to win every encounter. We have this fixation with strength, which we equate with "toughness," giving no quarter and "killing" the other side as we try to win even our phone calls. This fixation can consume us; so color our attitude we adopt an "offensive" defensive mindset where we distrust everyone, engage in snarling personal attacks and pit bull tactics as revenge for any perceived slight or to avoid the "humiliation" of losing. Have you noticed that backing down, conceding anything, being helpful, losing gracefully, walking away from confrontation are now tagged as "wimplike" behavior of someone who doesn't have the "fire in the belly" to win? We all know the lawyers who have to win even when arguing with themselves. Winning—the ultimate face-saver—becomes everything, regardless of what is accomplished. How often have we consoled ourselves about our own less-than-admirable behavior in such exchanges, saying that we have to "fight fire with fire," and return the nasty, a.k.a.

"tough," behavior of the other side? What does this accomplish for ourselves, our client, or society? Realistically: Zip, except for the ego flexing. Repeated behavior such as this numbs us to further nasty conduct. We see "in your face" bully behavior as the norm and it carries over into our everyday public behavior.[2]

Many Clients Love to Sue

What may be pushing our litigation crisis over the brink more than anything else is a client's penchant for suing another person over the slightest offense. The rampant materialism, hedonism, and secularism of today's society overwhelm many clients. If anything bad happens, many folks come to two immediate conclusions: (1) somebody else is to blame and (2) somebody else is going to pay. And these troublesome individuals often sue before they talk, rather than after. They hope threatening someone with litigation will bring an opponent to his or her knees. They seek to force payment of a ransom to avoid the expense of defending against an expensive lawsuit.

In New Hampshire, the parents of a nine-year-old sued their eighty-eight-year-old neighbor who refused to return the boy's ball after it rolled into her yard. Result? Litigation and valuable court time used to award damages of $30.20. In 1992, an Albright College student sued his football player roommate for negligence and breach of contract because he didn't study, played loud music, and partied late. A customer sued his Florida barber for more than $10,000 in damages because he believed his haircut was too short on top and too long on the sides. The customer claimed the "anxiety-producing haircut" deprived him of his right to happiness.[3]

As Lee Iacocca lamented in his book *Talking Straight*, "In the old days, if a neighbor's apples fell into your yard, you worked it out over the back fence or picked them up and made pies. Today, you sue."

Then there are lawsuits that defy logic, like the burglar who fell through a skylight while breaking into a school. He successfully sued the school for damages. Or the man who unsuccessfully attempted suicide by jumping in front of a train only to survive and sue the transit company for failing to stop the train in time to avoid inflicting the minor injuries he suffered. Another couple, hit by a train while making love on the tracks sued the New York Transit Authority for $10 million after escaping with no life-threatening injuries. An East Orange, N. J., boy, hit by a jeep while riding his bicycle at night, sued the company that distributed the bike for $7 million for failure to attach labels warning against night riding.

Timothy Anderson, shot and wounded by a security guard whom he threatened while making an armed robbery of a Milwaukee McDonald's, sued the security guard from his prison cell. Anderson's attorney told the

Milwaukee *Journal*: "The mere fact that you're holding up a McDonald's with a gun doesn't mean you give up your right to be protected from somebody who wants to shoot you."[4]

Todd L. Johnson, serving time in a California prison for robbing Stephanie Lucero in June 1993 and stealing her car, filed a $2,794 claim against San Mateo County for clothing and other belongings he left in the stolen vehicle after its recovery. Lucero gave Johnson's clothes to charity when she received her car. Johnson charged that this was an unreasonable seizure of his belongings.[5]

In a case that went all the way to the Wyoming Supreme Court, Richard Osborn sued a local video store because Busty Belle appeared for only eight to nine minutes in an adult video he purchased. Osburn claimed damages of $29.95 for the cost of the video, $55.79 in medical costs for an asthma attack that he suffered due to the "stress and strain of being ripped off," $50,000 in compensation for suffering, and punitive damages.[6]

Get instant riches! Jump on the lawsuit bandwagon! Don't blame yourself—hold someone else responsible. This is the attitude of many clients today. But mean-spirited litigation like this is a two-way street. Many clients bent upon revenge have discovered that their lashes at others with legal whips quite often end up in stripes across their own backs.

Many Clients View Themselves as Victims Demanding Their Rights

America prides itself on being a nation of hard-working, ingenious people. But too many clients abuse the justice system by seeking compensation for injury or damage arising from their own actions, regardless of their fault. Many today mourn the America that has become a nation of victims without personal accountability. Selfish people use race, religion, gender, nationality, sex, or disabilities as smoke screens and subterfuges for manipulation to collect undeserved compensation.

American Alliance for Rights and Responsibility President Roger Conner provides penetrating insight into this serious problem:

> The tension between individualism and community has always been with us. However, in the past twenty years the values associated with mutual obligation, voluntary restraint and civic responsibility have declined sharply. Law and public policy have reinforced these trends in a powerful way, led by a phalanx of lawyers and non-profit organizations, [leading to] a veritable rights industry without any sense of the need to balance community needs with individual wants. Underlying many legal arguments is a seductive theme, that rights are individual, absolute and disconnected from any sense of social obligation. That idea has escaped from courtrooms and now dominates the way Americans

think about themselves and their relationships to their family, community and nation. The resulting self-centeredness is corrupting an entire generation. . . . Thinking Americans increasingly sense that the rights explosion has gone too far, that it has become an expression of self-absorbed individualism which is weakening our country. . . . At this time in American history, we need to hear a more complex message about rights: that a society with all rights and no responsibilities is a society in which individual freedoms cannot flourish.[7]

———

Steven Luck of Salt Lake City, Utah, echoed this sentiment: "I feel our government, and we as a nation, are becoming less and less what our founding fathers wanted us to be."[8]

Some Clients Are Frequently at Odds with Their Lawyers

From a lawyer's perspective, some clients are often very demanding and extremely difficult to please. These curmudgeons on the prowl are insecure people who are equally obnoxious to everyone—not just lawyers. Attorneys are always on guard against clients who come into the office with a hand truck of file boxes. They convince themselves that the three or four different unpaid lawyers who represented them before were "no-good thieves who didn't deserve a dime from me."

Clients often work at cross-purposes with their lawyers. This is especially true with business clients who are used to calling the shots at work, or those who have watched *Matlock* and *L.A. Law* and believe they know how to practice law. Instead of concentrating on being available, articulate, and eager to cooperate with their attorneys and respecting the truism that a little knowledge can be dangerous, too many clients believe they can sail their own ship. Usually they end up sabotaging a lawyer's carefully prepared case. They want to control the entire process—even third party witnesses and opposing counsel. This leads some attorneys to envy brain surgeons because they can anesthetize patients before they operate.

Some lawyers capitalize on client pride such as this. One law school dean at London University remarked, "Always encourage your clients to write their own wills. . . . If you write the will, you will get a fee; if the client writes the will, you will collect for a generation."[9]

A very common problem is the client who harasses his or her attorney, wanting to know when work will be done. Some become irate bullies. They have the attitude that being obnoxious enough will force the lawyer to work faster, in order to avoid incessant telephone calls or faxes. Even after this barrage, many of these clients deafen themselves to requests for payment of a reasonable fee.

Clients may complain long and loud about legal fees. To be sure, a lawyer's fees should be fair and reasonable. But what is reasonable? Discussing this issue alone could fill a book by itself, and some are already on the shelf!

What is the value of legal service? Clients must consider the problem that is solved by the lawyer and the benefits that are gained. But lawyers have an amusing modern parable that provides one answer: A factory owner once had a very valuable machine. But the machine broke down. After many efforts by various repairpersons, the machine would not work. The owner became frantic thinking of how this crisis would cause shutdown of production, factory layoffs, and even bankruptcy, as creditors pressed for payment on past due bills. Just when all seemed lost, in walked a stranger who offered to fix the machine. "Please," cried the owner, "Do anything you can! Everything I have worked for all my life is in jeopardy." After walking around the machine for a few minutes, the stranger took out a dime, bent down and turned a single screw. In a flash, the machine worked! Later the stranger sent the owner a bill. It read: "Fixed the machine. $50,000." The owner immediately called the miracle worker. "Don't get me wrong, I am indebted to you for saving my business. But would you itemize your statement?" A day later the owner received the itemized statement that read: "Turned the screw in the machine, $50. Knowing which screw to turn, $49,950."

Conflicts over legal fees between clients and their attorneys keep everyone at odds with each other in the justice system. Attorneys and clients have mismatched perceptions of what legal services are worth. Clients view value-billing for merely turning a screw as a lawyer ploy to reap larger fees (although they are not happy with hourly billing practices either). Lawyers, on the other hand, see value-billing as additional compensation for exceptional service and results. Nevertheless, the result is often the same. If the client and attorney are not fighting their adversaries, the attorney is in court suing the client for unpaid fees, while the client is countersuing the attorney for alleged malpractice. Even if it is a totally unfounded malpractice claim, the client's goal is to intimidate the lawyer into settling for a fee less than what is rightfully due.

Some Clients Can Be Notoriously Fickle

A general fickleness in how a client views the work and success of a lawyer is legendary in legal humor.

Some lawyers, through bitter experience, can predict client fickleness and virtually plot their client's reactions on a linear "graph of gratitude." First, a client suffers a loss. After calling the insurance agent, the client exclaims, "You mean my policy *doesn't* cover it?!?" The client then calls the lawyer (usually at home around 10 P.M.) with the urgent plea, "I need to see you right away!" At the first appointment, the frantic client wails, "I'll lose *everything* if they sue me!" After receiving the court papers filed against him or her, the client confesses, "This looks bad. Can you get me out of it?" As the attorney prepares his case, the client marvels, "There's a lot of work in a lawsuit, isn't there?"

Just before trial the client praises the hard-working lawyer: "You're doing a great job!" After securing a verdict for the client, the lawyer hears: "No one else could have done it!" After the trial, the elated client shouts, "You saved my business. I don't know how to thank you enough!"

But then, after a few days of enjoying the thrill of victory, the client reflects, "Wow, I really was great on the witness stand." A week or two later, the client thinks, "You know, the other side really never had a chance because I had a great case." A month later, the client concludes, "It was a snap. I could have handled the entire case myself!" Later still when the lawyer sends a reminder that the legal bills remain unpaid, the client is indignant. "What a presumptuous jerk that lawyer is!"

When the lawyer finally has no choice but to file a collection suit for the unpaid fees, the client screams, "That shyster!" When the collection action is successful and the client finally must pay up, he vows: "I'll tell the world about that crook!"

Client interference goes beyond merely having second thoughts about a legal action or settlement agreement. Some clients resist reasonable settlements simply to get even with opponents. They urge their lawyers on with the promise, "I'd rather pay you than that turkey!" But in the end, the "turkey" and the lawyer are left gobbling together as the client skips out on payment to both.

Then there are clients who cry, "Please get this nightmare over with right away so I can get on with my life. Settle for whatever you can!" After accepting a deal, the client feels the pinch of payments or loss of property and blames the lawyer who "caused this entire mess."

Even the best lawyers in the country are vulnerable to nuisance actions. Clients may file a grievance action against lawyers with state bar associations or sue them for malpractice in retaliatory harassment. Unhappy clients who suffer because of unwise personal or business decisions, made even against an attorney's instructions, will often make a scapegoat of that lawyer who gave them "rotten advice."

As one commentator noted, "When the result is a bad deal or lost profits, the client's attention usually shifts to the lawyer's neck. In the absence of documentation [confirming a lawyer's advice in writing], clients second-guess the actions of attorneys and often have selective memories as to what was disclosed to them at the crucial juncture of the transaction. . . . Clients frequently claim that they were not aware of certain risks involved with the transaction and had they been told of those risks, they would not have gone forward."[10]

Some Clients Are Just Bad News

Sometimes the signs are obvious, like the case of New York City traffic scofflaw, Leroy Linen. New York City police arrested Linen in November 1994 after he mistakenly offered his real name during a traffic stop for having only a crudely hand-lettered license plate on his car. Police computers reported that Linen's driver's license had been suspended 633 times since 1990. It took an hour and forty-five minutes to print out all the traffic violations![11] And yet people like Linen need to be defended to make sure that the penalty for his crimes is reasonable. Even so, there are more than a few individuals who become a menace to society and then seek legal protection to escape punishment. And, unfortunately, there are an equal number of hungry lawyers who are ready to take their cases. We all pay for this.

But for all the lawyer games and hard-hearted attitudes and fickleness of clients, the problem in our court system does not begin and end when war-like attorneys and vindictive clients rush into court. Litigation crises then fall into the laps of judges who often have many of their own problems and shortcomings.

JUDGES: GUARDIANS OF SOCIAL ORDER

America has been a nation of laws from the beginning. Lawyers at the Constitutional Convention framed the critical social, economic, and political questions of the age in legal terminology, with the intent that lawyers would help define the problems of social order. But it is up to our judges to arrive at an ultimate resolution of all issues—even if reasonable (or unreasonable) lawyers and clients might disagree with the result.

Judges have long had the trappings of civil high priests of the law. Think of the many similarities between judges and religious priests—black robes, the way we address the judge as "Your Honor," the "All rise . . . Hear ye" opening address that resembles a processional when the judge enters the courtroom, and the solemn taking of oaths by witnesses in front of the judge using the Bible.

In court, judges seem almost omnipotent and godlike, sitting robed in black on high, lofty benches with sober, stern expressions. This creates an aura and mystique that is intended to intimidate those deserving of rebuke and discipline. Judges are special people. They have a vital function in society and deserve our full attention and respect. We address judges as "Your Honor" because anyone who puts aside personal freedoms and pleasures to serve the public in these ways is a man or woman truly worthy of respect and double honor.

What should we expect from the judges in our courts?

Integrity and Independence

This is vital to justice in our society.

Respect for the Law and No Hint of Impropriety

A judge should not allow personal relationships to influence his or her judicial conduct or judgment; lend the prestige of his or her office to advance the private interests of others; or convey the impression that anyone is in a special position to influence him or her. Due to public scrutiny, judges should willingly accept restrictions on their personal conduct above and beyond those applicable to ordinary citizens to preserve the honor and integrity of their office.

Impartial, Competent, and Diligent Fulfillment of Judicial Duties

A judge's duties must take precedence over all other personal activities. Judges must rise above and not be swayed by partisan interests, public clamor, or fear of criticism. Judges must exercise professional competence while maintaining order and decorum in the courtroom; they must be efficient, prompt, and businesslike in exercising justice. In doing so, judges must also be patient and deliberate in hearing argument from every person who is legally interested in a proceeding. Judges should step away from any proceeding that raises questions about their impartiality due to personal bias, prejudice or personal knowledge of disputed matters in a proceeding.

Precise, Concise, and Incisive Orders and Rulings

Judges should attempt to demystify the law. They need to bring high-minded legal argument down to earth and breathe some life into formal law codes.

The best judges also remain aware that they are temporary surrogates for the great Judge of all the earth. U.S. Court of Appeals Judge Irving Goldberg was well-known for using humor and religion in many of his opinions. In *Golden Panagia S.S., Inc. v. Panama Canal Commission*,[12] involving an attorney who stole settlement proceeds that arose from a shipping accident and who later died, Judge Goldberg glibly noted: "A Higher Court thus has jurisdiction over Henry Newell, and we are confident that any sins he may have committed will be dealt with appropriately there."[13]

There are many excellent, honest, and trustworthy judges in our country. They are not creating the problems in our courts. But there are those few individuals wearing judicial robes who are unable or unwilling to fulfill the duties of their office. These troublesome judicial officers are tearing down our courts of justice through mismanagement, personal laziness, and even dishonesty.

"THERE'S A ROGUE AT THE END OF MY CANE!"

That's what the notorious Judge Jeffreys, known as "Bloody Jeffreys," remarked as he pointed his cane at a man who was on trial in court. The man looked at the judge and replied, "At which end, my lord?"

This anecdote about the judicial process from James V. Bennett in the Journal of American Judicature Society is not far off the mark. Going to court with an adversary brings bickering and complaints into a public courtroom. Each adversary, personally and through attorneys, blames the other. Each tries to put the other in the worst possible light.

The mission of the courts is to stand between the government and individual citizens, interpret the law, and resolve disputes in matters where a particular court has jurisdiction. Simply put, we need honest judges who will do their duty. Unlike the lawyers in their courtroom, judges do not have clients to deal with. Their responsibility is to the audience in their courtroom and to the public who is watching from a distance. But quite often judges get their priorities confused, creating further problems in our justice system. Here are a few examples:

When You Are in My Courtroom, I Am God

Judges do appear godlike in court and receive attention and respect for giving justice to all. But it is another matter for a judge to believe that he or she *is* God or can act like God. Sometimes judges act in ways that are hostile, demeaning, or humiliating to lawyers, parties, or witnesses.[14]

I've Heard Enough, so Don't Say Another Word

Responsible judges realize that lawyers have a right and a duty to present a case fully and properly as part of every litigant's right to a fair and impartial hearing. Allowing lawyers to present proper arguments provides a complete and accurate record of the controversy for future review. This requires reasonable patience and experienced wisdom in knowing when to stop a proceeding. But sometimes judges rush and make a ruling before hearing all opposing arguments. This defeats the purpose of our adversarial system.

I Can Give You a Trial Date in About Three Years

Cases backlog in our courts. This is certainly not the fault of most judges. However, there are some judges who are working in chambers cluttered with cases that are waiting for rulings simply because of judicial neglect or laziness. Judges who do not work diligently on their cases when the need is great are anathema to lawyers and litigants alike; they obstruct justice.

The other side of this problem is being too tough and rigid in following legal rules when survival depends on cooperation between judges and lawyers. Dade County Florida Judge Thomas Spencer found this out the hard way. He refused to approve lenient criminal plea bargains with defendants. But this created a major crisis and threatened gridlock in Spencer's court when he already had the highest caseload backlog by far of any Dade County criminal court judge. His tough stance swamped state prosecutors and public defenders with cases. This threatened to sabotage some cases due to Florida's speedy trial rule and delays in coming to trial. The controversy prompted Chief Judge Leonard Rivkind to reassign Judge Spencer to family court effective in Fall 1994 against his wishes.[15]

I'm Going to Take this Matter under Advisement

There is a place for judges to give all issues in controversy impartial and studied analysis without having to rule on the spot. But an experienced trial judge should rule immediately on many matters, particularly routine court matters, without extended delays and formal legal briefing or argument by attorneys. We cannot spare any more court time for frivolous disputes. If judges do not rule promptly, it affects court schedules for everyone concerned. Once again, everything gets backlogged.

I Won't Penalize You for Failing to Follow the Rules

The rules of procedure used in every court set deadlines for certain events to occur. But many times people miss these deadlines. Sometimes this occurs by agreement of the attorneys. At other times, however, an attorney refuses to obey the rules in a timely manner. He or she comes to the judge, repeatedly in some cases, for additional time. Complacent judges tolerate this practice, which delays the case unfairly for the other party, who may be diligent and wants the litigation to end quickly. If judges held firm to these deadlines and consistently applied penalties as a deterrent to violations, there would be less delay in our courts, attorney time would be reduced, and everyone would have fewer attorney's fees to pay.

Efficient justice requires better management, control, and participation by judges at all stages during a case. The key to lowering litigation costs and reducing court time comes from setting strict case deadlines, sticking with firm trial dates, and consistently encouraging the parties to settle if possible. To do this, judges must take control of their courtrooms, while not going too far (as Judge Spencer allegedly did).

Many times judges allow lawyers to decide when they are ready to go to trial rather than using their own discretion and urging lawyers to prepare their cases diligently. Because many judges do not closely watch their caseloads, it falls to the attorneys to tell the judge when they are ready to go to trial. However by then, any delay may be unavoidable. The opposite is also true. Sometimes the judge will set a case down for trial, but the date is far into the future. Or he or she sets it too early, before each side has a full opportunity to prepare for trial.

Our court system is failing us. But it is not solely because of unprofessional lawyers, clients bent on revenge and greed, and judges who will not actively manage the judicial process properly. "We, the people" fall short ourselves as we participate in the process as jurors.

JURIES: UNINFORMED CITIZENS DECIDING COMPLICATED CASES?

Our U.S. Constitution and almost every state constitution in America guarantee a right to trial by jury in criminal proceedings and in suits at common law. Although England (which originated the jury system) and most countries in Europe limit use of juries, the founding fathers believed that a trial by a jury of one's peers was essential to justice.

No less than three constitutional provisions guarantee this right on a federal level:

- Article III of the Constitution requires a jury trial in all federal criminal cases.

- The Sixth Amendment states, "In all criminal prosecutions, the accused shall enjoy the right to a speedy and public trial, by an impartial jury.

- The Seventh Amendment grants the right of trial by jury in suits of common law when the amount in controversy exceeds twenty dollars.

An impartial jury usually is a panel of legally competent individuals who know little or nothing about a legal case in question. Courts select them from a representative cross-section of the community, without discrimination by race, sex, or nationality. The Constitution does not guarantee a particular mix of jurors, only impartial selection of jurors promising to reach verdicts in the same manner.[16] Jurors satisfy these legal requirements if they competently understand the issues in a case and if publicity or other undue influences do not sway their viewpoints and judgment.

Potential jurors come to court so the lawyers can interview each one at a time in a process called *voir dire* (French for "to see, to say"). The lawyers can ask the judge to dismiss any number of individuals for cause, due to any bias or prejudice showing that the juror candidate cannot, or will not, serve impartially. In addition, each side has some *peremptory challenges*, which allow the lawyers to excuse a juror for any reason except those prohibited by law (for example, race or gender).

In jury deliberations, each juror discusses the evidence that has been submitted at trial and considers all the issues before reaching a verdict. No juror should change an opinion or vote because of the pressures of time, undue influence of other jurors, or otherwise. Each has the responsibility to test his or her own viewpoint in relation to those of everyone else. But sometimes these safeguards break down, as we shall see.

DOES OUR JURY SYSTEM REALLY WORK?

Almost from the date of our Constitution, critics have scorned jury panels as "twelve illiterate and perhaps ignorant people," "twelve bodies without a head," or "a group of twelve people of average intelligence." But even the best jurors taste these bitter fruits in public service:

Pressure Due to Being Away from Family or Work

Jurors might serve in a trial that could be over in a day or two—or it might drag on for months. This scares many people away from performing their civic duty.

In December 1994, Judge Lance Ito advised the O. J. Simpson jurors to get their affairs in order over the Christmas holidays. Beginning in January, they should expect isolation from the world for a long trial period in 1995. This is not at all untypical. (Also, this handful of Simpson jurors are unable to follow the commentary and analysis on one of the biggest trials of this century.)

For many jurors, there is a real fear that jury duty will adversely affect their job or source of income. Their very livelihood could be in jeopardy.

In 1971 a U.S. judicial conference concluded that employers sometimes coerced, threatened, or intimidated prospective jurors, discouraging their civic service or forcing them to seek an excuse from such service. Some years later, Congress passed the Jury System Improvements Act of 1978,[17] prohibiting an employer from discharging, or even threatening to discharge, or intimidating or coercing any permanent employee who is summoned for jury duty. Even so, prospective jurors may lose their regular pay for each day spent away on a jury. Loss of work is a serious concern that affects a juror's attitude in serving on a jury panel.

Indoctrination by Lawyers—Even during Jury Selection

The purpose of jury selection is to weed out anyone who cannot serve impartially. But many lawyers use much of their *voir dire* time to persuade jurors to consider the cases of their clients favorably.

Discrimination Due to Peremptory Challenges

Weeding out jury bias is vital to conducting a fair trial. Massachusetts law professor Harold Sullivan made this point very clear in 1940: "The minds of a jury may be likened to twelve test tubes. What scientist would commence an experiment with twelve test tubes, soiled and discolored by the deposits of repeated experiments."[18] Since challenging a juror for good legal cause is no easy task, many lawyers believe that unrestricted peremptory challenges are essential to securing a fair and impartial jury. Some juror candidates cannot or will not acknowledge personal bias or prejudice or other predispositions against parties on trial. Sometimes attorneys use these challenges based on no more evidence than lack of eye contact, body language, gestures, or other impressions.

How do you discover juror bias? Trial lawyer Bobby Lee Cook of Summerville, Georgia, tried an arson case in a small country town a few years ago where everyone knows everybody else. He ran into trouble during jury selection: "I asked the potential jurors if any of them knew Little Johnny, my client. Nearly all of them raised a hand. So I inquired as to what they knew about my client. They all started looking at each other, and one old gentleman on the back row spoke up: 'We all know Little Johnny,' the man said, 'and we all know he's a firebug.' I knew at that moment I was in trouble and it was time to plea bargain."[19] But many other cases are far from being that obvious. So peremptory challenges allow attorneys to dismiss jurors on only a suspicion of bias or prejudice.

However, critics argue that such challenges are discriminatory. Attorneys dismiss one prospective juror for another. This unrestricted power allows attorneys to reject jurors subtly on the basis of race,[20] ethnicity, age, gender,[21] or religion, even though the law forbids it. Improper and discriminatory challenges like this falsely assume that members of a certain group are unqualified to serve as jurors or unable to consider a case impartially involving a member, or nonmember, of their own group.

Discriminatory challenges against jurors also creates another obstacle for our courts—finding jurors to serve. A New York jury commissioner wanted to increase minority representation on juries and mailed invitations for jury registration to fifty-three African-American churches. Fifty-two churches did not respond. The last church declined, stating that the commissioner would be welcome as soon as the court system became fair to minorities. In a 1993 study, the Capitol District Bar Association in Albany, New York, verified that almost 70 percent of juror qualification questionnaires that were mailed to predominantly minority and low-income zip codes were returned as undeliverable, compared to about 30 percent in areas with more affluent and Caucasian people.[22]

Confusion in Trials that Hinders Reliable Findings of Fact

Many believe that trials proceed in ways that are intended to manipulate, confuse, or confound juries. Courts assemble juries who know nothing about a case in a strange and unfamiliar courtroom. They are tense and uncertain about what they should do. They hear evidence at trial that is presented in a jumbled-up order. If a witness testifies, frequent objections by attorneys are distracting. Items that lawyers take for granted frequently remain unexplained to jurors. For rulings on some objections, juries must even leave the room—many times a day in some cases. Highly technical expert witnesses who are unaccustomed to using layman's language are often hard for many jurors to understand.

As if these factors were not enough of a challenge, jurors cannot ask questions of witnesses or take notes while all the trial information is thrown at them in complex cases for days, weeks, or even months of court action. Their passive role in the court process can hinder the truth-finding process. They may not have heard an important response. A complex piece of evidence may confuse them, but they must remain silent and passive. They are to remain detached observers of the courtroom drama.

Allowing juror questions could help clarify confusion about testimony of a witness or other trial matters and better inform the jury. But jurors might ask legally improper questions that could adversely influence other jurors, prejudice the case, or cause a mistrial. If there were no limit on such questions, it could drag the trial on much longer than necessary. And this would put attorneys in the difficult position of possibly objecting to a juror's improper question at the risk of offending this decision maker.[23]

Taking notes may help refresh a juror's recollection of trial matters, aid concentration, and keep his or her mind from wandering. But problems could arise if a juror misses important points or fails to notice the demeanor of witnesses while taking notes, or if the jurors who take notes dominate the deliberation process over the non-notetakers, or jurors rely too heavily on what selected notes stated as opposed to each juror's overall independent recollection.

Whatever the reasons, putting inexperienced jurors into a courtroom with little or no help in fulfilling their duties jeopardizes many important points in a trial.

Incomprehensible Jury Instructions

A judge's instructions to the jury at the end of a trial on how to apply the law to the facts *should* clarify matters for them.[24] In reality, however, this frequently makes the jurors even more confused. Unfortunately, no one advises the jurors of these matters at the beginning of the trial to give them some frame of reference in hearing the case. It is even more frustrating for them not to have a written copy of the judge's instructions to refer to in the deliberation room. How can they understand, much less remember, pages of complicated legal instructions?

Unpredictable Fellow Jurors

Juries do not always deliberate in a rational way or arrive at conclusions based on the law. In 1993 after a high-profile trial concluded in Miami, the *Miami Herald* reported this assessment after interviewing various jurors:

> Every day in America's courtrooms, jurors weigh crucial evidence. Witness testimony. Circumstantial clues. Charts and diagrams. Important stuff. But in the wild world of trial deliberations, the verdict often turns on the real nitty-gritty: Squabbles over candy in the jury room. Spats over five-card draw. Raucous debates over who gets the window seat. Like rambunctious seventh-graders, jurors form cliques, appoint bullies, pass notes,

snicker and flirt with each other all the way through trial. . . . In theory, juries dole out justice pure and sweet, delivering impartial verdicts untainted by petty personality clashes. In reality, jurors often do the best they can, but personal disputes sometimes erupt in a jury-room showdown and, ultimately, help swing the outcome of a case. . . . Picking a jury is a little like playing the lottery—you never know what you're going to get.[25]

———

In theory, jurors should be competent and qualified to listen to a case and reach a verdict. But in practice, jurors frequently lack such competence. As one judge remarked: "Would any sensible business organization reach a decision, as to the competency and honesty of a prospective executive, by seeking, on that question of fact, the judgment of twelve men or women gathered together at random—and after first weeding out all those men and women who might have any special qualifications for answering the questions?"[26] One juror went even further in response to a California survey in the late 1980s: "Jury trials are archaic and unfair. Justice does not always prevail in jury trials because the general public is not sufficiently experienced and/or educated to understand the law and evidence presented. Jury verdicts should not be left in the hands of such people."[27]

Many legal observers today marvel at how much time and effort that lawyers and judges put into a case, paying attention to minute details of evidence, only to turn the whole process over to a jury of strangers who mysteriously deliberate behind closed doors and conceivably could sabotage their best efforts. But then, being a juror is no picnic either. An oft-quoted *New Yorker* magazine cartoon some years ago said it best: "We the jury find the defendant guilty, and we sentence him to jury duty."

THE REAL WORLD OF COURT LITIGATION

The philosopher Voltaire once remarked, "I was never ruined but twice: once when I lost a lawsuit, and once when I won one." There's a lot of truth to that astute observation.

By now you may be wondering how our justice system has survived as long as it has with all its flaws and imperfections. The public wants, needs, and must have an efficient and effective court system that decides disputes in a prompt, efficient, and fair manner. But there is a pervasive feeling of hopelessness and apathy about our judicial system today. The reality of modern justice is that hundreds of attorneys must fight for even a three-minute hearing before the same overworked judge who has not had time to read the pleadings of their cases. Most major law firms will not even take on civil cases involving disputes of $50,000 or less because running these lawsuits through the court system incurs legal fees and expenses that often exceed the amount in controversy. Our Constitution and body of laws are enormous. Our judicial system, overburdened with the responsibility of having to wade through it all for hundreds of millions of clients, cannot handle the load.

Judicial reform is a high priority for many attorneys, judges, and legislators as we move into the next millennium. But reform will not be easy. To think that we can change this system quickly is as unrealistic as thinking that an aircraft carrier can be stopped on a dime rather than its usual ten-mile course. It will take time, money (*lots* of it!) and a renewed commitment from all of us—the people—to follow the rules that make the system fair for *everyone* concerned and not just for the privileged few. If we fail to plan for quicker, less expensive, and more fair ways of securing justice in this country, we plan to fail.

But there is an even more basic and troublesome hurdle to jump. The public remains skeptical of lawyers, the gatekeepers of justice. They already believe that attorneys consistently twist the truth to serve their own purposes. They look at the laws coming from Congress and their state legislatures, and whom do they see? Lawyers. Who judges violations of the law? Lawyers. Who defines who can practice law and who may not? Lawyers. Even when a client suffers a grievous wrong from a lawyer's practice, who disciplines the lawyer? Other lawyers. This just feeds the conviction of many people that the "fox is guarding the chicken coop!" Many lawyers believe they have a monopoly on access to the justice system, that belongs to the people. But now that the people have little or no access to the courts, they are ready to stand these gatekeepers before a firing squad for dereliction of duty.

Sure, there is a contradiction at work here. Americans love to sue each other, but hate the ones who make it possible. Nevertheless, many times people hate lawyers out of abject fear of the legal nightmare that could come upon them in a flash. Walter Olson, author of *The Litigation Explosion,* explains:

> Government grants enormous coercive powers to lawyers. If you're an ordinary American with a house, child or business to lose, you know that any day a licensed attorney can come around and dump a pile of paper on your front lawn. While you're trying to dig your way out from under it, your rights will be up in the air; terrible things will be said about you; you'll be compelled to yield your privacy by answering intrusive questions; and you may shovel years of time and attention, as well as your family savings, into defending yourself. Then, when you finally show that you've done nothing wrong, the lawyer can simply walk away.[28]

Despite all the gloomy news about our justice system and lawyers, the Bible, given by the Lord of the universe, and our Declaration of Independence, Constitution, and Bill of Rights survive to give us hope for a better tomorrow. These precious words reflect our souls as human beings and as free Americans. They also help us see better ways to serve each other and uplift our mutual, God-given rights.

Fortunately, there are also people in high places who are sensitive to the problems we all face. In 1993, American Bar Association President R. William Ide III told the Bar's 532-member House of Delegates:

> What we need today is nothing short of a revolution in our administration of justice—a peaceful "shot heard round the legal world."... Although a myriad of societal factors contribute to the crisis in our justice system, the bottom line appears to be that our system of justice is slowly, but surely, grinding to a standstill.... [America needs] bold and new ways of thinking to create a multidisciplinary justice system that will encourage . . . resolving disputes without bringing them into the courts. . . . Scholars can study the problems. Lawyers can advocate change. Judges can render verdicts. But in the end it is the public that must decide what is best for them.[29]

————

Private dispute resolution—now that is a revolutionary action plan! But it began almost two thousand years ago with Jesus of Nazareth, as we shall see in Part Two. Why did we not listen to Him? If there is a lesson that history teaches us many times over, it is this two-fold truth: First, life is always changing. Second, we are always going to forget the first part of this truth.

Our reliance on the courts of justice has, regrettably, turned us into a nation of victims and responsibility-shifters—far from the industrious and neighborly heritage of early generations of Americans. If the litigation process becomes an end in itself, the choices we make in life become inconsequential. Our failure, neglect, or refusal to accept personal responsibility and to face the logical results of our decisions is breaking down governance by the people. The freedoms our founding fathers willed for us and future generations of Americans evolve to nothing more than an empty dream if our continued existence hinges only on a formal legal system to govern our disputes. Each of us needs to work together to govern ourselves.

❧

Questions for Personal Reflection

1. Do I have enough confidence in America's present justice system to believe that it will decide my legal matters consistently and fairly?

2. In what ways have I added to this crisis by acting, or failing to act?

3. Have I examined my own motives for engaging in litigation?

4. Am I open to considering alternative means of resolving my disputes—even if it means more personal involvement and responsibility in achieving a just result?

5. Am I willing to commit myself to using litigation only as a last resort in trying to resolve my disputes?

Chapter 8

The Coming Litigation Apocalypse

Litigation is a blazing fire. It is a winepress of fury that assumes God's wrath as its own. Those living by the sharp sword of lawsuits quickly fall to the sword themselves. Litigation becomes an iron scepter in the hands of legalists and the uncompassionate—destructive to those on both sides of this weapon.

ଈ

Family litigation in divorces and child custody disputes destroys families. Church-related lawsuits undermine the credibility of the Christian witness in America. Increasing legal challenges to religious freedoms weaken First Amendment protections. War-like attorneys and vindictive clients find courtrooms staffed with overworked judges and juries that use questionable procedures. What will happen next?

> It was the best of times, it was the worst of times, it was the age of wisdom, it was the age of foolishness, it was the epoch of belief, it was the epoch of incredulity, it was the season of Light, it was the season of Darkness, it was the spring of hope, it was the winter of despair, we had everything before us, we had nothing before us. —Charles Dickens[1]
> ———

Dickens' description of revolutionary Paris two centuries ago could just as well have applied to the modern American judicial system.

We can claim that America's judicial system is a shining example of democracy and the envy of the world. It surely is. But having justifiable pride in calling our courts the best in the world doesn't convert these arenas into an oasis of fairness, justice, and reason any more than putting a saddle on a duck makes it a racehorse.

We are facing a litigation apocalypse in America. Webster's dictionary defines *apocalypse* as "an imminent cosmic cataclysm in which God destroys the ruling powers of evil and raises the righteous to life in a messianic kingdom" in the manner described in Revelation. But it also means, "to reveal," "to uncover," and "something viewed as a prophetic revelation." Rest assured, I am no prophet. But there are some very disturbing trends in our justice system that merit our full attention and concern before it is too late.

SIGNS OF THE TIMES

Jesus told the Pharisees, "When evening comes, you say, 'It will be fair weather, for the sky is red,' and in the morning, 'Today it will be stormy, for the sky is red and overcast.' You know how to interpret the appearance of the sky, but you cannot interpret the signs of the times" (Matt. 16:2–3). What are the signs of our times? Is a litigation apocalypse coming our way? What is the biggest crisis facing our legal system today? Why should this concern you?

There is good litigation that serves a useful public purpose. Some lawsuits help protect us from potentially dangerous products, root out corruption and injustice, and investigate hazardous problems such as asbestos, the infamous Dalkon Shield, or faulty automobile fuel tanks. But the primary complaint about our civil court system is that litigation today costs too much, justice takes too long, and our courts remain inaccessible to far too many people. There are simply too many nuisance cases of little or dubious merit clogging our courts—cases that are better suited for private settlement. This is unacceptable in a society where crime, violence, drugs, dysfunctional families, severely disadvantaged children, and racial and gender bias threaten to overwhelm us.

An even larger fact of life is that litigation too often takes on a life of its own—many times beyond anyone's ability to stop it. Business productivity suffers. Litigation depletes business capital and personal finances. Creative and resourceful people must put aside their talents to deal with disputes in the stressful and anxiety-ridden environment of the judicial process.

We read in our newspapers and magazines accounts like this 1991 comment:

> How bad is this system that Americans love to hate? The competing studies fly like subpoenas. The system is slow and expensive. The average lawsuit filed in court languishes for 19 months. Last year plaintiffs and defendants paid out $22 *billion* in attorneys' fees. While most civil cases are settled out of court, defendants who go to trial are at the whim of increasingly gener-

ous juries. In 1962 there was just one personal-injury jury verdict over $1 million; in 1989 there were 588 verdicts over $1 million, according to Jury Verdict Research, Inc. (Many of these verdicts are reduced or overturned by judges on appeal.) . . . Once everyone has sued and been sued, perhaps there will be enough empathy in the land to work on this problem and solve it.[2]

As these serious problems plague America, we also find incomprehensible anomalies from case to case. Consider the California jury award of $3,816,535.45 in April 1994 to Rodney King, the videotaped victim of a beating by Los Angeles police, to pay him for his trauma. Did this award ignore evidence that King's total estimated lifetime earned income is $500,000 at most?[3] Certainly he deserved payment for his medical costs, reasonable lost wages, and re-establishment of his pre-arrest quality of life as a result of this horrendous abuse of police power. But what justifies such a large award? And who will pay the damages, court costs, and lawyer fees? Taxpayers like you and me! This means less money spent on other vital community projects like providing medical care to the disadvantaged, building better schools, hiring high quality teachers, and upgrading roads and utilities to meet growing population needs.

It doesn't stop there. We can already see signs of a much larger problem.

LETHAL DOUBLE WHAMMY: RISING CASELOADS AND FALLING FUNDING

It has been said that one way to drive someone crazy is to put the person in a round room and tell him or her to sit in a corner. With all the lawsuits filed each year, we tell our courts to take care of the load without providing enough money to do the job. It is a crazed existence! Something has to give—either we must pay more taxes, or our courts must turn away more cases.

COURTS IN CRISIS: THE LITIGATION EXPLOSION

The National Center For State Courts (NCSC), based in Williamsburg, Virginia, conducts an annual national study of state court caseloads.[4] Many legal authorities widely respect its statistics as the most authoritative and comprehensive available. What are the NCSC findings? Here's a sample:

- In 1990, for the first time since the NCSC began reporting in 1984, cases filed in state courts exceeded *100 million*—up from 98.4 million in 1989.[5] These figures represented a five percent increase in civil filings and a four percent increase in criminal filings over 1989.

- In 1990, only eight states among the forty who reported comparable data reduced their overall civil caseloads by completing more cases than new filings. In addition, only nine of forty-three states reporting criminal caseloads lowered their number of pending cases. This means that with new case filings and noncompletion of existing cases, the overall load on our courts increases from year to year.
- In 1991, over 93 million *new* cases were filed in state courts, with increases in civil cases, criminal caseloads (primarily felonies), and juvenile cases.[6] (The overall number of new cases declined from 1990 because civil administrators, rather than the courts, handled many traffic court cases. The total caseload figure does not reflect this additional work.)
- In 1991, people filed more than 31 million civil and criminal cases in the nation's state trial courts, compared to 253,500 new cases in the U.S. district courts (the federal trial courts). The report concluded that over one hundred times as many civil and criminal cases began in the state courts as in the federal courts.
- In 1991, state trial court case filings for torts (a private or civil wrong or injury), contracts, domestic relations, estate, and small claims grew by 3 percent compared to 1990.
- During the eight-year period between 1984 and 1991, civil caseloads rose by 33 percent, criminal caseloads by 24 percent, and juvenile caseloads by 34 percent, while the national population increased by only 7 percent over the same period. The NCSC Report for 1990 concluded that the caseload for that year was equivalent to one court case for every other adult in the United States.
- The volume of appeals from state trial courts reached a new high in 1991, with 245,103 filings—more than three percent higher than in 1990.[7]

What themes emerge from the NCSC report and its analysis of state caseload volume? The authors issued these findings in the report overview for 1991:[8]

The 1991 increases in state caseloads "are part of a continuing upward trend." Extrapolating trends from prior years suggests that "many trial and appellate courts are likely to see their caseloads double in size before the end of the decade."

Many courts "are having difficulties in keeping up with the growing volume. They dispose of fewer cases than they take in each year, thereby adding to the size of their pending caseloads. This suggests that the public's demand for services in many courts is outstripping the available resources."

Criminal cases represent "the greatest caseload increase during the past five years . . . ." Felony cases and appeals are increasing even faster. "As a result, more resources and innovative management procedures are necessary to respond to these specific trends. Unless trial and appellate courts are able to meet these demands, they will find it difficult to avoid civil case backlogs." This is inevitable if we must redirect limited court resources from civil cases to handle criminal cases.

———

The NCSC's 1992 report included similar warnings:
- The volume of appeals from state trial courts reached the highest level ever—259,276, which is up 5.8 percent from 1991.
- Civil, criminal, and juvenile caseloads continue to escalate.[9]
- Felony cases have increased more than 65 percent since 1985 and reflect the greatest growth in recent years.
- Domestic relations cases comprise more than one-third of all civil case filings nationally and represent the most rapidly growing segment of the civil caseload, increasing at a rate of more than 43 percent since 1985.[10]

How do these statistics affect you and me? It shows that too many of us—"we the people"—file too many lawsuits. Our courts face the same situation that our banks would face if everyone withdrew their money at the same time. If we do not find a cure for this onslaught, some states could put a freeze on new case filings, delay pending trials, or even collapse into bankruptcy. Otherwise, your state property taxes, sales and income taxes, and court filing fees will have to increase to pay for more courtroom buildings, staff, and law libraries. Either way, this affects you and your neighbors in an economically painful and personal way!

Because many Americans are unable to pay more taxes, many families and companies are pushed into bankruptcy. As state caseloads exploded in the early 1990s, the assets of bankrupt public companies skyrocketed an estimated 4,876 percent from $1.7 billion in 1980 to about *$84 billion* in 1990![11] And as more people are unable to pay their fair share of these increasing public costs, everyone else is forced to pick up the slack.

Are the federal courts doing any better than the state courts? Not so, according to the Administrative Office of the U.S. Courts. For the period ending September 30, 1992, federal district trial courts across the nation had 6.4 percent more bankruptcies, 3 percent more criminal cases, 9 percent more civil cases, and 9 percent more appeals than during the same period the year before. During the same reporting periods, federal appellate courts were the targets of a 9.3 percent increase in the number of appeals filed, with a 7.9 percent increase in the number of already pending appeals.[12]

After a survey of more than 80 percent of our federal judges about their caseloads in 1992 and 1993, the Federal Judicial Center (a research arm of the federal judiciary) reported its findings in July 1994.[13] Among the results: Almost 47 percent of the federal appeals court judges who responded believe the volume of civil cases is a "large" or "grave problem" in our federal courts. Almost 73 percent of the same federal appeals court judges believe the volume of criminal cases also present a large or grave problem. More than 57 percent of the federal district court judges who responded agree with this assessment.

J. Clifford Wallace, Chief Judge of the 9th Circuit U.S. Court of Appeals, noted that the number of cases filed in the federal appellate courts between 1981 and 1991 increased by nearly 60 percent. In addition, the number of criminal cases filed in the federal district courts increased by nearly 50 percent during the same period.[14]

There is another trend that also merits serious concern. Between 20 to 25 percent of most state and federal cases filed in the 1940s and 1950s went to trial. However, by the late 1980s and early 1990s, these trial rates dropped to 3 to 4 percent—even as the number of case filings increased dramatically.[15] To be sure, many judges in recent years are more actively encouraging litigants to settle their disputes. But this also could mean that many cases going to trial in earlier decades would not do so today because of the huge backlog of cases.

Even the U.S. Supreme Court is reducing the number of cases it accepts for review. The number of petitions for certiorari review on the Court's docket for the October 1993 term increased dramatically to 6,896 (compared to 3,888 in 1978, for example). Of that total, less than 100 cases received a full opinion by the Court, the lowest total since 1955, and a 37 percent reduction from full opinions issued by the Court in 1988.[16] One reason is that the vast majority of the increased petitions came from federal and state prisoners who challenged their convictions, prison conditions, or other court proceedings. (This is a major abuse of our judicial system, as we shall see.) But this increased activity at our nation's highest Court ties up our justices and keeps many other cases of national importance from receiving full consideration.

Prison Lawsuits

Inmate lawsuits are a major factor in America's litigation explosion. According to the Federal Bureau of Prisons, the average number of federal prison inmates per institution rose from 699 in 1950 to 1,015 in 1992—even with twenty-three new prisons built over the last ten years.[17] This means more men and women in prison with a lot of time on their hands, and free access to taxpayer-supported law libraries at each institution. What happens? Each year thousands of prisoners file tens of thousands of frivolous lawsuits—all at your expense!

In 1993, inmates filed more than 33,000 lawsuits, with each jury trial costing taxpayers an average of $50,000. In Arizona and Iowa, prisoner lawsuits accounted for 48 percent of all civil litigation in Federal Court. This figure was 46 percent in Wisconsin and 42 percent in Arkansas, according to a July 1994 report on ABC's *20/20* news program. To make matters worse, most of these prisoners claim they cannot pay the court filing fees on their petitions. So you pay for this litigation nightmare from start to finish!

And what are the prisoners complaining about? The same *20/20* program profiled one Florida prisoner who filed more than three hundred lawsuits over such mundane matters as receiving only one salad or a single dinner roll at meals or receiving no television privileges. An Illinois prisoner sued when guards barred him from attending chapel in the nude. Another inmate sued because his prison served only creamy peanut butter, rather than the crunchy kind. In a 1982 case costing taxpayers more than $60,000, a Florida inmate filed a complaint alleging police brutality because a guard hit him with a flashlight. But he cleverly failed to mention that he was stabbing the guard repeatedly with an ice pick at the time!

Other accounts include a New York inmate filing a million-dollar lawsuit claiming cruel and unusual punishment. For what reason? Because of events surrounding a guard's refusal to refrigerate the prisoner's ice cream! Then there are prisoners suing to protest limits on Kool-Aid refills or lack of a prison salad bar. One even sued a county government for damages because he broke his leg trying to escape from jail.

Commenting on these inmate lawsuits, Missouri Attorney General Jay Nixon remarked: "It's a huge drain on the system. We have as many as 60 lawyers working on these cases at any given moment. . . . I appear to be the most sued person in the state of Missouri."[18] New York Attorney General G. Oliver Koppell, estimating that it takes 20 percent of his department's resources to defend inmate lawsuits, complains: "These cases are burying us."[19]

To prisoners, these lawsuits are great fun. They are a form of recreational litigation used to intimidate and punish others. The time and expense of litigation that keep many of us from filing suit is no deterrent to inmates. They enjoy years of free time researching their cases and filing fee-free lawsuits. As a bonus, each suit provides them with a "field trip" from prison and a chance to go to court and hassle officers and other governmental officials. You and I may see this and demand a stop to this outrageous practice. But these abusive individuals hide behind their constitutional rights. They also are part of "We, the people." But selfish and destructive people like this do great damage to America's legal system, and we all suffer for it. This intolerable situation begs the question: "*Why* can't we mediate some of these silly disputes quietly within our prison walls?"

Dwindling Judicial Resources

In years past, our federal courts handled a limited range of cases. The various state courts handled most legal disputes. But in the 1980s and 1990s, Congress has been enacting numerous new federal criminal statutes and civil claims as part of its war on drugs and similar legislative measures. In doing so, it is federalizing penalties for matters such as carjackings, drive-by shootings, stalking, and abortion clinic blockades.

This action shifted many cases, otherwise handled in state courts, into the federal courts. The number of drug cases alone in federal courts has increased 270 percent from 1980 to 1990.[20] In the 1994 Federal Judicial Center report mentioned earlier in this chapter, 69.7 percent of federal appellate judges and 75.1 percent of all federal district judges were strongly in favor of restricting federal criminal prosecutions to reduce the number of cases for ordinary street crimes in the federal courts.[21]

The number of cases increases year by year, and there are never enough judges available to handle all the cases. The number of federal judgeships has more than tripled from 264 in 1948 to 829 in 1990.[22] But this represents only judgeship positions—it does not mean judges are in those positions and hearing cases. In recent years, many judgeships remain vacant, some for as long as four years, because either the President has not made enough nominations for consideration by the Senate Judiciary Committee or the positions lack full funding by Congress. As of April 20, 1994, there were only thirty-one nominees pending for 137 vacancies on the Federal Courts of Appeals (21), District Courts (85), and Court of International Trade (31).[23]

In 1993, 11th Federal Circuit Chief Judge Gerald Bard Tjoflat blamed that Court's 18 percent increase in backlogged appeals and decline in output on long-standing judicial vacancies—with one vacancy being open for nearly three-and-a-half years.[24] Result? They adopted shortcuts to cope with the rising caseloads—fewer oral arguments, publication of fewer opinions, and a heavier reliance on law clerks and staff attorneys who may not have enough skill and experience to move the case to a proper conclusion.[25]

Some federal courts use a stopgap measure to deal with the resource crisis and to keep the system from collapsing. They use retired federal judges as senior judges to handle the caseload. In 1990 the work of senior district court judges equaled that of 79 active judges, which covered the vacancy loss in that year. In 1992 these judges did the work of 92 active judges. But the courts needed the equivalent of 109 active judges that year to cover the workload that was lost due to vacancies.[26]

The 1994 Federal Judicial Center report states that more than 58 percent of all federal appellate and district judges responding to the survey found delays in filling judicial vacancies to be a "large" or "grave problem" in our federal courts.[27] The dwindling resources in our federal courts mirror the problems in many state judicial systems as well. There just are not enough judges to cover the increasing caseloads in our courts.

In addition, the time and attention required per case differs radically. Consider how many months, and even years, that high-profile cases like the Manuel Noriega or O. J. Simpson trials require. But even this time drain is not unique in our court system. Stanford Law Professor Deborah L. Rhode recalls a California judge who spent ten days handling a $100,000 commercial dispute. During the same time, a typical domestics relations court judge in California could handle one thousand cases involving children.[28]

If cases increase and judges have too little time, the priority shifts to criminal cases. Civil cases get tossed aside. Judges in the federal district court in Miami, Florida, saw their average caseloads of pending civil and criminal cases rise from 355 in 1987 to 478 in 1992. Also, the average number of trial completions plummeted from 56 in 1987 to 39 in 1992. Part of the reason were the mega-trials that tied up various judges. Federal Judge Ursula Ungaro-Benages confessed, "I've been a little frustrated because it's impossible for me to conduct any civil trials. The criminal docket is so heavy there's no time to do it."[29] As Judge Aaron Ment, State Court Administrator for Connecticut, remarked: "When the cases come in by the hundreds of thousands and the judges are numbered by the tens, you can be the best managed court in the world and not, simply by management or hard work, abolish a backlog or stay timely."[30]

Can you see what is happening here? Our government has been cutting back on judges and court resources as more people file suit against each other. This is a bit like trying to squeeze just a little more air into a balloon that is already stretched to its maximum limit and ready to burst. To keep this from happening, you will see your legislators and other governmental officials yelling for emergency measures and funding to hire more judges and other court personnel. If the choice comes down to raising your taxes or letting the court system self-destruct, much as the legislators dread doing it they must (and will) raise your taxes to pay for these measures. And more taxes means less income for you and your family.

The Cash Crunch

An old Yiddish proverb says: "With money in your pocket, you are wise and you are handsome, and you sing well, too!" Many states today would love to have money in their pockets to support their court systems. And they are singing a very sad song. It almost has become an annual joke—if it's springtime, the federal judiciary must be in a cash squeeze. Our federal court system is a huge monster that needs *billions* of dollars each year to operate. This is especially true as the amount of litigation rises rapidly.

In 1992 Congress appropriated $2.4 billion for the judiciary, but this was about $400 million short of what the courts requested. Result? According to the Administrative Office of the U.S. Courts, the federal judiciary had to operate with only 79 percent of the support staff that is necessary to function properly.[31]

Due to federal budget shortfalls, courts made plans in April 1993 to postpone all civil jury trials across the nation beginning May 12 because there were not enough funds to pay jurors.[32] On Monday, June 22, 1993, for example, lawyers for both sides showed up in federal court to begin trial preparations on a police brutality case in Miami. But Judge Lenore Nesbitt sent them home. Federal funds for civil jurors ran out before the weekend. (Jurors receive $45 per day plus a 25-cents-per-mile travel allowance and free parking. The law does not permit them to work for free.) Everyone had to wait until Congress passed a $1.9 *billion* supplemental appropriations bill that included $5.5 million to pay jurors weeks later that summer.[33]

By July 1993, ABA President J. Michael McWilliams noted:

> The federal civil and criminal justice systems in this country once again are threatened by a virtual shutdown of operations.... This is the third year in a row that the federal judiciary has faced a funding crisis and the attendant likelihood of delayed civil trials and dismissed criminal prosecutions. Congress has historically provided the requisite supplemental appropriations to meet such shortfalls. Nonetheless, payments for court-appointed panel attorneys under the Criminal Justice Act were suspended for six weeks last year. This is but one symptom of the chronic underfunding from which the federal judicial branch has suffered for years.... Demands on the system, many of which are beyond the control of the judiciary, have grown tremendously. Yet federal resources devoted to the system have remained static—less than one cent of every federal dollar spent.[34]

By 1994 the courts wanted $3.1 billion. Each year the figure rises. Where will it end? How much longer can Congress budget for these demands and make emergency appropriations to fund shortfalls? Where will the money come from—education, defense, or social security? And if the funds do not come quickly enough and cases are put on indefinite hold, will some people ignore the courts and take matters into their own hands?

Part of the problem is that Congress and state legislatures do not make funding of the justice system a high priority. The U.S. Justice Department's Bureau of Justice Statistics reports that altogether, federal, state, and local governments in America spent about $74 billion in 1990, or about 3.3 percent of their budgets, on their respective justice systems. By comparison, social insurance payments accounted for 20.5 percent, education and libraries were 14 percent, payment of debt was 10.7 percent and transportation was 3.5 percent.[35]

Many state courts grapple with their legislatures for more funds. For example, the Dade County Florida grand jury surveyed Miami's criminal justice system in 1993–94 and determined, "Our system of justice is truly broken, but, like Nero's fiddling over a burning Rome, our state Legislature has historically pretended it is not." They described the situation as being like standing on the edge of an abyss due to the failure of state legislators to raise taxes to build enough prison beds to remedy Florida's chronically crowded state prison system. Though the legislature provided funds for constructing 17,033 new prison beds in April 1994, the grand jurors insisted that this did not come close to meeting the demand. Result? Fewer felons go to prison and end up on probation because of limited prison space. Other serious offenders win early release and victimize citizens once again.[36] This strikes fear into our society. Problems like this, immortalized in the infamous Willie Horton ads of George Bush, helped cause Governor Michael Dukakis to lose the 1988 presidential election.

On the civil side, in 1992 the courts and the Florida Bar used their maximum effort to lobby for additional state court judges to attack the burgeoning caseload. For the first time in many years, the Chief Justice of the Supreme Court of Florida appeared before the legislature to appeal for the needed judges.[37] The Florida Legislature's response? While the budget for state government tripled between the 1984–85 and 1994–95 fiscal years to $38.8 *billion*, the total budget for state courts merely doubled to $179.9 *million* as inflation (at 42.7 percent for the 11-year period) devoured much of that increase and caseloads escalated in increasing pressure on the judicial system.[38]

In 1993 a budget crunch in Louisiana forced the government to stop payments to more than five hundred private lawyers who were defending the state in various civil lawsuits. These attorneys turned over their files to the state attorney general's office because the state could no longer pay the bills. Result? Almost four thousand civil actions sat dormant in the courts. Meanwhile, the attorney general, who originally hired the lawyers to ease the overload, had to cope with these returned cases *plus* nearly seven thousand other pending lawsuits and two hundred new lawsuits filed each month.[39]

Matters were worse in Connecticut. A 1992 ABA study found that that state's court system was on the verge of financial bankruptcy in 1991. There were employee layoffs, forced vacations without pay, increases in civil and criminal fees, nonpayment of per diems to jurors, and even a brief suspension of civil trials. Response by the Governor and Connecticut Legislature? They cut the 1992 budget appropriation for the courts by almost 4 percent![40]

Because the specter of raising taxes strikes fear into the hearts of legislators and taxpayers alike, some states resort to other fund-raising measures. In 1994 Florida Supreme Court Chief Justice Rosemary Barkett vowed to break the family court logjam by adding various intake and case managers to each state judicial circuit. The goal was to steer domestic disputes into counseling and mediation without requiring judge time. The estimated cost for this staffing alone was $8 million. But how would the state get the needed funds? Hiking marriage license fees to $100 from $63.50 was one solution, but that would only reap $4.5 million. Another proposal raised divorce filing fees by $60, but that still would not generate enough funds. In addition, it could severely increase the financial burden on many hurting spouses in dividing households.

After lengthy debate, the Florida Legislature finally agreed to a compromise proposal in April 1994. They raised marriage license fees by $25, accounting for funding of about $3.25 million.[41] This left everyone unsatisfied, but it was better than nothing.

The situation in Florida is a typical example of how state courts and legislatures must scramble for funds during the 1990s and into the next century. Somehow you and I will have to pay to help out our courts. And this means less money for our families.

Questionable Litigation

Overwhelming caseloads, coupled with limited judicial resources and inadequate funding, are serious enough problems. But it does not end there. There are countless examples of vexatious or unnecessary litigation clogging up our courts, as we have already seen in part 1 of this book. Why don't "We, the people," as citizens and neighbors, realistically evaluate our cases and settle disputes privately instead of contributing to the pressures that are breaking down our justice system by filing unnecessary lawsuits?

For example, in a 1987 Florida case, a trespasser who had been drinking climbed over a private pier railing at a South Miami Beach oceanfront motel and dove twelve feet into shallow waters at a public beach next to the motel. When others pulled the diver from the water, he smelled of alcohol. When he discovered his dive left him a quadriplegic, he brought an action against the motel owner for negligence in maintaining the motel property. The court held that the motel owed no duty to the diver, who was trespassing, except to avoid willful injury to him and to warn him of known dangers not open to ordinary observation. Satisfied that these prerequisites were more than met by the motel owner, the court concluded that the diver's negligence was the sole proximate cause of his injury.[42]

Certainly this was a tragic injury. But was it right for the diver to sue the motel owner for his own negligence? Do we need trial and appellate courts to tell us this?

Or consider the case where ducks and rats invaded the balcony of a condominium owner in the Village of King's Creek in Miami, Florida. To resist the onslaught, the owner installed metal screening around the balcony. The condominium association demanded that the owner remove the screening and filed suit. The trial court ordered removal of the screens, but allowed the owner to plant shrubs and bushes around the balcony. Not satisfied with the result, the association appealed the decision. The appellate court affirmed the lower court's very common sense ruling and praised it as a "Solomon-like compromise."[43] But why must we clog up our courts with such trivial matters? Isn't this the type of case that disputing parties could (and should) resolve in private mediation?

In a case that captured national attention in 1992, Stella Lebeck of Albuquerque, New Mexico, sued McDonald's for burns suffered when she accidentally spilled a cup of hot coffee, received from a drive-through window, into her lap while sitting in her car. She argued that the coffee was too hot, although the serving temperature was the same as that served by most fast-food restaurants. Nevertheless, in August 1994, she won a verdict for $2.7 million in punitive damages and $200,000 in compensatory damages, reduced by $40,000 for her own negligence (although the judge later reduced the award to $640,000, and McDonald's quietly settled the case in December 1994 rather than fight an appeal of the decision).[44] In the past, cases like this would be settled quietly. The restaurant would pay any medical expenses and the customer would feel stupid for mishandling hot coffee. Not so today. I make a mistake—you pay!

Another case of national prominence was the lawsuit filed in November 1992 by eighty descendants of an all-but-vanished Paugussett Indian tribe. They laid claim to most of the land in Downtown Bridgeport, Connecticut and four suburbs, thereby clouding the title to more than $10 billion in real estate owned by many hundreds of property owners. Did they really want to recover ancestral lands? No. They used the lawsuit as leverage to gain federal recognition and lucrative casino gambling rights![45]

Then there is the case of Arturo and Vivian Tezanos of Miami, Florida, whose car bumped into the back of the hearse carrying their daughter's casket during a funeral procession. Since the casket was knocked slightly askew because of the collision, the Tezanos sued Caballero-Woodlawn Funeral Homes and the limousine driver for more than $500,000. Referring to the deceased, who died in a fiery car crash in December, 1991, the lawyer for the Tezanos remarked, "She can't even rest in peace. Not only did she have a violent death; she had a violent funeral." The family-owned funeral company owner apologized profusely, noting that it was the only time in many decades that an accident occurred during a procession. This case should have been settled peacefully among the parties and dismissed as an unfortunate accident. But it did not. The Tezanos are taking the case to trial in February 1995.[46]

But most cases are just neighbors suing neighbors, like Kevin Foley of Key Largo, Florida, who sued neighbor Dayami Diaz in 1993 because Diaz's Chihuahua, Rocky, somehow impregnated Canella, Foley's Rottweiler. Foley documented the amorous interlude on the deck of his house with photographs that were submitted to the court. Diaz countered by presenting testimony of other dog-owning neighbors who hinted that Canella did not have the highest morals, even by canine standards. But after hearing all the testimony, Monroe County Judge Reagan Ptomey issued a two-page order requiring Diaz to pay Foley $2,567.50.[47]

There are *many* other case examples of neighbor lawsuits that one could cite, such as the 1989 case at the Lake Wildwood Association in California, in which a home owner spent more than $40,000 in legal fees in a dispute over a $750 fence. After losing the decision, the home owner also had to pay the association's legal fees of $61,000.[48] No doubt you have heard of many similar travesties in your state as well.

A crushing caseload. Limited judicial resources to cope with the massive number of lawsuits. Fewer funds to pay for vital services in our judicial system. Unnecessary litigation. And our nation's law schools graduate more hungry young lawyers each year! This is a formula for courting disaster in our country before the end of this decade.

Is there any hope on the horizon? The answer depends on each American—you and me. What can we do to manage this crisis before it is too late? I believe it begins in our homes. Family, friends, and neighbors must become more of a national priority. And Christians know, as did the founding fathers, that this responsibility begins with God. "Unless the LORD builds the house, its builders labor in vain" (Ps. 127:1).

The Source of the Crisis: Family Breakdowns

Our court crisis is a symptom of a deeper and more troubling cause: family breakdowns. Former First Lady Barbara Bush said it well in her Wellesley College address some years ago: "At the end of your life you will never regret not having passed one more test, not winning one more verdict, or not closing one more deal. But you will regret time that you did not spend with your husband, a friend, a child, or a parent. If you have children, they must come first. Our successes in this society depend not on what happens in the White House, but what happens inside your house."[49]

In a pioneering study on family strengths, outlined in her 1983 work *Traits of a Healthy Family*, Dolores Curran found common traits among the strong families she surveyed and studied. Her conclusions? Healthy families communicate and listen to each other. They affirm and support one another. They teach respect for others. Healthy families develop a sense of trust; know how to play and enjoy good humor; have a sense of shared responsibility; teach the difference between right and wrong; develop family traditions; enjoy balanced interaction with each other; value service to others; foster communication; share leisure time; and admit failings while seeking help for problems. As Christians, we would add to the top of this list that the strongest families acknowledge and worship Christ as Lord, with proper respect for the roles and responsibilities of each family member.

But these are ideals. What is the reality today in America? Since we are not achieving the success in society that Mrs. Bush alluded to, how are we doing in our homes?

Unhappy Families

Florida Judge Herboth Ryder once quoted Tolstoy's *Anna Karenina* in a family property dispute: "All happy families resemble each other; each unhappy family is unhappy in its own way."[50] This is tragic, but true. And when unhappy families break apart, splits in our communities develop as well. Whenever division occurs, to paraphrase Abraham Lincoln, "A house divided against itself cannot stand."[51] The family breakdown occurs parent-to-parent and parent-to-child.

What Is Happening to Our Children?

It is better to build children than to repair adults. But we as Americans are failing in this task. We have full schedules; the children will just have to wait. The Census Bureau reports that over 1.6 million youngsters aged five to fourteen remain home alone each day in America. Population expert Martin O'Connell says this absence of supervision forces "these kids who are seriously looking for guidance or leadership, to go out and seek it on their own."[52]

A common theme of this book is that our government needs more money to address our nation's problems, which means higher taxes for all of us. And this means less money for our families. What happens then? As Walter Russell Mead explains it:

> Most people's paychecks aren't rising as fast as their bills—
> and they know it. As they cope with a generation of falling wages,

most American families have adopted a simple strategy to cope with rising expenses and stagnant or falling incomes: They work more. Specifically, women work more. Only one type of family saw its average incomes rise in the expansionary '80s: married couples with working wives. It didn't come from the men—80 percent of husbands saw their incomes fall during this period. . . . American wives in two-wage-earner families increased their hours of work by an average of 32.3 percent between 1979 and 1989.[53]

———

But as mothers and fathers work more at the office, the children suffer neglect and harm. This is precisely the dilemma that has been created by the overwhelming crush of cases backlogging in our courts today. It all comes back to each of us needing more work to make more money while ignoring our families. This exacerbates the whole cycle of national woes.

In April 1994, John Wilson, acting administrator in the Juvenile Justice and Delinquency Prevention Office of the Department of Justice noted: "We are paying a heavy price in society for neglecting our families and children, a price paid in violence in our streets, in our schools and in our homes."[54] Florida Coalition Against Domestic Violence President Mary Nutter would agree: "I believe the violence that's in our streets has spilled out of our homes."[55]

Broward County, Florida, Judge Kathleen Kearney sees the wreckage of families in the faces and eyes of children who come into her courtroom for child dependency proceedings. "The public should see everything that occurs . . . The problem is so bad that I really am frightened for the future of our country from what I see in our courtrooms every day."[56] Others have described the cause as a breakdown in nurturing of children by parents, resulting in a generation of people with low self-esteem—people who are insolent and undisciplined, selfish and uncaring, and unwilling to accept responsibility for their actions.

Problems stemming from the breakdown of the family cause our entire nation to fear and distrust each other. On September 14, 1993, the entire world grieved over the slaying of British tourist Gary Colley and the attempted murder of his girlfriend, Margaret Jagger, at a remote Florida highway rest stop. Who would do such a heinous act? Four teenage boys, two of whom are brothers. They had faced more than one hundred criminal charges in their young lives before this slaughter. The youngest of the four, a thirteen-year-old, received a ten-day suspension from school on the day of the shooting. He had fifteen prior arrests on more than fifty charges.

Meanwhile, among the 2,600 residents in nearby Monticello, Florida, the boys' hometown, three mothers grieved over their sons and their sons' mistakes. That is tragedy enough. But this thrill killing caused worldwide reactions, affecting the tourist industry for the entire state of Florida. The emotional and financial cost is without measure. All because of a family breakdown and a random, senseless act of violence by troubled children.

In his 1994 address to the ABA's Seventh National Conference on Children and the Law, John Wilson pointed out that, over the previous five years, violent crime arrests of juveniles increased by 50 percent, double that for adults. Juvenile arrests for murder increased 85 percent during the same period, in contrast to a 21 percent increase for adults. The reasons? Single-parent homes, availability of drugs and guns, and rampant gang activities.

Wilson pointed out that 11.9 percent of our children lived in single-parent homes in 1970, but this jumped to 24.7 percent by 1990. This means "less consistent discipline and moral and spiritual guidance for children, more after-school and evening hours without mom and dad, and more opportunities for involvement in drugs and alcohol, teenage sex, gangs and delinquency."

A July 1994 National Law Journal poll of 250 juvenile court judges across America backs up these alarming statistics. Most of these judges believe today's youth are more depraved than the youth of fifteen years ago. The most significant factor for this delinquency? Single parent homes and family breakdown. The side effects of increasing delinquency will not surprise you: 68 percent of these judges described their caseloads as "hectic" or "crushing." Almost half of the judges who responded admit outright that the juvenile justice system is failing because the judges don't have enough time to give most cases the consideration they deserve.[57]

As we abdicate our parental responsibilities, we are endangering the future of our nation. Our children are becoming more depressed and stressed-out because they are not being taught moral values and responsibility. They are vulnerable to evil influences. By the time the child first enters a criminal court, the child's life is already scarred. As juvenile cases increase each year, this further burdens the entire court system. Unlike civil litigation, criminal cases cannot be ignored. When tax dollars are used to put more cops on the street and for more judges and court staff to handle the flood of juvenile cases, civil court disputes inevitably come up on the short end as funding resources strain.

What Are Parents Doing to Each Other?

Divorces are not only destroying families; they are a major reason for the crisis now facing our courts. The National Center for State Courts reports that domestic relations cases make up over one-third of all civil cases nationally. In Florida, traditional criminal and civil cases account for less than 42 percent of all court filings. The bulk of the caseload? Family-related matters (dissolution, juvenile, or dependency cases), which account for 48 percent of the filings. To make matters worse, 54 percent of the dissolution cases being filed are made by husbands and wives without any legal representation, which require even more administrative court supervision and inevitable delays.[58]

In 1991 Florida's circuit courts received 26,749 new domestic violence cases—7 percent of all cases filed. In 1992 this number rose to 35,597—9.7 percent of all case filings. "[In 1992] 109,449 domestic violence instances were reported to the [Florida] police. The number of domestic violence cases has grown so much the Center for Disease Control in Atlanta is studying domestic violence epidemiologically, like any other cause of death and disability."[59]

The family breakdown is a symptom of the way our culture is losing touch with vital morals and values which are needed to keep order in our society. People want government—civil and criminal courts, law enforcement, and schools—to bring us back to a saner society. But government cannot block divorces or be a substitute parent and instill the vision and moral absolutes needed to mold a child into a responsible adult. As National Law Journal Editor Doreen Weisenhaus noted:

> Domestic relations cases, which comprise one-third of the civil caseload, are the fastest-rising part of the civil docket. But legislatures can double the ranks of the family court judiciaries, and the caseload still would grow. What's at work here is the increasing "legalization" of American society, a process of which court caseloads are merely a symptom, not a cause. The domestic relations caseload is a mirror of disintegrating families and stresses outside the home that directly or indirectly lead to such horrors as child and spouse abuse, skyrocketing divorce rates and young people in trouble. The courts, unfortunately, are being asked to be surrogate families, schools and legislatures. . . . Instead, other societal institutions—schools, families, companies, legislatures—are unable or unwilling to make hard decisions, and the problems are dumped on the court system, which after all serves as the arbiter of last resort.[60]

————

BECOMING A NATION OF DOERS ONCE AGAIN

Given that many parents cannot, or will not, provide the nurturing and guidance children need, there is something we can do to meet the critical needs we face today. We can create an environment in which mediating institutions—alternative dispute resolution centers, counseling centers, church and private mediation providers—can flourish. We can begin by helping each other assume responsibility for the consequences of our decisions and personal failings. We can encourage parties in conflict to meet with each other face-to-face once again to resolve problems and receive help toward reconciliation instead of encouraging them to deal impersonally through governmental agencies and lawyers.

As one commentator expresses it, "The current judicial system has to a great degree turned us into a nation of victims rather than a nation of doers. We cannot govern ourselves if our choices become inconsequential and if process becomes an end in itself. We must be a people of substance leading creative lives. To that end, we must enjoy a freedom that cannot exist when a formal legal system comes to govern us, instead of our governing ourselves."[61]

Even more, we serve one another best by pointing each other to the One—Jesus Christ—who truly has the answers to life's problems. He gives us the wisdom and power to make the needed changes that transform people into spiritual, healthy, joyful, and productive human beings.

Questions for Personal Reflection

1.   Do I know how the current crisis in America's judicial system affects me and my family?

2.   What have I done, or not done, to make this present crisis worse?

3.   What personal disputes or conflicts risked involving me in a lawsuit?

4.   What can I do to provide information to others about the crisis in our courts and the alternatives to litigation?

5.   If I become involved in a dispute, will I seriously consider mediating the matter with the other party before considering litigation?

Part Two:

God's Solution—Mediation

The first to present his case seems right, till another comes forward and questions him. (Prov. 18:17)

৯৯

Everyone should be quick to listen, slow to speak and slow to become angry, for man's anger does not bring about the righteous life that God desires. (Jas. 1:19–20)

৯৯

What causes fights and quarrels among you? Don't they come from your desires that battle within you? You want something but don't get it. You kill and covet, but you cannot have what you want. You quarrel and fight. You do not have, because you do not ask God. When you ask, you do not receive, because you ask with wrong motives, that you may spend what you get on your pleasures. (Jas. 4:1–3)

৯৯

If your brother sins against you, go and show him his fault, just between the two of you. If he listens to you, you have won your brother over. But if he will not listen, take one or two others along, so that "every matter may be established by the testimony of two or three witnesses." If he refuses to listen to them, tell it to the church; and if he refuses to listen even to the church, treat him as you would a pagan or a tax collector. (Matt. 18:15–17)

৯৯

*I*n I Chronicles 12 we learn of the "mighty men" who came to help David at Hebron. They sought to turn Saul's kingdom over to him. One of the crowning glories of these men was that they *understood the times,* and they knew *what should be done* (1 Chron. 12:32). They knew *why* there was a problem (discernment), and knew *what* needed to be done (action). Like these mighty men, we too must open our eyes and understand these critical times in America. It is time for us to focus on what action to take to cure the problems we share.

What do our times tell us? America's courts will not service everyone with disputes. God has a better way of dispute resolution—mediation by wise, competent and spiritual believers.

Consider this comment of former Supreme Court Chief Justice Warren Burger:

> One reason our courts have become overburdened is that Americans are increasingly turning to the courts for relief from a range of personal distresses and anxieties. Remedies for personal wrongs that once were considered the responsibility of institutions other than the courts are now boldly asserted as legal "entitlements." The courts have been expected to fill the void created by the decline of church, family and neighborhood unity.[1]

––––

Supreme Court Justice Antonin Scalia expressed similar thoughts:

> I think this passage [1 Cor. 6:1–8] has something to say about the proper Christian attitude toward civil litigation. Paul is making two points: first, he says that the mediation of a mutual friend, such as the parish priest, should be sought before parties run off to the law courts. . . . I think we are too ready today to seek vindication or vengeance through adversary proceedings rather than peace through mediation. . . . Good Christians, just as they are slow to anger, should be slow to sue.[2]

––––

It is time for us to take these wise words to heart, for the sake of ourselves and our country. Taking personal responsibility for resolving disputes privately challenges each party to deal with anger in a constructive way, exercise biblical forgiveness, and promote genuine repentance from sin. Will you commit yourself to do it?

In the Sermon on the Mount, Jesus tells us, "Blessed are the peacemakers, for they will be called sons of God" (Matt. 5:8). Will you be one to restore peace to a broken relationship in your life? Will you bring wisdom and insight in mediating the disputes of others?

Chapter 9

LET THE WALLS COME DOWN!

What is the best way to resolve disputes with others? Mediation opens the way for many creative and practical solutions for overcoming problems. It is the best option for reaching agreement on a fair and reasonable settlement. The key is to mediate—not litigate—with your neighbor in conflict.

ॐ

"Mr. Gorbachev, tear down this wall!" That was the cry of then President Reagan to President Gorbachev of the USSR as he stood by the famous Berlin Wall. For many years the wall had stood, cold and gray, as a division between the German people. Twenty-six miles long and ten feet high, it was topped with barbed wire and policed by guards with every incentive to shoot border crossers without hesitation. It was an icon of tension, hatred, and division.

Then, in November 1989, with the decline of Communism, people came from everywhere wielding pickaxes, hammers, and stones to bring the wall down. What a joyous event it was! Germans from the East met and mingled with those from the West for the first time in decades. Families rediscovered one another. Friends hugged each other warmly. Reunion. Celebration. It was a very special time.

Today, all that remains of that awful wall is one short stretch left up as a reminder of what once kept loved ones apart. On that section, artists have painted a colorful mural in sharp contrast to the colorless, drab gray barrier it once was. Visitors to Berlin see this concrete and steel monument and remember. Traffic now freely passes beneath the 200-year-old Brandenburg Gate that closed after World War 2. Barriers have given way to open gates that symbolize the unity of the people.

Who doesn't rejoice when loved ones, once divided, reunite? We can see this same joy in the father who greets his wayward prodigal son in Luke 15. Whenever reconciliation sweetens the air, it is intoxicating!

How about you? Why not bring peace to your broken relationships? By filling our hearts with reconciliation, we open ourselves to many new options. But how can we remove the foreboding walls of hostility between neighbors and others in conflict? How can we encourage and prepare for reconciliation? Before we take any action, we must know our limitations. And, for some who love to litigate, it means realizing . . .

WE HAVE A SYSTEM FAILURE

We have questions that need answers. We have problems that need solutions. We have conflicts that need resolution. But so many of these important matters simply do not fit into our traditional adversarial system.

If this is true, why do so many of us love to litigate? Because we Americans have always been a scrappy people who won't give up without a fight. We love the Revolutionary War banner with the coiled snake above the words, "Don't Tread on Me!" Logic succumbs to emotion. When an opportunity arises to draw a line in the sand and challenge others to a duel, it is too thrilling to pass up. Reason is overpowered by strategies for winning. Too many of us yearn for the time when we can stick our noses in the air and spit out, "*I'll* see *you* in court, pal!"

If we have the money to fund a litigation war, what an ego boost it is to have the resources of a large law firm reassuring us, "You are absolutely right in your complaint," "This is an open-and-shut case," or "We're going to put this guy in his place *real* fast—don't worry about a thing!" It is like a field general who surveys acres upon acres of tanks and soldiers lined up in rows while pridefully wondering, "Can anyone beat me?"

If we know we are wrong in a dispute, litigation gives us a chance to postpone judgment day. We use delay tactics and questionable litigation rope-a-dope ploys, much like Muhammad Ali's famous boxing defense of lying on the ropes and covering up while the other fighter flails away and eventually burns out. We simply sit idly by and let our opponents spin their wheels while trying to achieve a result. Who knows? Maybe something will happen, or a mistake by the other side will allow us to slip out of our weak case and escape personal responsibility for our conduct.

The truth is, many Americans *like* to fight it out. Clients send lawyers into the court arena like gladiators. Strategy is the name of the game—hide or obscure important information; ignore or stonewall communication; use diversions; set up stumbling blocks on trivial or tangential issues; build walls of separation.

But deep down all of us know better. Our consciences tell us that this is not right or fair. The time has come for us to admit that this is not justice. It is control and manipulation of the worst kind, where the strong exploits the weak. If we see the evils of litigation, as many of us do, why do we continually return to these destructive ways?

You may now have the impression from Part One that our courts are malfunctioning because of a lawyer problem, a client problem, a judge and jury problem, or some combination of these elements. But it is much more than that. We have a breakdown in our *system* of dispute resolution. Sure, lawyers, clients, judges, and juries may make the crisis worse in our courts. But the primary failure is the way so many unnecessary disputes clog up our present adversarial system with its inherent flaws and problems. Litigation limits the review of important evidence, encourages delays, multiplies expense, and promotes (rather than discourages) conflicts until a final decision maker says, "Enough already!"

Attorney John C. Susko made this observation (in a divorce litigation context): "[We have] a *system* problem. The issues, the questions and the problems which must be answered and solved in the processing of [marriage] dissolution matters do not fit the traditional adversarial system as we know it. To paraphrase a recent commentator, the present adversarial 'forum' does not 'fit' the modern dissolution 'fuss.'"[1]

ABA President R. William Ide III once reminisced about an old episode of the "Andy Griffith Show" in which Deputy Barney Fife revived a dispute between Floyd the barber and one of his long-standing customers. The nature of the conflict? Whether the man paid for his haircut seventeen years earlier. Barney learns the case technically never closed. He launches a renewed investigation. The result is predictable—fist fights, bad feelings, and animosity that divides the entire town of Mayberry.

Fortunately, Sheriff Andy Taylor faithfully restores peace in his quiet and simple way. He brings the combatants together, face-to-face, and sits them down to talk to each other. He reminds them of their long-time friendship. He tears down the walls of hostility dividing them.

Realizing that they allowed their emotions to run rampant in the spirit of the fight, Floyd and his customer resolve their dispute privately and peacefully. They reconcile their differences, neighbor to neighbor, without interference from others.

Ide then marveled at how this episode capsulized the essence of mediation (and other forms of alternative dispute resolution) in its simplest and purest form—neighbors coming together privately to resolve their problems without the adversarial clash of our traditional court system. He then surveyed the litigation scene in 1993 and reported:

> However these disputes were resolved in the past, it has become evident that for too many years we Americans have relied too heavily on our adversarial justice system to resolve disputes. We have lost the community connection whereby we once turned to one another to resolve disputes. And we have used the courts and legal system to fill the void. Today we can no longer do that.

The National Center for State Courts tells us that the average civil case in a state court takes nearly 14 months to reach some conclusion. Cases in federal courts typically take seven to 11 months from filing to disposition. Our justice system is overburdened and underfunded. It is deluged with criminal—mostly drug-related—cases, so much so that civil cases are being squeezed out of the system. Ten states have had to close their courthouse doors—at least temporarily—to civil cases because of the huge caseloads. And we in the legal profession have to shoulder some of the responsibility for the mindset of turning to the courts as a panacea for every dispute. . . . As lawyers, we must rid ourselves of that mindset that prompts us automatically to turn to the adversarial court proceedings as a first resort. In analyzing problems for our clients, we must return our thinking to being conciliators first and adversarial advocates only if necessary. Even Abraham Lincoln . . . admonished his peers: "Discourage litigation. Persuade your neighbors to compromise whenever you can . . . As a peacemaker, the lawyer has a superior opportunity of being a good man [or woman]. There will still be business enough."[2]

———

One commentator recently remarked, "There are two problems with expanding the use of alternate dispute resolution: lawyers and clients, and not necessarily in that order."[3] You and I are holding viable alternatives to litigation—such as mediation—at arm's length. Why? Because we do not understand the process. Or we may harbor anxiety over putting aside old ways of litigating everything in preference to an unfamiliar procedure in an informal environment. Or we may fear trying something new.

New Wine in New Wineskins

Resolving conflicts neighbor to neighbor, face-to-face, in a peaceful manner with the goal of reconciliation is a taste of new wine to many of us. But it is the way we used to do things in this country. And it is the way God wants us to do now. Even so, we cannot put the new wine of empathy, compassion, brotherly love, and reconciliation into the old wineskin of an adversarial litigation system. We need new wineskins of dispute resolution.

Jesus knew the value of timing and how to help people distinguish between old and new concepts. He was masterful in sharing this parable with a large crowd of lawyers and Pharisees during a great banquet at Matthew's house: "No one tears a patch from a new garment and sews it on an old one. If he does, he will have torn the new garment, and the patch from the new will not match the old. And no one pours new wine into old wineskins. If he does, the new wine will burst the skins, the wine will run out and the wineskins will be ruined. No, new wine must be poured into new wineskins. And no one after drinking old wine wants the new, for he says, 'The old is better'" (Luke 5:36–39).

In this passage, Jesus makes a comparison between the incompatibility of the old Law of Moses and the new covenant of Christian grace and mercy. He uses an illustration highlighting the futility of sewing a patch of new cloth onto an old garment. The new cloth shrinks in the wash and will tear a hole in the garment. Similarly, no one puts new wine into old wineskins. The new wine, while fermenting, expands old wineskins until they burst. New patches and old garments do not mix. Neither do new wine and old wineskins.

The Pharisees saw no need to change the old ways of the Law. Jesus, the Son of God, offered them a taste of new wine, but they could not receive it. They wanted no part of Jesus' ministry of new faith, new life, and spiritual renewal (John 3:3–5; 2 Cor. 5:17; Eph. 4:22–23; Col. 3:10; Titus 3:5). They trapped themselves into old legalism and rigidity. This kept them from going where God wanted to lead them. They satisfied themselves with the old wine of formal religiosity and self-righteousness that fermented faster than they imagined. While resisting the Son of God, they measured Jesus using the short rulers of man-made traditions and laws.

Some make changes in their lives by chasing after the newest fads. But making changes that are made to please and glorify God is vision. Enlightened souls who are willing to yield themselves, their logic, systems, and syllogisms to faithfully and fully follow God's way of dispute resolution do exist. They trust Him who knows better.

New wine. New wineskins. There is a certain irony to it all. But we worship and serve a God of ironies—One who comes to us as a child born in a manger, lives as a street person rather than a conquering hero, and dies on a cross in our place. And our God gives us ironical challenges to our faith. One such irony is that it is better—much better—to meet face-to-face with those whom we offend, and with those who offend us, rather than succumb to our natural inclination to avoid them (or sue them). He calls us to honor reconciliation of relationships and to make that a priority over the possessions and rights of this world.

So for those who love litigation and hold to its established ways in the traditions of humankind, perhaps it is time to open your mind and heart and receive a taste of some new wine.

Lawyers used to the old wine of litigation also feel threatened by the new wine of mediation. We fear it. As psychotherapist Benjamin Sells, whose practice specializes in working with individuals and groups within the legal profession, says: "On one level, it would be nice if we could just chalk up the litigators' reluctance to bureaucratic intransigence or a kind of genteel foot-dragging. But I think it is more than this. I think it is fear. The litigious mind-set sees the possibility of alternative dispute resolution as a direct threat to the system of values that underlie the litigation process itself. In particular, the concepts of mediation and compromise are anathema to a system that seeks to define itself in terms of militaristic conquest. Compromise is not Victory, says litigation. Mediation is for sissies."[4] But, as Sells also says, "We act badly when we act blindly." It is time for lawyers to open their eyes to other ways of resolving disputes and truly *serve* their clients' best interest.

For many, litigation is old wine. They don't want to give it up. But they forget that our courts are old wineskins. Mediation is the new wine. Informal forums for dispute resolution in which persons in conflict sit down with each other face-to-face, discuss the issues, and reason with each other are the new wineskins. Mediation also allows parties in conflict to put into practice the spiritual principles that we will review in chapter 10.

ALTERNATIVE DISPUTE RESOLUTION

What do we mean by alternative dispute resolution or ADR? You may have heard the term used over the past few years. If not, you will hear it during the rest of this century and into the next one. It is merely a legal phrase for various methods of providing people in conflict with alternatives to suing each other in court—mediation, arbitration, mini-trials, early neutral evaluation, and other hybrid procedures.[5] The emphasis is on conflict resolution rather than adversarial litigation. It is a means of encouraging constructive communication and information-sharing for parties in conflict. It provides a forum for people to reason together in working out a fair and mutually satisfactory settlement.

Widespread public recognition of ADR really began in earnest with the 1976 Roscoe Pound Conference which brought together a think tank of judicial officials from all over America to discuss "Perspectives on Justice in the Future." At that conference, Harvard Law Professor Frank Sander proposed a courthouse screening process directing disputing parties into the most appropriate conflict resolution process. Ideas like this have sparked frequent use of mediation by many state courts.

Over the past fifteen years, most state legislatures have enacted ADR legislation for use in the courts or through statewide commissions. State bar associations now have ADR committees. The American Bar Association recently created the Section of Dispute Resolution—its first new section in twenty years. Over one-third of the federal courts had ADR measures in place by 1990 as well—principally as a result of the Civil Justice Reform Act of 1990 (CJRA)[6] that requires every federal court to reduce the delay and expense of litigation. In 1992 the National Center for State Courts determined that more than 1,200 ADR programs existed across the nation receiving referrals from various state courts.[7] This is a good start but only a beginning. We need even more mediation opportunities.

Just what is this new wine of mediation? How does it remove walls of hostility?

WHAT IS MEDIATION?

Mediation literally means "to be in the middle." It conveys the idea of stepping into a conflict to stop discord and encourage reconciliation. By contrast, litigation springs from the root meaning, "to carry on strife." Fighting does not cease until someone prevails.

By definition, mediation is a process whereby a neutral third person, a mediator, acts to encourage and facilitate the resolution of a dispute between two or more parties. It is an informal and non-adversarial process with the objective of helping the disputing parties reach a mutually acceptable and voluntary agreement. In mediation, decision-making authority rests with the parties. The role of the mediator includes, but is not limited to, assisting the parties in identifying issues, fostering joint problem-solving, and exploring settlement alternatives.[8]

Mediation is an informal, but structured, nonadversarial process. A third party facilitator actively encourages resolution of a dispute. It is different from arbitration (in which arbitrators are decision makers) or a trial (in which a judge or jury decides the case). Mediation offers more flexibility in considering creative solutions to disputes. The parties have more control over the outcomes of their disputes. There is a big difference between a judge telling you, "You will do it," and voluntarily agreeing in mediation to a settlement by saying, "I am willing to do it."

The role of the mediator is to guide the parties toward an acceptable settlement of a dispute. He or she helps those in conflict by providing information that is vital to settlement, clarifying and organizing facts, identifying issues, highlighting those needs critical to a solution of the dispute, aiding discussion and cooperative communication, managing conflicts, and exploring alternative ways for the parties to achieve their goals. The mediator is not a fact finder, but he or she does try to ensure that those who are involved in mediation make adequate disclosures to each other and have enough information to make informed decisions in reaching agreements.

The mediator makes no rulings. The parties involved decide what is best. The mediator manages mediation sessions so the parties can deal with each other in a neutral environment with balanced bargaining power and clear communication. The mediator continually reminds the parties of the purpose, procedure, and scope of mediation so that everyone involved remains focused on positive progress toward a mutually acceptable settlement. The mediator helps the parties test the consequences of their own choices and decisions and produces a written memorandum of understanding to memorialize points of agreement.

Most mediation proceedings are confidential. The mediator is bound to secrecy unless statements relate to commission of a crime. Mediation usually is not legally binding unless the parties reach a mutually acceptable agreement, made in writing, and signed by the parties.

Civil law mediation has a good record of resolving disputes. The Florida Dispute Resolution Center confirmed successful resolution of more than 70 percent of all Florida family mediation cases in 1989. Other mediation centers around the country experience settlement success rates of 85 percent to 90 percent. Considering that mediation is less expensive and less risky than litigation, and that parties can schedule mediation conferences more quickly than court hearings, the advantages are obvious.

WHY USE MEDIATION?

Some will ask, "Isn't mediation really just negotiation of issues?" True, there are similarities. Like mediation, negotiation brings together disputing parties with the best working knowledge of the dispute. One might think this would be opportunity enough to convince those in conflict to deal directly with each other to avoid the enormous costs of litigation and formal proof. But it is not as simple as that. There are important differences between negotiation and mediation. Consider the following points:

Disputing Parties Need a Referee

Each party to a conflict has interests and positions. Interests are desires for ideal results. Positions are benchmarks in negotiation that may or may not be a means to achieving a person's interests. Negotiation zeroes in on the stated positions of the parties more than on their actual needs and desires. It does not promote or evaluate possible imaginative solutions to the fullest extent. Parties entrench into their respective positions. Hearts harden. The conflict grows.

In negotiating face-to-face without help from a neutral party, the contest of wills and competition between sides puts people on the defense. And defensive people are not empathetic or creative in considering views of others. Left to themselves, few conflicting parties properly assess their personal weaknesses or the strengths of those in opposition. Ego turns a resolvable dispute into unending competition. Both parties want to win, and neither is willing to lose. Walls go up. Having lawyer-advocates step in to voice the one-sided positions of their clients, thereby raising the adversarial tone, only compounds the problem.

Volatile situations like these where the parties lock bumpers in an issue demolition derby, cry out for a traffic cop. They need to hear a voice of reason, moderation, and balance. They need a guide to lead them into a valley of reason rather than to destroy each other by vying for who will be king of the mountain. A neutral mediator brings these elements into the conflict and sets a more positive problem-solving tone.

Disputing Parties Need Creative Input and Options

Ideally persons in conflict will be candid with one another about complaints and competing claims. However, candor can be a double-edged sword. Too often it weakens one party's negotiating position while encouraging the other to go too far. To protect themselves, it is very natural and common for people to raise defenses, use gaming techniques, and to ignore their own shortcomings and weaknesses. This severely hinders any creative solutions.

The competitive nature of negotiation escalates when lawyers or other representatives conduct the negotiations without the direct participation of the real parties in conflict. Use of advocates like these mitigates personal accountability and responsibility. The parties focus on the negotiating skills of their representatives rather than on a realistic assessment of their complaints. It is tempting to listen to the arguments of professional advocates, who frequently seek to reduce the conflicts to cold, hard facts and the bottom line economically. So too often negotiation defines success in dollars instead of workable solutions and reconciliation of the parties.

But mediation is *reasoning* together. In a neutral environment that promotes problem-solving, the parties eventually learn to lay down their legal weapons and circle around the campfire of even-handed discussion. They review options and alternatives. A think tank forms, with the additional input of a mediator's fresh insights and ideas. The conflict shifts from you against me, to *us* against a common problem.

This is where negotiation falls short and mediation really works. If the mediator has some personal expertise in the area of the dispute and is familiar with how a court might rule on the issues, the mediator can help each party understand the weaknesses and strengths of his or her respective positions. It is not uncommon for a mediating party to exclaim, "Gee, I never thought of that before!" or "You know, now that you put it that way, I'm beginning to see this situation from an entirely new and different perspective."

A good mediator manages the conference forum. He or she works hard to keep the discussions on a level that is less adversarial and more solution-oriented than simple two-party negotiation. Rather than having the parties jump back and forth in many skirmishes on different issues, the mediator organizes the negotiation issue by issue. As a nonadvocate, the mediator is free to explore the real interests of the parties, separate and apart from their negotiating positions, and to identify reasons why a party balks at settlement.

WHAT MEDIATION IS NOT

Mediation is more than simple negotiation. It also is different from other processes of resolving conflicts and reconciling parties. For example:

Mediation Is Not Litigation

If parties need to set up a public precedent in a case, need a full public record of proceedings, want to establish a uniform policy governing many people, or want to secure a ruling that will affect many different third parties, then nonbinding, voluntary mediation is not going to provide the results that litigation can. If one or both parties want vindication of their positions, cooperative mediation will not be as useful as litigation. For people who cannot or will not accept a win-win situation, but instead want someone to win and someone to lose, a trial court will rule on *who's* right or wrong. But mediators focus on *what's* right for everyone concerned. Those in conflict and who have a litigatory mind-set usually react by walking away in frustration from an offense if they believe they cannot win or by becoming enraged enough to file a lawsuit. Mediation is an interim measure that offers parties a moderate alternative.

Mediation Is Not Arbitration

Arbitration is a different form of ADR whereby a neutral third person or panel, called an arbitrator, considers the facts and arguments presented by the parties and makes a decision intended to resolve the dispute. This decision may be binding or nonbinding on the parties as they decide among themselves or as applicable law requires.[9] By contrast, mediation encourages the disputing parties to make the decisions that will lead to settlement. Arbitration was really the first form of nonjudicial dispute resolution used as a litigation alternative. More recently, however, people are moving toward nonbinding mediation and away from the more rigid, and at times more expensive, arbitration process that is laden with legal rules.

One major complaint against arbitration, as opposed to mediation, is its quasi-judicial nature. The parties are given a decision in their case, rather than making the decision for themselves. Result? Some will not be as inclined to "own" the result as they would in mediation.[10]

Mediation Is Not Counseling Therapy

While mediation does provide some measure of therapeutic benefit, the primary goal is to resolve issues in dispute between conflicting parties. Reconciliation of the parties and emotional growth are important by-products of the mediation process. But mediation is definitely a problem-solving exercise—not individualized counseling therapy. It will not delve into a person's past or family relationships to help him or her cope with the present. Parties who need therapy are best served by seeking the services of a specialist. An impartial mediator cannot provide counseling without sacrificing neutrality to some degree, even if the mediator is a qualified counselor.[11]

Mediation Is Not Education

Parties who participate in mediation will learn a great deal about the facts of their dispute, options, and procedures for resolving their conflict. In the process, they also learn more about each other. Mediation is an eye-opening experience. It sheds light on the underlying causes of conflict—the walls that divide us. But education on the issues and discovery of facts are not the primary goals of mediation. Litigation also can satisfy this goal, but in a much more expensive and time-consuming manner. Mediation is much more than a consciousness-raising opportunity. Mediation is completely successful when it brings parties to resolution of the conflict *and* achieves reconciliation.

How Does Mediation Work?

In civil law mediation, the process usually begins when either party files an application for mediation with the court, or by a pre-trial court order for mediation entered to promote settlement. The application or court order notes the issues requiring mediation, assigns a mediator to the case, and schedules a mediation conference (usually within forty-five days). (In private mediation, the parties voluntarily begin the process by contracting with a mediator to set a conference for discussion of a particular dispute.)

If mediating parties have attorneys, they may bring them to the conference. But if one party has legal counsel and the other party does not, the mediator encourages the party with a lawyer to consult outside the meeting room or by telephone so no one feels intimidated or at an unfair disadvantage. The mediator tries to put the parties on equal footing.[12]

Most mediation conferences begin with all parties attending an orientation session. The mediator makes introductions and explains the confidentiality rule. Then a general session begins with each party making an opening statement that outlines positions on the issues. Once the parties define the facts and issues, the general session may continue, or private sessions with each party may occur as needed.

Since flexibility is a key element of legal mediation, the mediator has discretion to meet privately with each party. If one party becomes entrenched in a position and is not negotiating effectively, the mediator may seek a private session or caucus with that person. One of the mediator's functions is to explore the strengths and weaknesses in each side's arguments and to search out alternative approaches to break a deadlock. If dispute resolution is more likely in private sessions, the mediator will shuttle offers back and forth rather than continue a general session.

The mediation process continues for as long as both parties are willing to participate. Disputes typically settle in one or two mediation sessions. Even the most complicated cases can settle after five or six two-hour sessions if all parties cooperate with each other. Some states impose a maximum time limit of three hours on any one mediation session, unless both parties agree to the contrary. If the parties reaches a settlement, the mediator helps them prepare a Memorandum of Understanding or Settlement Memorandum. If they fail to agree, the mediator declares the mediation at an impasse and concludes the session.

ADVANTAGES OF MEDIATION

Mediation has many advantages. Here are just a few:

Mediation is a flexible process that can occur anywhere. Legal standing and the amount of money that is necessary to participate in mediation are much less of a problem than they are in litigation. Discovery of facts and documents becomes information-sharing rather than an adversarial, disruptive, and costly clash of litigatory roadblocks and maneuvers.

Mediation allows the parties to choose the mediator. Unlike having an unfamiliar and often inaccessible judge who is assigned to a case in litigation by a blind lottery or appointment, in mediation the parties can choose mediator(s) in whom they have some confidence and trust by personal interaction. This allows people to consider not only good training and experience, but also gender and cultural influences as well.

Mediation honors the needs and desires of each party. As each party makes known his or her needs, interests, and positions, and why a particular result is so important, all other parties can try to understand and appreciate these needs and desires. This allows a resynthesis of thinking. Maybe the parties overlooked some facts. One party may have unfairly assigned wrong motives to the other party. As the parties sensitize themselves to their respective interests and re-examine their positions on the issues, workable agreements occur.

Mediation provides a confidential forum. Private forums for dispute resolution have an inherent advantage—they drastically reduce the posturing and publicity that too often plague litigation and impede settlement. Some parties desire confidentiality more than assurances that their disputes will receive full consideration. They may not want the public to know how they settled a case out of concern that others might exploit them in trying to gain a similar settlement on copy-cat complaints. Mediation keeps private settlement discussions private. This frees parties to discuss, test, and consider various options and alternatives, both good and bad.

Mediation promotes better *communication.* Because mediation is a non-binding, confidential procedure that is entered into voluntarily by both parties, it provides an excellent environment for improving communication. The mediator is present to remind the parties to cool off or take a break if emotions run high; to attack the problem rather than the person involved without name-calling, put-downs, blaming, cursing, or screaming; to help each party express clearly how he or she is feeling, why he or she is feeling that way, and to articulate needs, interests, and positions; to listen to each party's side of the dispute and monitor discussions so that each party speaks one at a time; and to encourage mutual appreciation and gratitude for the mediation process and for any mutual successes that are gained. Adversarial measures of dealing with conflict cannot offer these vital techniques.

Mediation helps resolve cases close to settlement. Quite often disputing parties are close to agreement except for a few issues. Why should they push each other into litigation over these limited issues and risk disrupting the agreements that already have been reached on other issues? Meeting face-to-face in mediation encourages reason and compromise. It has a better chance of a quicker and more satisfying settlement. As one commentator noted:

> Empirical studies of mandatory mediation programs in family courts, small claims courts, state civil trial courts, U.S. district courts and U.S. circuit courts of appeals all have reached the same conclusions: Litigants ordered to participate in mediation are more satisfied with both the outcomes of their cases and the way their cases are handled than are litigants in non-mediated cases in the same court. . . . Depending on the court, mediation has been found to have increased the settlement rate by an amount ranging from 50 percent to 500 percent more than the settlement rate in non-mediated cases in the same court. Savings brought about by mediation, as estimated by litigants and attorneys, ranged from an average of $1,000 per case in one family court to an average of $80,000 per case in one U.S. district court.[13]

____

Mediation encourages parties to create their own *settlement.* Mediation offers the parties in conflict an excellent opportunity for self-determination. Participants who create their own settlement agreements become involved more in the issues, understand the details and nuances of the settlement better, honor personal agreements made, and are less likely to go to court for interpretation of an agreement's provisions. This results in less court involvement because the parties do not need a judge to tell them what they agreed to face-to-face. There is an emotional investment in the process and a personal attachment to the settlement that is absent when an arbitrator or judge coldly and abstractly imposes a judgment. Mediating parties can consider pragmatic factors and intangible considerations in reaching a settlement a court might be unable to consider.

Mediation promotes *reconciliation of the parties.* Mediation provides disputing parties with an excellent opportunity to bring a closure to conflicts and to open new avenues of peace in relationships in a neutral setting. Since the parties do not confine themselves to issues and facts reviewed in a legal context, they can deal face-to-face with hidden sources of conflict that rise to the surface. By focusing on the *causes* of conflict, as well as the specific issues of the dispute, the parties can choose to preserve an ongoing relationship, or end it in a less destructive manner.

This is why mediation is also the best form of dispute resolution for disputing parties who need or desire a continuing relationship, such as landlords and tenants, business partners, or members of the same church congregation. It makes good sense to avoid severing a long-standing and fulfilling relationship, rather than to sever it and suffer the disruption and costs of protracted litigation.

Mediation costs less than litigation. By its very nature, mediation is quicker and much less labor-intensive than litigation. This results in significant cost savings to the parties involved. Often five to twenty hours of mediation costing $100 to $200 an hour (1994) in reaching a settlement will be a fraction of the litigation costs and attorneys fees for each party. The parties increase these cost savings if they agree to mediation *before* litigation begins. If nothing else, a prelitigation settlement reached in mediation could save the parties endless hours of preparation for trial, reviewing testimony, assembling documents as exhibits, and completing similar time-consuming and expensive requirements.

Mediation results are more predictable than litigation results. Litigation veterans will tell you that you can win a case but still lose after spending an enormous amount of money to prevail in court. And those receiving final judgment against them lose altogether. But the most frustrating part of the litigation process is the unpredictable results. Many times it is like gambling with your future—a risky roll of the dice.

Mediation empowers the parties, giving them more control over their own destinies. There are so many options and alternative ways to reach a mutually satisfactory settlement. This flexibility helps parties forge settlements they can live with and fulfill.

Mediation also offers true closure to a dispute. If the parties agree on a settlement, the dispute is over. The case ends. There is no further litigation of the dispute. This is not true in most litigation, where rehearings and appeals can drag on for years.

Even if mediation results in an impasse, the parties usually make significant strides forward in defining the issues. Usually they develop a more congenial attitude toward each other that promotes a greater willingness to settle later. The defining of issues and friendly relationship work well in reducing the natural acrimony and hostility so prevalent in the litigation process.

Mediation is the most useful ADR procedure in the widest variety of disputes. In 1993, Harvard Law School Professor Frank E. A. Sander and Northwestern University Law School Professor Stephen B. Goldberg developed a table compiled from the experiences of professionals to determine which ADR or litigation procedures (as between *nonbinding* procedures of mediation, mini-trials, summary jury trials, early neutral evaluation, and *binding* procedures such as arbitration and litigation) are most likely to satisfy participants' goals while also being most likely to overcome settlement obstacles. They concluded:

> Mediation receives top scores on the goals table for achieving the goals of low cost, high speed, maintaining or improving the relationship, and assuring privacy—an interest that is present in many business disputes. Procedures other than mediation are preferable only when the client's primary interests are in establishing a precedent, being vindicated, or maximizing (or minimizing) recovery. . . . Mediation scores higher on the impediments table than any other procedure for overcoming impediments to settlement. . . . Because mediation is so often the preferred procedure for overcoming the impediments to settlement, we suggest a rule of "presumptive mediation"—that mediation, if it is capable of overcoming the barriers to settlement, should be the first procedure used.[14]

———

In general, mediation is much easier than litigation, and more effective and comprehensive in resolving disputes. It avoids the potentially enormous cost of tying up otherwise productive assets in litigation. Usually mediation ends in a win-win situation with no real losers.

Disadvantages of Mediation

Mediation can result in damaging delays. Since mediation is usually a nonbinding procedure, skeptics of the process view it as another time-consuming hurdle to engaging in litigation. If the parties are unable to reach a settlement, it can add time and expense to the cost of litigation. But this fails to acknowledge the excellent success that mediation has had in helping parties reach settlement. Usually the parties will know from the first or second mediation session whether any substantial progress can be made in mediation. If an impasse is likely, they can end the mediation and return to litigation. Also, the time in mediation is not a wasted effort if the parties define issues and share information that would otherwise require formal discovery procedures in litigation.

Many perceive mediation as second-class justice. Many mediators are not judges or even attorneys. Some fear this encourages a seat-of-the-pants type of justice that avoids careful examination due to the confidentiality of mediation. Will the parties have a neutral mediator who can professionally, realistically, and fairly evaluate the strengths and weaknesses of their positions? Can the mediator provide guidance on likely litigation results without giving legal advice? Some mediators do not have the skill or experience to provide this help. Nor will nonlawyer mediators be as able to communicate effectively with lawyers on legal concerns. For this reason, I strongly recommend team mediation using a knowledgeable and experienced lawyer and a sensitive and perceptive mental health therapist as mediators. This co-mediation team provides the best resources for assisting the mediating parties through almost every type of dispute.

On another front, many parties to litigation seek a definitive and firm court decision that becomes a matter of public record. Unlike a public court decision, since mediation settlement agreements are private and confidential, anything binding the parties is of little value to others in similar cases. There is no record of background discussions and process of agreement in a mediation settlement. But the goal in mediation is settlement and reconciliation of the particular parties—not to provide a court transcript. If the parties resolve the dispute, the means of resolution become less important. If they cannot resolve their differences, the mediating parties can always return to litigation.

It is difficult to secure *cooperation from unwilling opponents*. If a person in conflict files a complaint after a period of mulling over the dispute and formulating charges and requests for relief, usually he or she is not going to have a conciliatory mind-set. Therefore any offer to mediate the dispute meets with understandable skepticism and doubt about motives. Some perceive a mediation request as a ploy to secure an advantage in litigation by causing the disputing party to drop his or her guard.

This is why it is a good idea to have parties agree to mediation *in advance* of the dispute whenever possible. More businesses and professions are addressing this by inserting a mediation clause into contracts and agreements. Many churches and workplaces have written policies that encourage mediation of all disputes. The parties then know what to expect when a dispute arises. Mediation becomes a strength—not an after-thought.

Mediation lacks some safeguards offered by litigation. For all its faults, litigation does offer helpful features such as judge-monitored confrontation and cross-examination of witnesses, detailed rules of evidence to ensure accuracy and reliability, and court-enforced discovery procedures. For litigants trying to hide a "smoking gun" or withhold relevant evidence, mediation may not be as effective without the same safeguards. If relevant facts escape the notice of mediating parties, it keeps them from making an informed decision in reaching settlement.

It is also true, however, that litigation can obscure and complicate rather simple and straightforward cases. Facts can become garbled and contradictory after months or years of rehashing the same matters through interrogatories and depositions. Memories fade. False or erroneous facts can seem true when the same issues are revisited many times over.

The solution is to have clear, evenhanded rules and guidelines for mediation that the parties agree to in advance. If there is any question about the veracity of certain statements that have been made or as to disclosures and documents that have been produced, the parties could exchange affidavits confirming the accuracy or completeness of the matters that have been shared in mediation.

If a mediating party suffers abuse, a *power imbalance occurs*. Mediators will do everything possible to create a level playing field for the parties. They try to empower each person so that everyone negotiates on equal terms. But strong and uncompromising emotions, intangible control issues, and a power imbalance occur if one mediating party is abusing the other physically or emotionally. Abuse destroys equality between the parties and hurts many mediation opportunities.

But some believe that mediation still provides an excellent, controlled forum for addressing issues of abuse as well. The parties use the mediation forum as a "demilitarized zone" where specific instances and nature of the abuse can be discussed. This can educate the parties about the consequences of the abuse and show how it is affecting each of them and third parties. In mediation, the parties can set boundaries and agree upon penalties for violations. But this can only happen if the mediator is willing and effectively able to challenge and manage the abuser, rather than the other way around.

Is mediation appropriate in cases when abuse exists? It can be *if*: (1) each party feels absolutely free to express opinions and ideas; and (2) each party has adequate protection from abuse after a mediation conference. Some mediators also require that the abuser acknowledge incidents of abuse and show a genuinely repentant attitude as a prerequisite for mediation. But abuse situations are a serious concern. This is why mediators try to screen out instances of domestic violence and other abuse in premediation questionnaires and initial orientations.

Obviously no procedure for resolving disputes is without its flaws. But mediation is still an outstanding vehicle for settlement. It also offers an excellent setting for establishing peace and *reconciliation* in ways that litigation never can.

Preparing for Reconciliation

The missionaries to the Auca Indians in South America had a real problem. There was no equivalent word in the Auca language for *reconciled.* Struggling with how to share the concept of Christian reconciliation with these people, one day a translator traveling with some Aucas through the jungle came to a narrow, deep ravine. The missionary thought they could go no further, but the Aucas quickly took out their machetes and cut down a large tree so it fell over the ravine. This bridged the gap, permitting everyone to cross the chasm safely. Then the translator learned that the Aucas had a word for "tree across the ravine"—a very appropriate term to describe reconciliation.

A tree across a ravine. Is there any way to bridge the gap between adversaries? How willing are we to put our machetes to work to span the chasm separating opponents?

Consider the effort of Robert and Linda Bernecker of South Florida, who divorced after four years of marriage. A year after their son, Wesley, was born, Linda was fed up with Robert's long hours at the family nursery and at church. She packed up and left with their son in March 1991. Eleven months after their divorce, Robert still hoped for some sign of reconciliation from his ex-wife. Then, on January 30, 1992, he received one—a huge billboard by U.S. 1 that read: "Robert, we want our family together. Can we come home? Linda & Wesley." Linda had spent $1,200 for the sign, put up that morning at 9:15. By 11:30, Robert was on Linda's doorstep. Two weeks later the sign was still up by the highway with Robert's response nailed across the top in big letters: "Yes. Yes. Yes."

I like that story. But reconciliation in many other conflicts seldom occurs this way. Even so, we must be ready for it to happen, just as the father was in the parable of the prodigal son (discussed in chap. 10).

Reconciliation tears down walls of hostility to restore friendship and fellowship. Our love for Christ should compel us to follow His example as the ultimate peacemaker: "For He Himself is our peace, who has made the two one and has destroyed the barrier, the dividing wall of hostility, by abolishing in His flesh the law with its commandments and regulations. His purpose was to create in Himself one new man out of the two, thus making peace, and in this one body to reconcile both of them to God through the cross, by which He put to death their hostility. He came and preached peace to you who were far away and peace to those who were near. For through Him we both have access to the Father by one Spirit" (Eph. 2:14–18).

This passage refers to the way Christ reconciled Jews and Gentiles, fulfilling the Law of Moses with His sacrificial death on the cross. It speaks beautifully about reconciliation. Read the passage again. This time, imagine that you and your adversary are the ones spoken of in these verses. Christ wants to reconcile parties that are in conflict. This also is why He died on the cross!

We are to emulate God (Matt. 5:48). If so, are we ready to forgive and reconcile (Rom. 5:10; 12:14–21)? And how can we prepare ourselves for reconciliation in a godly way?

Reconciliation Begins with Commitment

Do you sincerely desire reconciliation with your adversary because it is a righteous action? This is not a weak or cowardly act. We commit ourselves to submission rather than trying to overcome our opponents and the situation. It is a commitment that requires the utmost courage and graciousness. The easy way out is to keep our distance from others and build walls of bitter division. It is a heroic and faithful act of obedience to tear down the walls, open doors, and restore a broken relationship once again. Are you ready?

Reconciliation Flows with Forgiveness

What kills reconciliation? Intense, unresolved anger with a failure to forgive.

Reconciliation is a two-step process that involves: (1) confessing and forgiving personal wrongs that led to conflict and division in a relationship; and (2) negotiating a mutually satisfactory resolution to the issues in conflict in the spirit of Matthew 18:15–17 and 1 Corinthians 6:1–8. Anger and resentment build a wall of stone between adversaries, a dividing wall of hostility as foreboding as the Berlin Wall once was. But Jesus tells us,

"Love your enemies and pray for those who persecute you, that you may be sons of your Father in heaven" (Matt. 5:44b–45a). If that is how we are to treat our enemies, how much more so our spouses, friends, and neighbors!

Our Lord is compassionate and gracious, slow to anger, abounding in steadfast love. He will not always accuse, nor will He harbor His anger forever. He does not repay us as our sins deserve (Ps. 103:8–10). Are we willing to do the same with our adversaries?

Tear down the wall! Give peace and reconciliation a chance.

Reconciliation Grows with Wisdom

Rejoice with any reconciliation, but take reunification slowly, with wise counsel. Healing a broken relationship requires transition and compromise. It may take weeks, months, or even years of adjustment, with lots of prayer, biblical counsel, and encouragement. Bringing back those old, close feelings that once bonded us to our former friends prepares us for good times again in the future.

In resolving a dispute, each person must commit to communicating with mutual respect. There must be mutual courtesy, honesty, and openness in discussing and resolving issues that create problems *as they arise.* Set a date to review the process of reconciliation so everyone can appreciate the progress that has been made. Define and allocate responsibilities in rebuilding the relationship as soon as reconciliation occurs.

Reconciliation Never Ends

Amen. Achieving reconciliation takes a heartfelt commitment and a lot of work. How do we get from conflict to reconciliation? What does the Bible tell us? In the next chapter we will examine specific and practical steps to resolve *any conflict.*

Questions for Personal Reflection

1. In what ways could mediation help solve America's current court crisis?

2. Are there instances when mediation would be helpful in disputes at work, at church, and even among my own family members?

3. Are there any people who have engaged in mediation that I can talk to about the process?

4. Do I truly appreciate how important reconciliation between adversaries is to God?

5. When someone offends me, do I feel the need to reconcile or to get even with that person?

Chapter 10

God's Answer: Three Keys to Resolving *Any* Conflict

Why are we so quick to rely on our own resources and ignore the wisdom of God in resolving conflicts? God has a better way. He focuses on restoring relationships rather than property. He points us to the most valuable aspects of life.

❦

Mediation is a wonderful process for resolving conflicts. But any book praising its virtues is incomplete without going to the *heart* of the matter—how we treat each other as neighbors.

What Is Our Responsibility in Life?

If you could sum up all God has to say to us in the entire Bible in one short statement on life, what would it be? A lawyer once asked Jesus this very question. His response? "'Love the Lord your God with all your heart and with all your soul and with all your mind.' This is the first and greatest commandment. And the second is like it: 'Love your neighbor as yourself.' All the Law and the Prophets hang on these two commandments. There is no commandment greater than these" (Matt. 22:37–40; Mark 12:31).

When the lawyer heard this, he asked Jesus, "And who is my neighbor?" Jesus then shared with this man the parable of the Samaritan who took pity on a stranger, who was stripped and beaten on the side of a highway after falling into the hands of robbers (Luke 10:30–37). Others turned away from this bleeding man, but the Samaritan went to the man's side and bandaged his wounds. He poured oil and wine on the wounds. He put the stranger on his own donkey and took him to an inn. He took care of the man. Who was the true neighbor? The one who exercised mercy and had compassion for his fellow man. Jesus then told the lawyer (and us), "Go and do likewise."

This brings us back to a theme we first mentioned in chapter 1—being neighbors to each other. When life is going great and we enjoy being with our friends, we love the idea of having good neighbors. We embrace it willingly. But what about during the times of conflict, sharp disagreement, and contention without end? With whom are we fighting? Our neighbors.

We have waged war against each other for too long without thinking about how we are neighbors to each other. We *are* our brother's keeper. We have strayed far from binding up each other's wounds and anointing each other's heads with oil in comfort and peace. We are the robbers now—beating up on one another and stripping each other of everything we own.

Stepping into our wars and destructive conflicts, Jesus comes to us to say, *"Stop!"* We cannot be in step with God and out of step with our neighbor. He calls us back to loving our neighbors *as ourselves.* Think of the one you love to hate. Put yourself in that person's place. That individual is a person with feelings, emotions, dreams, desires, family—one loved by God just as much as you are!

What are we to do when conflicts arise with this person? We can

- seek to even the score;
- walk away and forget about it;
- throw up our hands in exasperation and tell him or her, "OK, OK, do whatever you want. I give up!"
- capitulate and compromise on what we know to be true; or
- sensitively and humbly meet with the person while speaking the truth in love.

The first four options *avoid* conflict. Only the fifth option promotes conflict *resolution.* The last option springs from a solution-seeking mindset. Biblical resolution comes through confrontation—not avoidance— but with *gentleness* and respect for our neighbor. There is no room for hostility, cruelty, revenge, or retaliation. How the *messenger* acts, speaks, and loves is just as important as the *message* given to those who are confronted.

How do we resolve disputes with others in a biblical and loving way? The New Testament gives us three major keys on how to do it.

THREE KEYS TO CONFLICT RESOLUTION[1]

Many of us don't like conflicts. In fact, we do our best to avoid them. We see confrontation as a no-win situation that only takes time and delivers trouble. But Jesus, the Master of conflict resolution, puts the initial responsibility for resolving disputes directly upon us. In every way, He encourages us to use *quick* initiative in bridging the gap with our adversaries.

First Key—Go to the Offended

In the Sermon on the Mount, one of the greatest discourses on life and its problems ever heard by humankind, Jesus tells the multitudes:

You have heard that is was said to the people long ago, "Do not murder, and anyone who murders will be subject to judgment." But I tell you that anyone who is angry with his brother will be subject to judgment. Again, anyone who says to his brother, "Raca," is answerable to the Sanhedrin. But anyone who says, "You fool!" will be in danger of the fire of hell. Therefore, if you are offering your gift at the altar and there remember that your brother has something against you, leave your gift there in front of the altar. First go and be reconciled to your brother; then come and offer your gift. Settle matters quickly with your adversary who is taking you to court. Do it while you are still with him on the way, or he may hand you over to the judge, and the judge may hand you over to the officer, and you may be thrown into prison. I tell you the truth, you will not get out until you have paid the last penny. (Matt. 5:21–26)

———

What is the primary message of this passage? Urgency! The offender is to drop everything—even in the middle of worshipping God—and *go to* the offended to seek resolution and reconciliation.

Reconciliation precedes worship of God. Worship is a time of searching one's heart and life (Ps. 139:23–24). What will God find? Conflict? Division? Bitterness? This unreconciled conflict and broken fellowship with others adversely affects our fellowship with God. How can we say we love God, whom we have not seen, when we have not dealt lovingly with our brother, whom we have seen (1 John 3:10, 14–15; 4:19–21)? This is not a command to put off worship. It is a command to go the distance *with urgency*, reconcile with an offended brother, and then to *return* to worship.

Repentance and reconciliation with those we have offended is not meant to be done tomorrow—the Lord means for it to happen *now*. Why? Because if we are too busy with tomorrow, we will miss the things we need to do today. Because, by tomorrow, matters may boil over and become worse. Because tomorrow may never come (1 Thess. 5:3). *Today* is all we have for sure. Take it from a lawyer. If you do not act to neutralize problems when they first arise, these difficulties will take on a life of their own and steamroll over the people involved.

Who are the "offended" that are deserving of our response? Neighbors. Jesus is addressing these words to the multitudes hearing the Sermon on the Mount—the world at large. He repeatedly uses the words *anyone* and *brother* in verses 22, 23, and 24 in contexts that many in the audience— especially Jews (by reference to the Sanhedrin and leaving gifts on an altar)—would understand. All human beings are brothers to each other in the context of interpersonal conflict.

In verses 21–22, Jesus also points out the serious nature of sin. Don't miss the point He is making here, or in Matthew 5:27–30 immediately following. Jesus is not saying that some contemptuous words are more sinful than others anymore than He is advocating physical mutilation in verses 27–30. Why not? Because a person who says "Raca"[2] can hate another person as much as one who says "You fool!" A blind man can lust without sight, and a limbless person can sin as much as a whole person. Jesus *is* saying that, to rid ourselves of evil motivations and desires, our *hearts* must change through the spiritual transformation God offers each of us.

People violate God's Law not only by *outward* acts, but also by *inward* motivations of the heart which lead to those actions. Murder begins with anger (Matt. 5:21–22). Adultery begins with lust in the heart (Matt. 5:27–28). Jesus implies that the *desire* is as wrong as the act.[3]

Property disputes and money matters are secondary. The real motivation behind Jesus' command in Matthew 5 is to guard our hearts against roots of resentment, bitterness, and division. These evils cause us to brood over conflict, harbor malice, and think of revenge. They fester and eventually become uncontrollable. They crave self-justification by excusing wrongs we have committed or seeking revenge for the sins of others.

Root it out. Don't give anger a foothold in your heart. Don't let the day pass by without seeking some just and peaceful resolution. Do this as you are on your way to seek forgiveness from, and *reconciliation* (*dial-lasso*—exchanging hostility, hatred, prejudice, aggression, or rejection for goodwill, comfort, friendship, joy, love, and unity) with, your neighbor. Then you replace the chaos of sinful division with peace, order, and harmony in ways that honor God, keep the church intact, and reclaim offenders.

What if a person has no reason to feel offended? Must the alleged offender still take the initiative in seeking peace and reconciliation? Yes! Jesus addresses situations where we notice someone who has something[4] against us—not necessarily a valid complaint, but *anything* that could break fellowship or become a breeding ground for sinful thoughts. It may be an unfounded complaint or even a misunderstanding on the part of the other person. But we still have personal responsibility to take action and go to that person. If the complaint is valid, confession and repentance are appropriate. If it is not valid, we are to help the offended person understand the error and reaffirm the relationship in the process so that peace prevails (Rom. 12:18).

In every way, the primary goal in Matthew 5:21–26 is for one perceived by another as an offender to take the urgent initiative to bridge the gap with the offended. This is not a passive process at all. Very rarely will it occur on its own as people bump into each other by chance. It is the *active pursuit* of peace and reconciliation through negotiation face-to-face.

But Jesus did not stop with the urgency of settling conflicts quickly before sin takes root in the heart. He tells us *how* to settle our conflicts. This is the second key to conflict resolution.

Second Key—Go to the Offender

> If your brother sins against you, go and show him his fault, just between the two of you. If he listens to you, you have won your brother over. But if he will not listen, take one or two others along, so that "every matter may be established by the testimony of two or three witnesses." If he refuses to listen to them, tell it to the church; and if he refuses to listen even to the church, treat him as you would a pagan or a tax collector. (Matt. 18:15–17)

The first key sends the *offender* immediately to the offended to seek forgiveness and reconciliation. The second key sends the *offended* to the offender in the same spirit.

This second key addresses those who might say, "Wait a minute. I am not the offender here. He sinned against me. He must come to me." Jesus dismisses this rationalization quickly. The offended person also must take the initiative in pursuing peace. If these two keys are taken to heart by both sides in a conflict, the parties will meet on their way to see each other.

But Matthew 18:15–17 goes further. It outlines an important four-step process to follow for dispute resolution when others offend us. This is not optional—it is a command of Jesus. There is divine thought behind each step of this process and the importance of compliance in strict order. The key link between each step of the process is whether the offending person will listen to[5] the reason of others. This obviously requires time, patience, and *multiple attempts* at completing each step as appropriate to the particular situation.

Step 1—Meet privately with the offending person, one-on-one. Is the problem serious enough to pursue? It is a loving gift to overlook a minor offense (Prov. 19:11b, 10:12), but one cannot ignore a problem if it creates a lingering resentment or division. Begin with prayer for God's guidance in solving the problem and softening your heart in the process. Then go directly to the source of the problem. After all, by not addressing an offense quickly, the offender could make matters worse—especially if that person is not aware of the problem.[6]

Notice that Jesus does *not* say that if we find fault with our brother we are to challenge him to a public debate or write him up in a church bulletin. In fact, He emphasizes the need to talk face-to-face "just between the two of you," implying that we are not to tell anyone else at this point. This would hold true for public offenses as well. We are to seek out the public offender *in private.* Aquilla and Priscilla exemplified this when they invited Apollos quietly to their home to correct some error in his public teachings (Acts 18:26).

Keeping a problem "just between the two of you" is where most potential conflict resolution breaks down. Why? Christian Legal Society Executive Director Samuel E. Ericsson offers us a few reasons:

> In the church . . . we often do not follow the process as outlined in Matthew 18:15–20. We get the steps out of order. When an offense occurs, instead of going to the individual privately, we often tell it to the church first. This usually occurs at prayer meetings or other small gatherings. We mention that we're concerned about Jane or Jim because of what she or he has done against us or because of what we have heard about her or him. We then ask prayer for Jane or Jim and lay out all the details. Everybody's listening, because we all love to hear about the fallenness of others, except our own. After we've shared our prayer request, we are then bold enough to ask, "Is there someone here who will go with me to confront the wrongdoer?" And finally, when we've got the safety of numbers, with one or two "witnesses" on our side, we are then ready to go to the offender "in private."[7]

God gives us an early example of going to meet with offenders. When Adam and Eve offended God in the Garden of Eden, what did He do? He went looking for them and called out to them even while they hid from Him (Gen. 3:8–9). After finding them, He was careful to allow Adam and Eve to explain their situation (though, being God, He obviously knew the truth already) (Gen. 3:10–13). Only then did He begin to address the problem.

It is not timely or responsible for us to look the other way if another is in sin or to withdraw by avoiding the person out of anger, fear, displeasure, or neglect. Contain the problem in an informal and private manner. Keep the meeting as specific as the offense.

Approach the offender cautiously and sensitively. *Assume the best,* instead of the worst (1 Cor. 13:7). Will anyone really have all the facts before talking to the offending individual and considering that person's perspective? Perhaps a misunderstanding occurred. Matters are not always as we perceive them to be (Mark 4:12). This is not the time for suppositions, preconceived judgments, or reckless accusations. Instead, it is a time for constructive fact-gathering and enlightened, gentle confrontation— not for a bloodletting.

There is no room for gossip with others, self-justification, or self-vindication (Jas. 4:11). Talking about others promotes conflict and ill will. Talking *to* others directly is the pathway to peace and reconciliation. Keep matters confidential in a manner that is biblically consistent and appropriate to the circumstances. Why? To protect the reputations of others from any false accusations. Involving other people too early can complicate the problem.

This is not an opportunity to hit and run by venting anger and quickly dodging further conversation. We cannot rush up to others, demand our rights, and then take a relationship vacation. It is a time to make peace, rather than to say our piece. It is a time for understanding, reasonable compromise, and reconciliation, rather than a time to berate others for rude or thoughtless conduct.

Unresolved conflict that creates division among brothers is not acceptable to God. The point of Jesus' words in Matthew 18:15–17 is to unite, not divide, us. There should be no lingering problems. If an offender will not listen, it is imperative to go to step 2 rather than to leave the matter without resolution and closure so that division prevails.

Step 2—If no reconciliation comes from this private meeting, bring one or two others along. This shows that there is a deep concern and it engages a few others who desire to serve the disputing parties through aiding communication, determining the facts, exploring options and alternatives for resolution, and promoting reconciliation. They can also witness the efforts the disputing parties make in working toward a just result or can document a deadlock.

But watch out! This is not a gang or a hunting party. These other individuals preferably are neutral observers—not "yes-men," or a lynch mob that joines forces arbitrarily with one party in conflict against another. If that is loving your brother, it is only like a fox *loves* chickens!

These mature, wise, and unbiased persons should have a loving concern for all parties involved, preferably with no personal stake in the dispute. They should resist any effort by either party to lobby for particular positions in advance of a meeting. They must be on guard against rumors, unfounded or false accusations, and bad attitudes. Their role is to help conflicting parties bear their individual burdens and faithfully restore them to full fellowship in spirit and in truth (Gal. 6:1–2).

Step 3—If the meeting with witnesses fails to bring reconciliation, then bring the matter to the church for a decision. This does not necessarily mean publishing the news to everyone within earshot at a church service, including guests and out-of-town visitors. The goal is to rely upon more people who will exercise responsible and loving action in restoring an erring person who will not listen to reason and reconciliation. This is the last chance for repentance by a person who continues in open rebellion against the Lord before disfellowship occurs.

The same principle applies to nonchurch settings as well. At workplaces there are people in charge and administrative committees that serve similar functions to settle disputes. Getting help in a work-related dispute means following the administrative guidelines that are in place.

But there is a right and wrong way to put this step 3 into action. The offender should be a part of the church group or work environment before applying this discipline. If the offender is no longer present, the purpose of the larger group learning of the dispute and reasoning with that person may be lost. You may want to review some of the issues we discussed regarding the *Collinsville* case in chapter 4.

Also, step 3 will not be a viable option for some people. Why? Because their church is not prepared to handle disputes in a biblical manner. In those instances, the members needing help from church leaders in resolving disputes privately and biblically either need to change church ways of handling problems, or change churches. This is so important that it is better to be with Christians who take seriously the commands of Matthew 18:15–17 and 1 Corinthians 6:1–8 than to remain with those who do not! We cannot expect to please the Lord with our plea, "I can't do this." The failure of churches to fulfill their responsibilities in honoring Jesus' command in Matthew 18:17 is a major factor in pushing Christians into our courts. Take the initiative to get your church in line with God's Word, or go somewhere else where it is already happening!

Step 4—If even the church's decision does not bring reconciliation, the church is to treat the erring person *as* an unbelieving outsider. Note that this does not mean that a person always *is* an unbeliever. Only God knows a person's heart. He holds the key to that person's salvation—we do not (1 Sam. 16:7; 2 Tim. 2:19; Rev. 2:23).

But disfellowshipping the person and putting him or her out into the world has an eye-opening effect on the heart. It tears into anyone who is at all sensitive to how much God's love and fellowship means. If anyone chooses to act like an outsider, Christ's admonition is to treat the person that way—as an outsider, left alone and unbothered until he or she is willing to listen to reason and make the situation right.[8]

This is a logical result of disfellowshipping the person—removal from the midst of believers (1 Cor. 5:2, 5, 7, 13; 1 Tim. 1:20). It is social amputation of a person who might be introducing a serious, and possibly infectious, sin into a church community. The church is to withdraw (2 Thess. 3:6), not fellowship with the person (2 Thess. 3:14; 1 Cor. 5:9, 11), and not even share a meal with the individual (1 Cor. 5:11). Also, it is a period of mourning for those in the church, just as if the person were dead (1 Cor. 5:2a).

This may sound rather divisive and judgmental. But read the Scriptures cited. These are biblical commands. Sin is too serious to ignore. Left unchecked, it will cause even more division and heartache among many more people. After verifying the facts through steps 1–3, the church should no longer tolerate an offender who resists reason and repentance.

The clear goal of each step in Matthew 18:15–17 is not to win an argument or even to take a pound of flesh out of hard-hearted or unruly members. The focus always is to promote reconciliation of disputing parties and maintain peace within the family of God. In the meantime, this action purifies the church and reminds members that sin is so cancerous that no one should condone it among those who obediently seek to follow Christ.

Scripture clearly states that the church is a group of people for whom Christ died, to wash and cleanse them of their sins so they might be "holy and without blemish" (Eph. 5:25–27). Christians are a "chosen people, a royal priesthood, a holy nation, a people belonging to God" (1 Pet. 2:9). How each Christian lives is the general concern and responsibility of the entire spiritual family in Christ.

The apostle Paul commanded members of the church at Thessalonica to withdraw from every brother in Christ who does not live according to the teachings of the church and to not associate with that person (2 Thess. 3:6, 14–15). Elders in each Christian congregation are spiritual leaders who have been set aside to watch out for the souls who are in their care. The Bible clearly says they must give an account for those who are subject to their leadership (Heb. 13:17). It commands elders to support the weak, encourage the fainthearted and admonish the disorderly (1 Thess. 5:12–15). Civil law even grants them a qualified privilege against suit for defamatory statements made without malice in the process of doing so.[9] But how many leaders in America's churches today take this solemn biblical instruction to heart? Aren't there too many leaders who duck the sticky issues and abdicate their responsibilities, leaving Christians in their care to fend for themselves in the world?

The apostle Paul respected God's commands. He did not hesitate to order members of the Corinthian church to deliver over to Satan a brother guilty of fornication "so that the sinful nature may be destroyed and his spirit saved on the day of the Lord" (1 Cor. 5:5).

Discipline in the CorinthianChurch. Take a moment to read 1 Corinthians 5:1–5, 9–13. This was a shameful situation—a Christian having an incestuous affair with his stepmother.[10] The Law of Moses specifically prohibited this relationship (Lev. 18:8; Deut. 22:22). This matter was scandalous even in immoral Corinth. It also was illegal under Roman law. But the Corinthians, caught up in conceited self-satisfaction and indifference, were doing nothing about the offender in their midst! They enjoyed freedom in Christ (1 Cor. 6:12; 10:23), but this was never meant to be a license for sin. This disgusted Paul.[11] He called for immediate action against this obvious sin—expulsion of the man from the church assembly!

In verses 4 and 5, Paul challenges the Corinthians to use church discipline to rebuke this man for everyone's good if he did not repent. In commanding, "Expel the wicked man from among you," Paul exhorts the Christians to use urgency in separating themselves from this sinful influence. (This is the same type of urgency commanded under the Law of Moses in Deut. 17:7; 19:19; 22:21, 24, and 24:7 to purge evil from among the people of God.) It is a *very* strong statement indeed! The Law of Moses formerly commanded physical death for such sinners. God spared this man's life under the new covenant. We may think it harsh to disfellowship anyone, but God is graciously exercising personal discipline in this way to encourage repentance. He disciplines those He loves (Heb. 12:1–13).

Paul's disciplinary measure is a classic example of tough love—a very biblical concept. What is tough love? It is a *firm and measured response* to sinful decisions and ungodly actions of those we love. It helps them feel the full weight of responsibility and the inevitable consequences of their decisions and actions. Tough love sets limits on what God tells us is acceptable conduct. It enforces clear boundaries between lives that are splitting apart in broken relationships. It is the courage of speaking the truth in love. Tough love reinforces options for repentance and forgiveness rather than revenge. It often means letting go of someone who does not want to continue in a relationship. Tough love takes firm action in dealing with imbalanced and sinful situations, but it never loses sight of the *person* and his or her worth. It still loves the person despite the predicament.[12]

The focus of Matthew 18:15–17 is to promote personal accountability through loving but direct confrontations with the person in error. Each of the four steps described above encourage understanding and repentance. Each one attempts to achieve full reconciliation and restored fellowship. If necessary, each step escalates the disciplinary measures that are designed to pinch the conscience of the offender and bring that person to his or her senses. [13]

This brings us to the third key to conflict resolution. If you and a fellow Christian deadlock on resolving a conflict, what then? Consider the advice the apostle Paul gives to Christians in 1 Corinthians 6. He warns Christians *not* to sue each other, which is exactly what happens in too many disputes. God's counsel is to seek mediation within the church.

Third Key—Settle Disputes Privately

How did Jesus counsel believers and unbelievers alike on resolving disputes? "Settle matters quickly with your adversary who is taking you to court. Do it while you are still with him on the way, or he may hand you over to the judge, and the judge may hand you over to the officer, and you may be thrown into prison. I tell you the truth, you will not get out until you have paid the last penny" (Matt. 5:25–26). Settle matters privately, without going to court. This is even more imperative for Christians.

One Christian has been cheated by another. Is it time to go to court and sue for the loss? The Bible tells us no:

> If any of you has a dispute with another, dare he take it before the ungodly for judgment instead of before the saints? Do you not know that the saints will judge the world? And if you are to judge the world, are you not competent to judge trivial cases? Do you not know that we will judge angels? How much more the things of this life! Therefore, if you have disputes about such matters, appoint as judges even men of little account in the church! I say this to shame you. Is it possible that there is nobody among you wise enough to judge a dispute between believers? But instead, one brother goes to law against another—and this in front of unbelievers! The very fact that you have lawsuits among you means you have been completely defeated already. Why not rather be wronged? Why not rather be cheated? Instead, you yourselves cheat and do wrong, and you do this to your brothers. (1 Cor. 6:1–8)

———

Christians are to apply 1 Corinthians 6 to their disputes with each other.[14] Seek help and counsel from spiritual men and women in the church. It is biblical and right.

Paul uses a series of questions to argue against Christians suing each other in civil courts:

- Do you dare take legal disputes[15] with Christian brothers before the ungodly for judgment instead of before the saints?
- Do you not know that the saints will judge the world?
- If you are to judge the world, are you not competent to judge trivial cases?
- If you will judge angels, are you not able to judge the matters of this life?
- Is there nobody among you wise enough to judge a dispute between believers?
- Are you satisfied that a brother sues another brother in front of unbelievers?
- Doesn't having lawsuits among you mark you as defeated?
- Why not rather suffer wrong or be cheated?[16]

Paul is *very* forceful in demanding, "How *dare* you go to law against your brother!" Fighting over the spoils of this world, which ultimately will burn anyway, confirms that a Christian's priorities are all wrong. Just as there is a separation between church and state on the civil law side of justice (as we saw in chap. 5), Christians are to come out and separate themselves from the world (2 Cor. 6:17–18; Rom. 8:9, 13; 1 John 2:27). In 1 Corinthians 6, Paul addresses Christians who are locking horns and willingly going into the civil courts of unbelievers to battle out disputes. This shames them, their church, and Christ Himself. Instead of bearing each other's burdens and fulfilling the law of Christ (Gal. 6:2), each litigant seeks to shift burdens onto the other. One brother has something another brother covets. Or one sister keeps what another sister rightfully owns or deserves. This was merely a form of stealing between believers (Prov. 21:6; Jer. 17:11). But the deceit or theft leads to even greater sin and tragedy— believers engaging in civil lawsuits and dishonoring Christ among unbelievers. Paul saw this as a very worldly ploy (1 Cor. 3:3).

Why would believers seek relief from those who have no jurisdiction over spiritual matters? Christians seeking a verdict from the world against other Christians is like our president seeking a decision from a traffic court judge in an international trade dispute. The priorities are totally out of kilter.

As Paul correctly warns us, going to court against a fellow believer is a complete defeat for a Christian. From Part One, we know how parties to litigation suffer defeat in our civil courts. Why engage in the practice? Of greater concern is how unbelievers get turned off by a church of bickering believers. The church loses credibility by not resolving disputes internally with the power of God. And those who wear His name subject Christ to shame and embarrassment as they move far away from Him in seeking their own ends. Where is the believer who turns the other cheek (Luke 6:29)? Where is the practice of not returning evil for evil (1 Pet. 3:9; Rom. 12:13)? Where is the humility that leaves vengeance to the Lord (Lev. 19:18; Deut. 32:35; Rom. 12:17–19; Prov. 24:29)?

"But," someone will protest, "what about my civil rights as an American? Our laws allow me to enforce my rights in court if I choose to do so. Doesn't God, who sets up governmental authorities (Rom. 13), allow me to take civil action against those who wrong me—even if they are Christians?" Not so! The Word of God takes precedence over civil laws of our nation in matters of private dispute (Matt. 28:18–20; John 12:47–50; Acts 5:29; 2 Pet. 1:20–21; 2 John 9–11).

The primary goal in every instance of conflict resolution among Christians is to promote forgiveness and reconciliation between those who formerly loved each other but are now, unfortunately, divided. Reconciliation of people usually is more important than recovering property or protecting personal rights. There are few better illustrations of this than Jesus' parable of the lost son.

The parable of the lost son (or prodigal son) in Luke 15:11–32 is a lesson in dealing with conflict and broken relationships. By using the father's loving and gracious spirit as a model, we learn more about our God, receive comfort, and find the wisdom to handle our conflicts in a godly way.

Some readers will have great trouble with this parable, however. It will disturb them. Why? Because Jesus talks of doing something that they absolutely do not want to do—forgive their offenders. To those who feel this way, try to remain open-minded. Let God speak to your heart. Forgiveness appears to be an impossible task, but with God everything is possible (Mark 10:27)!

In the parable, there is deep dissatisfaction and rebellion in the younger son's heart. Like so many other tempting lies, it sounds good for someone to cry out that he must be in control of his own life and go his own way. But too often the dark underbelly of it all is a hotbed of manipulation and control, rebellion and selfish independence. If any relationship doesn't satisfy these needs, it gets axed! Isn't this how many marriages and other relationships end up on the chopping block as well?

The son acted selfishly and severed his relationship with his father. Result? Conflict. Estrangement. Division. The son wanted his share of what the father owned. He did not care about anyone or anything else. In doing so, he lost his perspective on the important treasures in life. Think about it. When selfishness like this creeps into any partnership and remains unchecked, how long can the relationship survive? The son sought wild living and the pleasures of this world. But in pursuing selfish gain and resisting his father's authority, he sold out his relationship with the one who loved him more than anyone else.

The son talked himself into believing that everyone and everything around him was the source of his own unhappiness. It was only logical that a change of scenery would bring joy to his heart, right? Wrong. Many counselors, with the best of intentions, counsel others to "Follow your heart," or "Do what feels natural to you." But Jeremiah 17:9 tells us the heart is deceitful above all things to the point that no one can understand it. We can quickly rationalize and convince ourselves that everyone else has the problem. We tie our unhappiness to our adversaries, other people, and outward circumstances. We really believe we know our hearts. God knows better! This follow-your-heart fallacy can lead us down some dangerous roads. What God asks of us may not feel natural—in fact, quite often it is unnatural for us to love and forgive as He calls us to do!

The parable (v. 14) shows what happens inevitably when a drunken, selfish spree awakens to the sober light of reality. Selfishness usually wears us out, bringing famine and degeneration. It may not come quickly in every instance. But a time of reckoning will come for the decisions we make for ourselves. Many choices have unavoidable consequences.

But what about the father? How did he react to the son's leaving home? Was it wise to give his son the inheritance early when he knew his son would probably blow it? The father (who is a picture of how God relates to us) gave the son what he asked for even though he neither earned it nor deserved it. This mirrors so much of the beautifully gracious nature of God. Yet we stop short of using this same spirit of grace with our neighbors. "God can be gracious, but don't ask me to do that with my friend after all I've been through!" Somehow we applaud God's grace, mercy, and forgiveness, but we want those who have hurt us to pay.

What was the father's attitude and reaction when the son *returned* home (vv. 20–24)? Could he have told the son to hit the road again? Sure. He could have said, "Come in, after you've wiped off your dirty feet, but you're grounded for eternity!" He could have laid a guilt trip on the son, telling him that he had disgraced the family. But he didn't. The father's attitude was, "Welcome home, son. I've missed you so much!" The father even *ran* down the road to greet the son as if he had been looking for him to come back! The father was *eager*, not reluctant, to forgive. It poured over into his actions. He didn't wait for his son to explain his repentance. He just loved him unconditionally. He treasured the relationship so much that he did not think of evening up the score of their conflict.

The point here is this: Sometimes we expect our adversaries and offenders to come to repentance for only the most rational and very sincere reasons from our point of view. Or we may demand that they admit we are the saints and they are the skunks as they grovel in the dirt for awhile. We may want them to do some penance at our bidding and suffer a little bit to balance matters out for troubling us in the first place. But geniune forgiveness doesn't work that way. And one's sincerity of heart is for God to judge—not us. Jesus tells us our task is simply this: "If your brother sins, rebuke him, and if he repents, forgive him. If he sins against you seven times in a day, and seven times comes back to you and says, 'I repent,' forgive him." (Luke 17:3b–4) Now that's *tough* to do! No wonder the apostles said to Jesus, "Increase our faith!" (Luke 17:5).

God's way is *active*, not passive, forgiveness toward those who wrong us. If they truly come to their senses in sincere repentance, we should be glad they desire reconciliation with us. After all, it's not easy coming back to say, "I'm sorry." Checking out the details of repentance can come later. Let their hearts speak to us and their actions show us the fruit of their repentance. Unconditional love accepts this response. It does not insist upon its own way. We must be ready to love them when they stand in our doorway, even if it is too late to restore the relationship fully to what it once was.

Was it wise for the father to kill the fatted calf and celebrate when his son came home? How about the ring, robe, and sandals (which symbolize restoration to sonship, honor, authority in the house, and freedom)? When the father saw the son's repentant attitude, he made *no* conditions. He just gave and gave! The son, lost and dead to the father, was now found and alive! That's all that mattered to the father. The son could have died in that foreign land, separated from his father and out of relationship with him. But the son repented and came back home. The father was ready to restore the relationship because forgiveness reigned in his heart.

If those who offend you want to start over, what will you do? What conditions will you set down?[17] Having the father's *attitude* of unconditional love and forgiveness guides us toward making right decisions.

THE DIFFERENCE BETWEEN FORGIVENESS AND RESTITUTION

Forgiveness is a two-way street. The lost son in the parable needed forgiveness as much as the father needed to give it (vv. 18–20)! There's no way to deal with that guilt and live joyfully without it. Both needed to experience release. Both the wrongdoer and the person who was wronged needed to let mercy reign in their hearts and free themselves of resentment. Freedom comes to a bearer of bitterness only when the choking yoke of resentment is cast off and the comforting oil of forgiveness is placed on the irritating wound.

If it is good for us to forgive others, why is it so difficult? One major reason is that we live in a world that is grounded on the principle of rewards and punishments. If we perform well, we receive a reward. If we fail, we receive punishment. Restoration requires a payback. Restitution is what the law requires! But God doesn't always require that the scales of legal justice balance.

Part of our problem is our failure to understand that restitution is *not* repentance. Restitution is a legal transaction. One returns or replaces what was taken or destroyed. But repentance is a change of will brought about by godly sorrow. It leads to a reformed *life*! Restitution comes from the pocketbook. Scriptural repentance comes from the heart.

God calls us to repent and turn to Him and to prove our repentance by our deeds (Acts 26:20). If one's *heart* is right before God, restitution flows willingly. Zacchaeus provides a beautiful example of this for us in Luke 19:1–10. God looks on our *hearts* and searches out those in the world who are fully devoted to Him (2 Chron. 16:9; Luke 16:15).

Restitution merely fulfills the requirements of the law. By itself, it doesn't make our hearts right. It does not reconcile relationships—it only makes injured people whole once again. And forgiveness does not *require* restitution. It does not put love on a ledger sheet. It searches for *repentance* and *reconciliation* on *all* sides of a broken relationship. As Dr. James Dobson so succinctly states on his national radio program, "Forgiveness is giving up my right to hurt you for hurting me." That isn't natural for us. It bothers us. But it is the gracious way of God.

What does it really mean to forgive someone? It means to "remember no more." It does *not* mean to "forgive and forget." There's a difference. If we really could forget life events, then we would never learn from our mistakes. We would lose some precious memories as well. But to "remember no more" means we will not seek out the memories of transgressions by others. We will not dwell on these slights. We will let these thoughts go out of our minds and instead focus on positive matters (Phil. 4:8).

The essence of responsible biblical forgiveness is to (1) *release bitterness and resentment* that is self-destructive; (2) *focus our anger* toward motivating repentance in those who have wronged us for *their* benefit; and (3) *offer to restore and reconcile* broken relationships whenever possible, even if others will not repent and accept it. If the person we forgive repents and desires reconciliation, then we should restore the relationship promptly if *reasonably* possible (Luke 17:3b–4). But biblical forgiveness encourages repentance from sin by offering the best incentives to restore fractured relationships.

And we should desire to forgive our offenders. Why? Because God has forgiven us. That's what the parable of the unmerciful servant is all about (Matt. 18:21–35). And the power of forgiveness does not fail even though the scales remain unbalanced. Forgiveness accepts scores that may never come out even for the greater victory of winning *people* over.

We may think forgiveness is our gracious act toward those who hurt us. We may think it is for *their* benefit. Not so! Forgiveness is primarily for *our* good! It allows us to lay down a relationship gently and move on. Releasing our resentments through forgiveness allows us to pick up the pieces of our lives and start over without requiring that others suffer.

FURTHER TEACHINGS OF JESUS ON CONFLICT RESOLUTION

Are you ready now for the ultimate test of your faith? Consider these words of Jesus: "You have heard it was said, 'Eye for eye, and tooth for tooth.' But I tell you, Do not resist an evil person. If someone strikes you on the right cheek, turn to him the other also. And if someone wants to sue you and take your tunic, let him have your cloak as well. If someone forces you to go one mile, go with him two miles. Give to the one who asks you, and do not turn away from the one who wants to borrow from you" (Matt. 5:38–42).[18]

There are more than a few individuals who believe that if preachers really preached what Jesus taught, the people would run them off. Those holding this view must have had this passage in mind. Too often we may have softened the words of Jesus with the familiar refrain, "Now He says this, but what He really means is . . ." This passage is a prime example that tempts us to ask, "Does Jesus really mean what He says here? Is He speaking literally? Can I accept this?"

This is not a natural way to live. It is the antithesis of how we normally respond to problems. It is an unnatural act. We have studied biblical forgiveness. That too is an unnatural act. It is not how we would respond to others who wrong us without God's guidance.

In so many ways Jesus works contrary to our thinking and desires in life. He says, "Blessed are the poor in spirit" (Matt. 5:3a). He must be wrong. We know the successful, the aggressive, and the resourceful people who gather an enormous fortune are the ones truly blessed. "Blessed are the meek" (Matt. 5:5a). Surely you're kidding, Jesus. The meek are the doormats of the world. They get walked over and spit upon. They're the wimps and weaklings.

But Jesus does know better than we do. This is no mistake. His teachings may conflict with our perspective of the world. And this conflict leads us to a choice. Will we live as Jesus challenges us to live, or will we go our own way? If we live the life to which Jesus calls us, it will be an uncomfortable fit for a while. It will not be easy. But, over time, we will feel ourselves adjusting and stretching, just like breaking in a new pair of shoes. Finally the fit feels good. Ultimately we will be *different* people, with God's help. Then we will truly be the salt of the earth and the light of the world.

Jesus tells us, "Do not resist an evil person." But James tells us, "Resist the devil, and he will flee from you" (Jas. 4:7b). Peter notes: "Your enemy the devil prowls around like a roaring lion looking for someone to devour. Resist him, standing firm in the faith, because you know that your brothers throughout the world are undergoing the same kind of sufferings" (1 Pet. 5:8b–9). We also know that Christians resist each other, as Paul did in opposing Peter publicly for his hypocrisy in dealing with the Jews and Gentiles (Gal. 2). How can we reconcile these verses? Through understanding the *nature* of the resistance.

First, the Old Testament principle of, "Eye for eye, and tooth for tooth" (Ex. 21:22–25; Lev. 24:17–22; Deut. 19:15–21) commands that punishment *by the authorities of God* (not persons in *private* disputes) fit the crime committed. It is a principle that guides legal action by the governing authorities for certain *criminal* activities—not private transactions between individuals. Nowhere in the New Testament does God give us the right to take vengeance upon others with whom we privately disagree. If it were otherwise, as some have said, we would be a world of eyeless, toothless people!

Second, Jesus' words do not deprive us of self-defense or self-preservation if others threaten us with bodily harm. Miami preacher Ancil Jenkins tells the story of an aggressor who challenged a man and wanted him to fight. Instead the man ran away. Later some of his friends approached him asking, "Weren't you ashamed? Didn't you hear the people say, 'Look at that coward run!'" The man replied, "Yes, I heard them. But it is far better to hear them say, 'Look at him run!' than to say at his funeral, 'Boy, doesn't he look *natural!*'"

We have the right to run. We can ward off blows against us without retaliation. But Jesus addresses the *attitude* behind resisting an evil person by using four illustrations.

If a person strikes you on the *right* cheek, it means a right-handed person has just slapped you with the *back* of their hand—an insulting blow. How should you handle the insult? Our natural reaction is to slap those who slap us—to retaliate and pay back harm for harm. But Jesus encourages us to turn the other cheek to this person. Do not retaliate.

Turning the other cheek is not symbolic or figurative. This is the way Jesus lived: "I offered my back to those who beat me, my cheeks to those who pulled out my beard; I did not hide my face from mocking and spitting. Because the Sovereign LORD helps me, I will not be disgraced. Therefore have I set my face like flint, and I know I will not be put to shame. He who vindicates me is near. Who then will bring charges against me? Let us face each other! Who is my accuser? Let him confront me!" (Isa. 50:6–8).

When they brought Jesus into the courts of evil men, how did He react? The Gospels record that for the most part, He gave no response. He offered no defense in the face of His accusers, who eventually condemned Him to death, spat upon Him, and beat and mocked Him (Isa. 53; John 18–19). When the authorities came to arrest Him, He did not resist. When they held His trial, He did not resist. When they took Him to be crucified, He still did not resist. He set us an example: "But how it is to your credit if you receive a beating for doing wrong and endure it? But if you suffer for doing good and you endure it, this is commendable before God. To this you were called, because Christ suffered for you, leaving you an example, that you should follow in His steps. 'He committed no sin, and no deceit was found in His mouth.' When they hurled their insults at Him, He did not retaliate; when He suffered, He made no threats. Instead, He entrusted Himself to Him who judges justly" (1 Pet. 2:20–23).

Jesus then moves on to a third illustration. If a man takes you to court and sues you for your tunic or coat[19], give him your cloak as well. Brothers made so by God have no right to be in court against each other, as we have seen from 1 Corinthians 6:1–8. But remember that in Matthew 5, Jesus is talking to a multitude of people—not just believers. He says that if *anyone* sues you, it is best to settle quickly. Why? Because if you battle it out with a skunk you're going to end up smelling like one! More than that, settle on unfavorable terms if necessary. If someone wants your tunic, give him the shirt off your back, as well, in order to settle. Fighting out matters in court is a losing proposition. For Christians, it is a spiritual defeat—a much greater loss indeed! Do everything you can to suffer wrong, before you do wrong (1 Cor. 6:7).[20]

There is practical wisdom in heeding this advice of Jesus. Pursuing our perceived rights at the expense of others, either by beginning our own legal actions or by aggressively resisting suits that have been brought against us by others, tends to steamroll and create more conflict. How? Christian Legal Society attorney and author Thomas Strahan describes it this way:

> Many Christians are as quick to start a lawsuit as anyone else and want to assert every legal right available to them if they get into some difficulty. However, if we are acting on the basis of some particular right, our action is actually based primarily on our own self-interest. Assertion of a "right" will often tend to cause alienation and division between individuals and groups. This division will first manifest itself between those contending for the "right" and those who believe that this claimed right will be gained at their own expense or diminish their position in some manner. A chain reaction is often triggered because other persons observing the struggle, but who were not initially involved, become worried that they are not getting enough for themselves and then they, too, begin clamoring for some "right" of their own to protect and enhance their position. It thus often ends up that people operate on fear or suspicion, resentment, envy, jealousy, or mistrust instead of faith, hope and love. Jesus tells us not to stand on our legal rights, but to take the further step of willingly giving the wrongdoer more than that which was taken from us.[21]

———

Think about it. In most instances, is peace ever promoted by filing a lawsuit? Isn't it more likely that lawsuits promote hatred (Prov. 10:12), pride (Prov. 13:10), quarrels and strife (Prov. 26:21), anger and division (Prov. 29:22), and an unhealthy interest in controversies and arguments that are a source of constant friction (1 Tim. 6:3–5)? Does one who pursues a lawsuit really want peace or a personal vindictive justice by wanting the other party to suffer?

One man not holding these truths in his heart once demanded of Jesus, "Teacher, tell my brother to divide the inheritance with me."[22] Asserting his rights consumed this man. He wanted a judge to see matters his way. He was thinking of selfish matters, putting property above his relationship with his brother. Jesus quickly replied, "Man, who appointed me a judge or an arbiter between you? . . . Watch out! Be on your guard against all kinds of greed; a man's life does not consist in the abundance of his possessions" (Luke 12:13–15). One wonders what Jesus' response to this man might have been if he had asked, "Teacher, how can I *love* my brother without letting property disputes separate us from each other?"

Jesus continues with one final illustration. If a man compels you to go one mile with him, go with him two miles. The Persians and Romans had the right to stop anyone and command that the person carry baggage for one mile. This was very insulting to the Jews, who were already struggling with the domination of Roman rule during the time of Jesus.

The Jews would not go one inch further than one mile when pressed into this bondage and servitude. The natural way was to carry the load one mile and dump it on the mark, while wishing for a reversal of roles someday so the masters would become servants. Jesus says to go two miles.

But mileage is not on Jesus' mind so much as the *attitude* of dealing with distasteful inequities and insults. He is almost saying that, short of a longer walk together for two miles, one cannot become acquainted with an oppressor and learn to love that person individually and unconditionally to win him or her over to repentance.

It is natural for us to say that relationships are a fifty-fifty proposition. But Jesus would say that true commitment to a relationship is zero-one hundred—you may end up putting everything into a relationship and receive nothing back! This does not mean being a wimp or stupid; it means strength under control. Going the second mile keeps marriages together. It keeps churches together. It keeps relationships together. Will you go the second mile—even if you have to go with no one but Jesus by your side?

If a person insults or hurts you in some way, what should you do? The Bible tells us:

> Bless those who persecute you; bless and do not curse. Rejoice with those who rejoice; mourn with those who mourn. Live in harmony with one another. Do not be proud, but be willing to associate with people of low position. Do not be conceited. Do not repay anyone evil for evil. Be careful to do what is right in the eyes of everybody. If it is possible, as far as it depends on you, live at peace with everyone. Do not take revenge, my friends, but leave room for God's wrath, for it is written: "It is mine to avenge; I will repay," says the Lord. On the contrary: "If your enemy is hungry; feed him; if he is thirsty, give him something to drink. In doing

this, you will heap burning coals on his head." Do not be overcome by evil, but overcome evil with good. (Rom. 12:14–21)

———

Pray for those who persecute you. Strive to identify with their interests and struggles in an even-handed search for common ground. Begin looking for opportunities to make peace with those who oppose you—in your home, at work, and in your church.

This means cultivating empathy for others. We are to *love* our neighbors. Talk with them face-to-face. Communicate with them. We should put ourselves in their place to understand them rather than force them to understand us. Love is more powerful than retaliation. And then, while loving evil people, we are to resist their evil conduct by not compromising the truth. "Turn from evil and do good; seek peace and pursue it" (Ps. 34:14). This means pursuing peace *actively*, like a hunting dog searches out game.

This does *not* mean that an evil person escapes judgment for injustice. As this passage clearly says, the Lord avenges the sins that are not repented of by an evil person. The Lord deals with this person directly (Ps. 34:16; Prov. 24:19–20). But we are to leave vengeance to the Lord. We need not concern ourselves with pronouncing personal judgment on others. What the Lord asks of us is to exercise grace, mercy, forgiveness, and love in doing to others as we would have them do to us (Luke 6:31).

How do we resolve conflicts with our neighbors—especially when they become enemies? It doesn't mean picking up the weapons of this world—guns, government or "gotcha" lawsuits—to assert our rights. A Christian's tools for conflict resolution are truth, righteousness, peace, faith, salvation, and the Word of God (Eph. 6:13–17). Sometimes this means not resisting an evil person. It may mean turning the other cheek. It may mean giving that person the shirt off our back. It may mean going the second mile. Or it may mean not turning that evil person away when he or she is needy.

Preoccupation with selfish defenses only gives the real evil one, Satan, an opportunity to uproot our faith. As we said in Part One, life is just too short to fall into this trap. Jesus tells us that the best way to resolve conflicts with our enemies is to love them, pray for them, and give to them as God does. Winning over an enemy through kindness is one of the most exhilarating experiences in life!

These are powerful principles in theory, but even more so in practice! Unfortunately, you and I know we cannot resolve every conflict, even by putting these principles into practice. Some conflicts defy resolution despite our best efforts.

We cannot manipulate or control others to seek the resolution and reconciliation we desire. This is when we must take Romans 12:18 to heart by striving to live at peace with our adversaries, as much as it depends upon us, and then turn the conflict over to God. But if opposing parties make the effort to go and meet with each other, face-to-face; if they allow wise and competent mediators to assist them in resolving their dispute and restoring the relationship without going to law against one another, the mediation will work. Mediation helps bring the "peace that surpasses all understanding" (Phil. 4:7).

※

Questions for Personal Reflection:

1.   How am I expressing my love for God and my love for my neighbor in practical ways on a daily basis right now?

2.   Do I know of someone who may have something against me? What efforts have I made to meet with that person and resolve the matter?

3.   Has someone else offended me? Does that person know of my irritation? Have I made an effort to meet privately with that person *face-to-face* to resolve the matter? Have I reached out to that person in friendship, even though I have no desire to be with him or her? Have I prayed for the person? Is there a need that person is experiencing that I can meet in order to bridge the gap between us?

4.   If I have a dispute with a believer in my church, am I willing to work within the congregation for a settlement while foregoing any opportunity I may have to enforce my rights in court?

5.   How do I feel about Jesus' command to turn the other cheek, give the shirt off my back, go the second mile, and not turn away an evil person?

Chapter 11

MEDIATION: TRIUMPH OF THE 1990s!

❦

At the end of the Civil War, President Lincoln entertained a group of hot-blooded, never-say-die Southern rebels in the White House. It was an uncomfortable time, but these visitors left with a new respect for their old enemy. Lincoln's gentle, conciliatory manner broke down the walls of hostility between them. Later, a Northern congressman criticized Lincoln sharply for befriending the enemy, suggesting instead that they should be shot on the spot as traitors to the Union. Lincoln listened thoughtfully to this charge. Then he smiled and quietly replied, "Am I not destroying my enemies by making them my friends?"

MEDIATION: RESOLVING CONFLICT PEACEFULLY

Mediation is a way to destroy your enemies by making them friends. Actually, it is a process of focusing on a common enemy—a *problem* or source of division—while building bridges between the *people* involved. Mark Twain once said that Adam and Eve's problems began because they ate the wrong thing. They could have saved all of us a lot of trouble by eating the serpent instead of the forbidden fruit! But we make the same poor choices today. We blame each other for problems instead of attacking the spirit of division that compounds our difficulties.

Resolving conflict takes courage and humility. But Jesus' challenge for us to turn the other cheek and to go the second mile in bridging gaps is so much against our nature. Texas attorney and religious leader William T. Dooling expressed the feelings many of us share: "The basic tension I feel is that I've taken vows and sworn to live a life that demands that I turn the other cheek, but I'm working in a highly adversarial profession. There are days when I just wish I could follow the Old Testament view of justice and get an eye for an eye."[1] And yet true Christianity in action often requires combining grit with grace.

For these reasons, resolving tense conflicts peacefully often requires help from others. When we face formidable challenges or adversaries, it is good to ask, "If only there were someone to arbitrate between us, to lay his hand upon us both" (Job. 9:33, author's paraphrase). A mediator lays his or her hand upon both disputing parties as a healer, comforter, advisor, and friend.

Mediation improves relationships between disputing parties. Alternative dispute resolution (ADR) reduces the cost of resolving conflicts, and speeds up resolution of disputes. It relieves the overwhelming demand of litigation on our courts and judicial resources. No less than twenty states and the District of Columbia have adopted ADR legislation or seriously reviewed the subject.[2] Court-ordered mediation cases in Florida alone increased from 34,000 in 1989 to almost 50,000 in 1991.[3] Mediation is taking root in other countries, such as Canada and England, as well.[4] It is a peaceful way to resolve conflict that is gaining momentum worldwide.

THE INCREASING USE OF MEDIATION

Mediation will touch your life in the 1990s. Here are just a few examples:

Neighborhood Communities

One widely-quoted Florida court decision captured the essence of nineties living: "Every man may justly consider his home his castle and himself the king thereof; nevertheless his sovereign fiat to use his property as he pleases must yield, at least in degree, where ownership is in common or cooperation with others."[5]

Communities today require even more give and take than neighborhoods of Americans before us. As a result, many condominium and community associations have mediation measures in place to resolve all types of neighborhood complaints.

The Community Associations Institute (CAI) in Alexandria, Virginia, is working with the American Arbitration Association (AAA) in offering mediation services and training to community associations in most states. Hawaii CAI Executive Director Leland Chang began a mediation service in Honolulu through the private, nonprofit Neighborhood Justice Center. Encouraged by the Center's 85 percent success rate in 1991, Chang noted: "Condominium association disputes lend themselves so well to mediation. You're talking a lot about relationships that need to be put back on a positive track. People are going to continue to live with each other, so any kind of an adversarial process just causes problems to worsen. There is a kind of healing that goes on that doesn't happen in any other process."[6] If more neighborhoods had dispute resolution centers like this, our litigation crisis would end.

Business Industry

There is a groundswell of increasing favor and use of ADR measures in corporate business. In a 1993 Survey of 246 legal counsel for Fortune 1000 companies, Deloitte & Touche's Litigation Services Group discovered that 72 percent of the respondents had some experience with ADR (including mediation), 10 percent used ADR extensively (20 or more times during 1990–92), while 80 percent expected to use ADR more frequently in the future. Of the respondents using ADR, 47 percent advised that they never pursue litigation after securing a non-binding decision through ADR. The survey confirmed that more companies are adopting policies that encourage the use of ADR, including use of ADR provisions in contracts with suppliers, customers, labor organizations, and business partners.[7]

The Center of Public Resources also tracked 406 companies using litigation alternatives in case disputes with more than $5 billion at stake and determined in 1993 that the savings in legal fees and expert witness costs exceeded $150 million.[8]

Many corporate officers see confidentiality of the process as the major benefit of mediation. This offers protection of valuable business information in an age of increasing public information and interference. Some court orders to reveal precious trade secrets horrify businesses. Coca-Cola Co. learned this the hard way when a court ordered it to disclose its formula in 1985. Rulings that order "disclosure of valuable commercial information can be catastrophic for a business party—far more damaging than the greatest exposure to a verdict in any single lawsuit."[9] As business owners adopt greater use of ADR and avoid much of the vexatious litigation that plagues America today, product prices should fall.

Banking Industry

Two of the largest banks in California, Bank of America and Wells Fargo Bank, began comprehensive ADR programs to handle consumer claims in the early 1990s. In July 1992, Bank of America announced that it would apply voluntary mediation and other ADR measures to all savings, checking, and credit card accounts, including disputes arising from existing account relationships. (It had previously experimented with non-binding mediation in lending disputes and found the results to be very positive.) Wells Fargo also uses a multi-step procedure to resolve disputes that begins with personal negotiation, followed by a mandatory mediation process. ITT Consumer Financial Corp., one of the nation's largest lenders, followed this lead shortly thereafter by putting ADR clauses in its consumer contracts in certain states.[10]

Bank of America has three hundred disputes a year. Each dispute has the potential of becoming a very expensive lawsuit. "One outrageous

$40-million verdict can sour your whole year," noted Bank of America Assistant General Counsel Arne Wagner. Executives agree with Wagner. They want to avoid any case with "once-in-a-blue-moon, unpredictable results of a jury going wild" and the unavoidable "mega-attorney's fees."[11] Being able to avoid such lawsuits should help lower bank fees and loan costs.

A 1994 study by the RAND Corp., a nonprofit public policy research company in California, backed up the value of ADR in the banking industry. It determined that banks could reduce their liability exposure "by limiting the risk of punitive damages and eliminating the unpredictability of juries, thereby reducing the incentives for plaintiff's attorneys to take cases."[12]

Check your banking agreement. See if it does not already have an ADR provision.

Building Construction Industry

The building construction industry was one of the first in the U.S. to use ADR measures (initially arbitration, but more recently arbitration and mediation) to resolve disputes. In 1991 the American Arbitration Association (AAA)[13] administered more than six thousand construction arbitrations. In a 1990 study of 142 companies in the construction industry that used ADR, as cited in the January 1992 issue of the *California Lawyer,* the estimated savings in litigation expense was more than $100 million.[14] The standard form of AAA construction contracts (widely used by contractors, owners, and lenders) contain ADR provisions governing any controversies or claims.

The construction industry also is on the cutting edge of ADR techniques, such as use of Dispute Resolution Boards (panels chaired by trained neutral facilitators that monitor work progress during a project and help parties resolve differences before they become disputes in a type of before-the-fact mediation)[15] and partnering (in which all parties involved in a project select a neutral facilitator and work together in formulating project goals, strategies, performance standards, and milestones).

If you build a home, it is likely that your contractor will use a contract with an ADR clause.

Governmental Agencies

During the unprecedented number of disputes that arose from bank failures in the late 1980s and early 1990s, the Federal Deposit Insurance Corporation (FDIC) and Resolution Trust Corporation (RTC) were responsible for overseeing many failed financial institutions. In 1992 alone, the FDIC and RTC faced more than 100,000 matters that involved troubled real estate loans, creditor's claims, and litigation against former bank officers and directors involving hundreds of millions of dollars. How was this mess handled? The FDIC and RTC used a wide variety of ADR programs designed to decrease costs, speed resolutions, and increase recoveries.[16] As a result, the FDIC saved $4.3 million in estimated legal expense in 1992.[17]

More state governments are using mediation in resolving conflicts and competing claims in state and local government planning. As early as December 1986, the Governor's Growth Management Advisory Committee issued its final report praising the use of mediation in resolving growth management conflicts in Florida. The city of Pensacola, for example, successfully used outside mediators for a conflict management session that allowed eight diverse parties (including the city) to present differing viewpoints on compliance with Florida's 1985 Growth Management Act.

Daniel W. O'Connell, Director of the Florida Growth Management Conflict Resolution Consortium, envisioned the great need for mediation in this area of government planning:

> Land use and water use disputes have increased in number and complexity as the State's population has grown. Growth management legislation has expanded citizen standing to contest local government land use decisions. Florida's integrated state, regional, and local planning system also presents new challenges for intergovernmental dispute resolution. In short, more people are involved in the process, providing greater opportunity for disagreement. The judicial system may be unable to absorb increasing numbers of new and complex land use disputes. Some alternative method of handling such matters could lessen the burden on Florida's courts.[18]

—

Labor Relations

In labor and employment disputes, many employers are changing how they defend themselves against allegations of unlawful discrimination under Title VII of the Civil Rights Act of 1964 (prohibiting employment discrimination on the basis of race, color, sex, national origin, or religion) or the Federal Age Discrimination in Employment Act (protecting those aged forty and up who face age discrimination).

Before November 1991, employers explained their decisions directly to federal judges in Title VII lawsuits. But with the passage of the federal Civil Rights Act of 1992, decision-making authority shifted from judges to juries. The Americans with Disabilities Act, which took effect in July 1992, also included jury trial provisions. This made employers very apprehensive about the court process because juries can be so unpredictable. Jury trials also are notoriously more expensive and time-consuming by nature than bench (judge only) trials.

With these new developments, many employers now use pretrial mediation and even pre-employment agreements to use ADR in the event of any post-employment disputes.[19]

Legal Practice

In 1991, 150 of the largest U.S. law firms voluntarily signed a Law Firm Policy Statement on Alternatives to Litigation prepared by the Center for Public Resources, Inc., a nonprofit New York organization committed to reducing litigation expense.[20] By executing the statement, law firms committed to educating their attorneys and advising clients of ADR options whenever appropriate. Also, signatories agreed to explore ADR first before engaging in litigation with any other signatory to the statement.

Also in 1991, the American Academy of Matrimonial Lawyers released a set of recommended standards for the legal practices of family law practitioners. These standards encourage knowledge and use of ADR in trying to resolve matrimonial disputes.[21]

Professional Relations

Unhappy clients, shareholders, and regulators have hit certified public accountants hard in recent years by trying to hold them responsible for various frauds and failures of corporate clients. Accountants face skyrocketing malpractice insurance premiums. This led to many of them practicing while uninsured. But the Florida Institute of Certified Public Accountants developed an innovative mediation plan in conjunction with the AAA and CNA Insurance, one of the largest insurers of Florida CPAs, to counteract these growing problems. Florida CPAs insured by CNA now include a provision for nonbinding mediation of claims in their engagement letters. Claimants must first try mediation. If anyone is unsatisfied with the result, that party is then free to take the case to court.[22]

There are some obvious benefits to requiring mediation as a first option: (1) nationwide, the average CPA malpractice award is less than $100,000, but the cost of defending an accountant sued for malpractice has escalated to more than $250,000, so the incentive is to reach settlement without litigation; and (2) a private and confidential mediation settlement of a malpractice claim avoids the stigma of a public malpractice lawsuit.

As this book goes to press, there are more accounts of various industries enlisting the aid of mediators to avoid self-defeating litigation. Public awareness is growing in this vital area. It is not unrealistic to foresee that many business contracts will have mediation clauses governing default remedies as we move into the next century. In fact, the publisher of this book included a mediation provision in its contract with me. My colleague and I even have a mediation provision in our agreement to help others privately mediate disputes.

Mediation Training for Grade School Students

We know that juvenile delinquency is a major problem in America. We live in times when students carry guns or knives in their backpacks along with their books. But educational institutions across the country are addressing this crisis in earnest by using peer mediation programs among grade school students.

Peer mediation involves kids who are trained in mediation, usually in teams of two, working with other schoolchildren to resolve disputes privately. Referrals to mediation are made by school counselors, teachers, or the students in conflict directly. These young mediators do not handle cases involving weapons, drugs, or physical abuse, but do mediate almost everything else. This responsibility also encourages mediators to be role models for other students. They learn to recognize different types of anger, how to identify causes of conflicts, and how to encourage communication with words rather than violence. Early involvement in mediation procedures like this resolves conflicts in the short run, while also training kids in conflict resolution procedures for later life.

In Dade County, Florida, peer mediation began with a conflict resolution program that was developed in the late 1960s by public school teachers (and sisters) Grace Contrino Abrams and Fran Schmidt. After Abrams died in 1980, peer mediation proponents in Miami formed the Grace Contrino Abrams Peace Education Foundation, a non-profit group dedicated to her memory. The Peace Foundation has been instrumental in providing peer mediation information,[23] including publication of *Win Win!*, a magazine distributed across the U.S. and Canada to students in grades 7 through 12 that extols the virtues of mediation. The goal is to achieve results where there are two winners in any conflict instead of one winner and one loser.[24] The Foundation also has been active in training mediator candidates in a twelve-hour course and in persuading many schools across America to organize peer mediation programs.

Dade County schools tried peer mediation in 1986. It proved so successful that, by 1992, at least sixty-four schools had adopted the program, including thirty-five elementary schools. In Broward County, Florida, all thirty-one middle schools use peer mediation.[25]

Other states also are organizing peer mediation groups. In 1993, seventy school-based mediation programs in Massachusetts schools achieved an 80 to 90 percent success rate. "Student Conflict Resolution Experts," an urban school peer mediation program supervised by the Massachusetts Attorney General's Office, was one of ten winners in 1994 of a grant from the Ford Foundation and the John F. Kennedy School of Government at Harvard for being a state government program shown to be effective at addressing public needs.[26]

Richard Cohen, author of *Students Resolving Conflict: The Complete Guide to School-Based Peer Mediation*, co-founded School Mediation Associates, a private company in Cambridge, Massachusetts, in 1984. He trained school systems around the world in building mediation programs. Cohen sees a great need for peer mediation programs: "There are economic pressures that exaggerate the pace of conflict so kids come to school angry, not well-fed and not having been taught certain lessons by their parents, so it's gotten to the point where educators are looking for ways to manage conflict. . . . Kids are getting into conflicts more often over issues of less significance, and when they act on these conflicts, they're often acting with more aggression and violence than kids in the past."[27]

Peer mediation is a concept you will hear more about in the coming years. It is a noble effort to help our children become responsible people during their early years.

The Desperate Need for Mediation in Divorces

It is one matter to desire mediation as a business decision for various economic and social reasons. It is quite another to need it in saving a family from the damage and chaos of separation and divorce. Then nonadversarial mediation becomes critical.

After experiencing how expensive and counterproductive litigation can be, especially in the context of a divorce, I became a firm believer in mediation.[28] Family mediation is the best way to cope with separation and divorce situations. To spouses tempted to run to attorneys and fight it out, I suggest that this may not be the best move for your family or future.

When I see frustrated litigants standing on the downtown Miami Courthouse steps with Day-Glo signs reading: "Divorce Lawyers — Family Butchers!" it offends me as a Christian and as a lawyer to have them unfairly generalize in this way. But as a divorcé, I can understand how these hurt people feel. I have compassion for them. I grieve over the ways in which their lives and families have been torn apart at the hands of strangers in the court system. I know that an expensive court process that often defies logic and their sense of fairness and bewilders them.

Mediation is the answer. It fosters healing and restoration of the marriage if reconciliation is possible and damage control if it is not. It promotes constructive communication between spouses with the help of neutral facilitators at a critical time of separation. It allows control over one's life, children, and property in a way that cannot occur in court. As we saw in chapter 10, biblical passages such as 1 Corinthians 6:1–8 mandate mediation for Christians.

There is a role for everyone in family mediation. Spouses should exercise restraint in putting aside the bitterness, resentment, and urge for revenge that pushes lawyers into action. They should consider participating peacefully in a mediation forum and quietly separate when their marriages hopelessly shipwreck. Counselors and mediators should use great care in keeping all consultations strictly confidential when they serve husbands and wives who are in distress. They must remain neutral, impartial communicators who are strongly empathetic (rather than sympathetic), while applying the proper balance and tension between affirmation and confrontation.

Lawyers should seek to be healers in *serving*, not exploiting, couples in crisis by providing constructive legal advice rather than continual advocacy. We lawyers must help spouses who are in crisis move on with their lives. We must use good judgment and be creative in helping them find constructive solutions to the problems divorce brings their way. We must make it easier for these desperately hurting people to have time to deal with the flood of emotions they are experiencing at one of the lowest points in their lives.

One of America's greatest challenges in fighting crime, battling the deficit, and restoring its strength and power in a turbulent world is this: We must stop helping others destroy their families through an adversarial legal system before we destroy ourselves and our great country.

Fortunately, more states are taking this message to heart. The Dade County, Florida, Family Mediation Unit celebrated its 15th anniversary of operation in February 1994. Dade County courts require all divorcing parents with minor children to accept mediation from the unit in working out their continuing parental responsibilities for their children.[29]

Even more encouraging are the studies that show great satisfaction with the results of mediation among those who mediate divorces and family disputes. Some researchers found that 92 percent would mediate disputes again in the future or recommend the procedure to a friend. Mediation also provides long-term relief by inspiring parties with confidence to work out future problems without litigation, remain satisfied with their divorce settlement agreements and custody arrangements, and forge better relationships with their ex-spouses.[30]

As new family cases that are filed in Dade County increase to more than 25,000 a year, the Florida Bar Foundation also provided a unique and innovative two-year grant in 1994 to the Dade County Bar Association for a family mediation project. The project assigns certified family mediators to guide middle income divorcing couples who, unable to afford legal representation by not meeting poverty requirements, usually proceed unrepresented and become lost in the morass of unfamiliar and confusing legal procedures. Family Court Judge Richard Y. Feder said that the pilot project is a "catalyst for expanded mediation throughout the state and will bring immediate relief to overburdened judges and unrepresented spouses."[31]

Does Mediation End the Need for Lawyers?

The short answer is a definite no. In mediation, attorneys must make sure that their clients:

- receive a complete, written legal evaluation of their case and discussion of the legal issues before mediation begins so the clients can make informed decisions;
- will not suffer harm or undue disadvantage by unequal bargaining power in mediation (especially in cases of mental illness, domestic violence, and abuse);
- have equal access to information available to other parties in mediation;
- understand the possible outcome of pursuing their rights in court compared to proposed settlements in mediation;
- are protected by all necessary court orders that support the mediation, and stop any end runs that circumvent the process (as when a divorcing spouse cashes out a joint savings account before reaching a mediated agreement on this issue);
- receive legal advice on evolving mediation issues before making any agreement;
- understand the fee and time requirements of the mediator and others involved; and
- will cooperate with the lawyer in mediation without undue adversarial posturing.

A classic problem between lawyers and mediating parties arises when an attorney, in good faith, advises a client against proceeding with a mediation settlement proposal. This is particularly frustrating when one party's attorney rejects a settlement as being too low, while the other party's lawyer aborts the same settlement for being too high. These post-settlement problems not only disrupt the mediation process, but also can create an adversarial relationship between attorneys and their clients. However, early analysis of issues in mediation with advance planning and preparation between an attorney and client guards against this possibility.

But lawyers can have a powerful effect in keeping mediation proceedings moving. If the parties hit a snag, creating an impasse in mediation, input from attorneys on legal requirements may help pull parties that are holding legally indefensible positions back on track.

For mediation to work at its best, lawyers must return to being legal counselors once again. Consider this wise observation of Chesterfield Smith, past president of the Florida Bar and the American Bar Association:

> While it is true that lawyers have always championed the causes of those clients they have served, . . . they primarily served the historic principles of a public legal profession: to accommo-

date and unify the body of law and their clients. Lawyers then were advocates. But more than that, they were counselors and mediators, bringing together the disparate, seeking just and expeditious resolutions, solving problems, making peace, protecting the innocent, striving for justice, and pursuing truth at all costs. . . . [Attorneys today must] keep clients informed in a professional way, an honorable and good way, and, if a particular course of action is ill-advised, alert that client of this fact forcefully at the outset. Tomorrow's dominant question from the client may well continue to be, "What is required here by law from me?" But the answer too rarely given to that question must be these noble yet wholly professional words from the lawyer: "This is what you ought to do, not because it is required, but because it is right and proper."[32]

Participating in mediation is the purest form of legal practice for attorneys today.

WHAT ABOUT CO-MEDIATION?

Co-mediation is the use of a team of mediators with different backgrounds and training. It is an interdisciplinary approach, such as when a lawyer-mediator pairs up with a mental health therapist-mediator to better equip themselves in meeting the various needs of the parties. I believe co-mediation by a balanced partnership of mediator-professionals brings out the best of different specialties in reaching settlement.

One reason for such co-mediation arises from the fact that so many legal issues spring from emotional needs. Not long ago, a couple in mediation fought vigorously over an old, beat-up yellow chainsaw. Seeing the futility of their fighting, the frustrated mediator went to the local hardware store and purchased an exact duplicate chainsaw to present to the wife so the husband could keep the other tool. The mediation resulted in settlement. But after everyone had left, the wife refused to take the new tool with her. Knowing how strongly she had fought for the other chainsaw, the puzzled mediator asked her why it was no longer important to her. "The chainsaw really meant nothing to me," she coolly replied. "I knew how much it meant to him, but I just didn't want him to have the satisfaction of getting it without a fight!"

This is why we blunder into litigation over so many issues. Pride and selfishness grip a person's heart like a vise and squeeze out the last drop of compassion, forgiveness, and sacrifice, leaving nothing but a dark, wrinkled, lifeless core of resentment and revenge. Restitution is not enough. We want adversaries to suffer and pay for wronging us. For those holding out on settlement due to underlying personal concerns, a mental health professional's experience and perception can break deadlocks by helping the party work through difficult feelings and emotions.

An attorneys' training is in advocacy and evaluating legal issues. It is natural for us to be skeptical of what anyone says, more guarded in what we say and do, and somewhat more reluctant to make full disclosures. We focus precisely on the facts of a case in achieving legal goals. We are less concerned with gaining a deeper understanding of a person's personal views and circumstances. At times we try too hard to learn what is wrong with those opposing our clients, rather than what is right for everyone concerned. Lawyers want the power to make legal decisions as their professional judgment dictates. Lawyers will be on guard against decisions that have an adverse legal or financial result.

In contrast, therapists encourage communication between disputing parties. They discourage withholding of personal information. They want to find root causes of any denial or self-deception. They help people see issues more clearly, discuss options, and then let them make their own choices as to future conduct. They allow clients to learn from the consequences of their own decisions without judging in advance whether an action is right or wrong.

For those who want to avoid face-to-face meetings with others in a dispute, or who have ambivalent feelings about their relationships, confining conflicts to a purely legal forum may never reach the real sources of problems. The law cannot deal very well with personalized justice tailored to the needs of particular parties. It needs objective, clearly defined and precise rules. It rejects anything that is vague or inconsistent across a large number of cases. But having input from a trained mental health therapist helps fill the gap in these areas. It really meets the needs of the people in the areas where they hurt the most.

All these issues of lawyers and therapists are important factors in mediation. Mediators help clients see other possible viewpoints. I firmly believe that, to use mediation to its maximum potential, an interdisciplinary collaboration using lawyers and mental health therapists is the best way to prepare for any number of legal and psychological issues that could derail settlement opportunities and reconciliation between the parties.

MEDIATION IS NOT THE PANACEA FOR ALL ILLS

Obviously it is overstating the case to argue that mediation will resolve all controversies, reconcile all people in conflict, and end the need for our court system. We must know when, and when not, to use mediation so it works to maximum advantage without being a waste of time or having an adverse effect on anyone's rights in future litigation.

Lawyers, clients, legislators, and judges alike need to embrace a new attitude of seeing opportunities to use mediation whenever reasonably possible. New Jersey Attorney Bernard J. D'Avella Jr. expressed the hope of many in this regard: "Litigation, as it is often practiced today, has gone far from the mark originally intended. While there will always be disputes that must be resolved by such means and that will need our litigation skills, many disputes are merely fodder for a large, ineffective machine that gives attorneys and the entire system a bad name. If we are to correct this situation, we must separate the disputes that do not require extensive litigation from those that do. The evolution of ADR is an opportunity to honor the basic tenet of our profession: doing what is best for the client."[33]

But mediation will be a major vehicle for resolving a broad range of disputes in the future. To ensure its success, our children are receiving early mediation training in our schools. In 1991 futurist John Naisbitt, author of *Megatrends*, predicted that "clogged courtrooms and skyrocketing legal costs"[34] would lead to increased use of ADR as a replacement for litigation. Today there are few who doubt the accuracy of this observation.

There is more to solving America's crisis than relying on mediation. That is where you and I come in. We need to help our country meet some significant challenges in the 1990s:

THE CHALLENGE FOR OUR COURTS AND LEGISLATURES

Solving the current crisis in our courts and neutralizing the threats to our religious freedoms must move beyond partisan politics. Some years ago, the National Council of Churches reminded then President Bush that God is neither a Republican nor a Democrat. But, as comedian Jay Leno joked, the devil is registered with both parties! Now is the time for us to torch the serpent of lies and division among us (as Adam and Eve should have done in the Garden of Eden), rather than to skewer each other politically.

Our courts and judges need the flexibility and training to shift from a heavily adversarial system to one that embraces the frequent and meaningful use of mediation and other forms of ADR. If we do not act to restrict trials for only the most complex or otherwise irreconcilable disputes, we will overwhelm our justice system and watch it crumble from the overload.

Our nation's judges need to apply the law fairly, equally, and consistently. They need to respect the source of their power: "We, the people." We need judges with clear, uncompromised moral values who are calm and steady in their deliberations and aware of how much our nation needs to turn to God at this critical time in our history. They need to use more legal craftsmanship and practical reason. They especially need to stop ignoring America's heritage of justice and religious freedoms as the founding fathers envisioned them to be almost 220 years ago. They need to be less creative in circumventing our nation's laws and our Constitution. It would not hurt if we had more judges who were churchgoing men and women.

Reducing litigation means instituting intelligent screening of disputes from the date a case first comes in the courthouse door, much like triage works in emergency medical situations. This requires all the "guardians of the process"—judges, lawyers, and court administrative personnel—to cooperate with each other. It means *guiding* claimants by moving them into the most appropriate resolution services of our court system rather than always resigning them over to adversarial litigation.

A 1994 Gallup poll asked respondents across America about ways to reduce costs of the justice system. An impressive 87 percent said that mediation and ADR should occur in certain cases. Highlighting the value of nonbinding mediation over binding arbitration, 63 percent of these respondents also believed that cases submitted to ADR should proceed in court if any of the parties did not like the result.[35]

Relief for the caseloads also may come from privatizing many cases now handled by our courts, in much the same way that private mail carriers and courier services have taken over much of the work formerly processed through the U. S. Mail. Our government needs to encourage potential litigants to use private resources, such as private mediation, to resolve disputes. This means educating the public through seminars, instructional videos at the courthouse, more user-friendly, high-tech instruments such as accessible computers to check on case management options, and menu-driven answer booths that respond to common consumer questions and complaints. Arizona QuickCourt is a good example of the improvements we need in this regard.[36] This interactive computer system provides legal information for those filling out forms for small claims and routine legal matters. It won a 1994 grant from the Ford Foundation and John F. Kennedy School of Government at Harvard.

THE CHALLENGE FOR LAWYERS

In 1990, Nova University Law Dean Roger I. Abrams asked members of the Florida Bar:

> Does this sound familiar? Obnoxious lawyers wrangle over a minor, irrelevant point. Disrespect, deviousness, and harass-ment—in short, sharp practice. Lawyers have become enemies. Associates work six days a week or more to amass billable hours. Physically and psychologically exhausted, some lawyers leave the profession and others wish they could afford to do so. Most came to the law to help people. They found instead that their work was valued by a number at the bottom of a time sheet. For them, the practice of law is not fun anymore. They see fellow members of the Bar who have turned to huckstering their professional services: "Come to me; I'll get you dough." Without the respect of their

fellow lawyers and the public they wanted to serve, without time to spend with family and friends, boxed into a pressurized work world without choices—these lawyers burn out. What have we done to our profession? What have we done to ourselves?[37]

Good questions. During the twentieth century the practice of law has evolved into a highly specialized venture as our society and its laws become more complex. As we learned in chapter 6, by necessity many lawyers now know more and more about less and less. The days of the general practitioner and family lawyer who handles everything are long gone.

Like never before, law firms and lawyers preoccupy themselves with profit and the financial bottom line. Overhead expenses rise and compensation demands escalate each year. Competing for a limited amount of dollars in the marketplace has become an increasingly competitive venture, particularly driven by the large number of students graduating each year from our law schools. These individuals enter law schools for any number of reasons—the intellectual challenge, social standing and public influence, civic virtue, and similar goals. But the common goal of most graduated students is to make lots of money.

As law firms hire these young men and women as associates, they are no longer discipled in legal discipline so much as exploited by their employers for economic benefit as cash cows. It is a rather evil, covetous, symbiotic, and economic, rather than collegial, relationship. To keep these associates busy, firms today accept cases with little or no merit that should be declined. Profit takes precedent over ethics and public service. Even in meritorious cases, too often the strong profit motive means fewer settlements and more litigation.

So we lawyers need to assume more responsibility for turning away clients who are out for blood. Falling for the money that is offered by these clients hurts the attorneys involved and the entire profession. Attorney Bill van Zyverden of Middlebury, Vermont, makes a excellent point: "More and more lawyers are finding out that being an attorney is detrimental to their personal health because of the adversarial, aggressive . . . me-against-you attitudes that set up walls between people. I don't blame lawyers for being the personalities they are, but it is time to start saying 'No!' when the public comes to them and demands, 'Be my gladiator.'"[38]

We have too many "cowboy" litigators who believe that civil suits must be a "shoot-out at the OK Corral," and that frontier justice works better than reason and cooperation. Former Supreme Court Justice Warren Burger sees this as a serious threat to the legal profession:

We have what has come to be called the *Rambo lawyer*, whose idea of counsel's function may have been influenced by the clownish performances seen on TV programs . . . When judges, even a few of them, put up with the Rambo lawyer's misconduct, the administration of justice suffers, and it leads to repetition of that conduct by other lawyers. Lawyers should not view themselves as a legal Rambo, or hired gun. On the contrary, lawyers must be legal architects, engineers, builders, and from time to time inventors as well. We have served, and must continue to see our role, as problem-solvers, harmonizers, and peacemakers—the healers, not promoters of conflict.[39]

How can lawyers turn this situation around? In his book, *The Lost Lawyer: Failing Ideals of the Legal Profession,*[40] Yale law professor Anthony T. Kronman sees the key to restoring the profession's identity and professionalism as being a new resolve by lawyers to stand by a commitment made long ago to serve the public and to make the sacrifices that pledge demands.

Those of us in the law need to embrace empathy, fairness, and an ethical morality once again as much as we embrace knowledge of the law and practical reasoning. This consciousness-raising experience ideally needs to occur throughout life—particularly in our families, neighborhoods, and churches during a future lawyer's childhood years. But certainly it also must be an integral part of our law schools from the first days of orientation through graduation. We need to feel the burden of hurting souls in society by more actively participating in pro bono legal services which are provided for little or no cost to the disadvantaged.

Meanwhile, law firms, clients, and judges must respect graduates who join the legal profession as human beings who have personal needs, family commitments, and interpersonal relationships outside the workplace. Job requirements should call for reasonable hours, rather than a sweatshop atmosphere. And we lawyers must do our part as well by not taking work attitudes home with us. "A hypervigilant lawyer may make sure every brief is letter-perfect and all deadlines are met, but at home, his or her children may be miserable if expected to bring home perfect grades and attend Ivy League schools. And a compulsive lawyer personality certainly can spark domestic fire if the lawyer arrives home after long hours fighting over a case to find the house a little messy."[41] Each lawyer's family that breaks down because of work at the office, means a bigger problem for all of us in America.

But one of the greatest challenges for lawyers during the decade of the 1990s and into the twenty-first century is to redefine *success*. Will we gauge our contributions to society in terms of task-oriented performance and dollars earned? Will we believe the lie that "We are what we bill"? Is our function to win more trials, or instead to be problem-solvers and creative, solution-oriented professionals who serve clients for a fair and reasonable fee? Lawyers today need a deeper sensitivity to true client needs and a renewed dedication to community service.

THE CHALLENGE FOR CLIENTS

There is a bias toward litigation today. But lawyers are not the sole cause of the litigation explosion. Chesterfield Smith spoke from years of legal experience when he said: "It is clear to me that lawyer ubiquity in and of itself has not led to America's sue-at-every-opportunity mentality. On the other hand, all of the blame for the unrelenting lawyer image cannot possibly be assigned only to client's cupidity, or even to an innately belligerent, in-your-face, American culture, bearing a monstrous chip on its shoulder. The problem rests equally with both."[42]

At ABA's Just Solutions Conference in May 1994, Supreme Court Justice William Rehnquist told those gathered, "In the same sense that World War 1 French Premier Georges Clemenceau said, 'War is too important to be left to the generals,' reform of the justice system is too important to be left to lawyers and judges."[43] ABA President R. William Ide III echoed this thought: "We created and built the best justice system in the world because the people it served were intimately involved. It can only be rebuilt by doing the same."[44]

Think about it. We already handle many of our conflicts privately, don't we? Who hires a lawyer for every dispute coming their way? Does a businessperson need an attorney to negotiate day-to-day matters with employees, customers, and suppliers? Is a lawyer necessary to settle a dispute with a barber, yardman, or a noisy neighbor? We can, and do, take care of many of these conflicts ourselves. Why not develop our problem-solving skills to settle differences in larger disputes with our neighbors?

How can we begin? By following the Golden Rule of treating others as we would have them treat us. This holds true for Christians and non-Christians alike. It defuses disputes ready to explode. Ken Sande, noted author of *The Peacemaker* and executive director of the Institute for Christian Conciliation, explains this universal life principle:

> If you speak gently to others (Phil. 4:5), they will usually speak gently to you. If you speak the truth (Eph. 4:25), others are more likely to do the same. If you believe the best about others (1 Cor. 13:7), they will be more inclined to think the best about you. If you admit your wrongs (Matt. 7:5), others will tend to admit theirs. If you look out for the interests of others (Phil. 2:4), they

will often show more concern for yours. And if you seek reconciliation with others (Matt. 5:24), they will usually respond in kind. Once these dynamics begin to take place, most conflicts will move toward resolution.[45]

———

When litigation becomes unavoidable, are we, as clients, urging our lawyers to win our case or to *resolve* the dispute? Will we embrace the role of peacemaker in reaching out to those engaged in a dispute with us or instead unchain a dispassionate legal warrior to fight our battles impersonally for us? Will we be forces for settlement and reconciliation, or further polarize the conflict (with an emphasis on the *polar*, as in very cold, part of the verb)?

Before pursuing or defending civil litigation, we need to ask ourselves a few questions:

Is it worth the turmoil to go to court and win?

Every civil case has the potential for becoming unmanageable. Litigation requires a lot of time and effort, coupled with restless nights. Is it worth it? If not, we need to take settlement opportunities more seriously. Even if we win in court, is it worth the bitterness and resentment that our opponents, family, and friends may feel toward us? To be sure: "If a wise man goes to court with a fool, the fool rages and scoffs, and there is no peace" (Prov. 29:9).

Is our cause just and reasonable?

Is it worth the time, expense, and trouble of litigation to win a few more dollars or to keep property of questionable value? Are we unjustly withholding or refusing benefits our opponents rightfully deserve? "Do not exploit the poor because they are poor and do not crush the needy in court, for the LORD will take up their case and will plunder those who plunder them" (Prov. 22:22–23). Imagine going through the struggle of court litigation and winning only to find the Lord standing against us at the end! Be wise, and compromise within reasonable limitations of tough love. Even if this shortchanges us to a degree, unquestionable fairness is what counts.

Have we fully considered the court issues in advance?

We may know matters about our adversaries that no one else but the Lord knows. If we wanted to be mean and vindictive, we could hurt and embarrass them. But this is a double-edged sword. They can do the same to us. What do we gain by revealing titillating information? Gossip makes us look exploitative and hateful. Witnesses to court conduct—family and friends—will never forget how each litigant deals with the other. "What you have seen with your eyes do not bring hastily to court, for what will you do in the end if your neighbor puts you to shame? If you argue your case with a neighbor, do not betray another man's confidence, or he who hears it may shame you and you will never lose your bad reputation" (Prov. 25:8–10).

Stick to the minimum amount of facts necessary to resolve the issues. Avoid personal attacks or innuendo against anyone unless the truth demands it.

Have we fully investigated the facts?

Never make decisions without first having the facts. It is reckless and unfair to make assertions that will harm someone without verifying the truth and making sure the charges serve a reasonable end. When in doubt, forget it.

Can we maintain self-control with a cool head and a warm heart?

"A fool gives full vent to his anger, but a wise man keeps himself under control" (Prov. 29:11). We must deal with personal anger and disappointment *before* going to court. If we are angry, let it be a controlled response concentrating precisely on the issues. Litigation is the time to be patient and willing to bargain without becoming compliant or retreating from tough love positions. Always keep the big picture in mind. What does each side want in court? Remember, God desires reconciliation if it is at all possible.

THE CHALLENGE FOR OUR CHURCHES

It does no good for Christians to read passages like 1 Corinthians 6:1–8 and go to their church leaders for help in a dispute with other Christians only to have these leaders turn them away. Our church leaders need to preach the Word of God, but they must live it out as well. Shepherding the flock in their care includes a readiness to handle disputes in a biblical manner at all times using correction, rebuke, and encouragement with great patience and careful instruction (2 Tim. 3:2).

Every church in America should have procedures for private resolution of disputes. Spiritual leaders or permanent committees must stand ready for that purpose at a moment's notice. If we do not do this for ourselves, we will push more Christians into the courts—to their personal detriment and to the shame of the cause of Christ.

Church members need to resolve internal congregation-wide disputes promptly in the same fashion. Otherwise, all our efforts at evangelism and our urging others to join God's family will be fruitless. After all, would you want to join a family that is caught up in weekly squabbles? Outsiders notice members who will not talk to each other. They see the hypocrisy. And they leave. For the sake of the lost; for the sake of ourselves; for the sake of our Lord; this must stop. Resolve any problems quickly.

The Challenge for Christians

If litigation is unavoidable, will we fight the good fight as Christians? Our shield in court—a civil law system premised on a search for truth and fair administration of justice—must be a *defensive* weapon. Attorneys are our defenders. We need to use this armor responsibly.

For Christians, the best armor comes from the Lord (Eph. 6:10–18). We may be in the courts of our peers, but we do not lay aside our spiritual armor. We buckle the belt of truth around our waist. We keep the breastplate of righteousness in place. We take up the shield of faith to extinguish the flaming arrows of evil sent flying at us. We take up the sword of the Spirit, the Word of God, and strengthen ourselves by moving forward with wisdom and grace.

To resolve disputes amicably without litigation, Christians should be loving and generous in pursuing settlement as a strong Christian witness to others. If you believe that God is prompting you to make a particular settlement proposal, and scriptural support exists for it, exercise faith and proceed unless a specific, valid legal reason exists for not doing so (beyond your lawyers' feelings and opinions). You have a higher allegiance to act in love and be gracious in following God's counsel over what the world tells you to do. Here are some other guidelines:

Be a person of integrity.

Be strong and act on the courage of your convictions. You will almost certainly be misunderstood, at least in the initial stages, if you go the second mile or turn the other cheek. But in the end, you and the Lord (and those sensitive to spiritual matters) will know you acted lovingly and responsibly. Be a faithful steward of your resources.

Begin with prayer.

Bathe yourself in prayer. "Do not be anxious about anything, but in everything, by prayer and petition, with thanksgiving, present your requests to God. And the peace of God, which transcends all understanding, will guard your hearts and your minds in Christ Jesus" (Phil. 4:6–7). Use no plan of action without first seeking the Lord's blessing.

"What would Jesus do?"

People are more important than property lost in any settlement. Possessions will come and go, but people last a lifetime. In the end, we have to answer to the Lord. Always ask, "What would Jesus do?" Then do it His way.

Believe in your plan.

Once you believe your plan is good for everyone concerned (not just yourself), set your sails and steer a straight course. "Do not those who plot evil go astray? But those who plan what is good find love and faithfulness" (Prov. 14:22).

Plan your work, and work your plan.

After you have prayed about your plan and sought good counsel about the details, commit yourself to following through with whatever you decide is best. But avoid being rigid and inflexible. Settlement requires negotiation. Allow for some flexibility in your plan of action.

Make no judgments where you have no compassion.

Keep the big picture in mind in considering settlement strategies. Don't focus on winning at all costs. Sometimes you win by losing on some issues. Sensitivity and empathy will help you know when to give in.

Above all, remember that there's a huge difference between weak Christianity infected with complacency, unspiritual compromise, and excuses, and strong Christianity, tempered with truth, mercy, and grace, that does not hesitate to fulfill the commands of God . . . no matter what.

WE CAN ALL DO SOMETHING TO EASE OUR CRISIS

Helen Keller once said, "I am only one; but still I am one. I cannot do everything, but still I can do something. I will not refuse to do the something I can do."[46] There is something you and I can do to help our country through this crisis.

We can discuss and consider various judicial reforms. We know we must reduce delay, increase funding for our courts, and improve access to legal and mediation services for poor and moderate-income people. It is clear we must take immediate action to simplify legal procedures, lower legal costs, and reduce existing incentives to litigate everything under the sun. We need to use ADR measures without delay in suitable cases. But the greatest contribution we can make in addressing this crisis is to assume personal responsibility for working out our disputes face-to-face with our neighbors using mediation.

§a.

Questions for Personal Reflection

1. How can I "destroy my enemies by making them my friends"?

2. How can I use mediation in my business, church, social clubs, and interfamily relationships?

3. Do I have the urge to run to an attorney whenever a legal conflict or dispute arises before considering other options such as mediation?

4. What are the advantages and disadvantages of settling a dispute privately versus litigating the matter? What legal expenses would I incur in both instances?

5. Have I tried using mediation? How can I use mediation to promote reconciliation with others?

Epilogue

COME, LET US REASON TOGETHER

Adlai Stevenson, former U.S. Ambassador to the United Nations, once observed: "Democracy is not self-executing. We have to make it work, and to make it work we have to understand it. Sober thought and fearless criticism are impossible without critical thinkers and thinking critics. Such persons must be given the opportunity to come together to see new facts in light of old principles and to evaluate old principles in light of new facts by deliberation, debate and dialogue."[1]

🍃

This book is a labor of love and concern for America. It is a call from one Christian lawyer beckoning his neighbors to examine new facts in light of old principles and evaluate old principles in light of new facts. The problems in our justice system and the solutions available to us are ripe for public discussion and debate. We desperately need more critical thinkers and thinking critics to make democracy, as our founding fathers envisioned it almost 220 years ago, work in the face of our conflicts and disputes. We need to put our creative minds together in finding ways to resolve our differences as neighbors rather than fall by default into so many contests where there must be winners and losers.

Whenever people exercise free choice, there will be conflict. Experts say that, since 3600 B.C., the world experienced only 292 years of peace. During all other years there were 14,351 wars, large and small, killing 3.64 billion people![2] After all, when there were only two people on this earth, they fought each other as one blamed the other for disobeying God's commands in the Garden of Eden. But the conflict for Adam and Eve began before they committed the first sin. It came with the choice to obey God or Satan. Sin was the result of how they mishandled this conflict. Of the next two people added to the world, one brother killed the other out of jealousy, anger, and depression. Cain slew Abel in disappointment that stemmed from his choice to offer God an inferior sacrifice (Gen. 1:27–

4:16). We've been fighting with each other ever since over the choices we make.

"I love humanity; it's people that I can't stand!" pronounced Lucy, telling it like she sees it as always in a Peanuts comic strip. Living peacefully with our neighbors, much less loving them, may make us feel like porcupines—togetherness can be a sticky situation! Maybe you can identify with the anonymous writer of these insightful words:

Oh to live up above with the saints that we love;
That will be glory!
But to live here below with the saints that we know;
That is a different story!

———

Yes, choices and conflicts are inevitable. It is hard enough to keep the peace with our neighbors as it is. But litigation capitalizes on conflict and makes it worse. Litigation cripples love, shatters hope, corrodes faith, destroys peace, undermines confidence, kills friendships, obliterates sweet memories, sabotages courage, invades the soul, and quenches the spirit.

Rushing to lawyers to file lawsuits without diligently pursuing alternative dispute resolution measures reverses the order of resolving conflicts. It places a period before the end of the sentence.

We live in an age when our modern legal system has made monumental shifts away from its Christian roots. America is in a moral free fall. Pumping more money into our judicial system solely to meet the selfish demands of an overly litigious public overcome with groundless prejudices and unrealistic expectations strikes me as a cure worse than the disease.

Every generation blames society's ills on the generation before it. But no one before us filed lawsuits like we do today. We are the *Litigation Generation*.

The crisis we face today in our judicial system is our own doing. If we, each one of us, do not assume our individual responsibility to become peacemakers rather than peacebreakers, we are truly courting disaster. To paraphrase Chekhov's rather jaundiced view of justice in his story, "In the Court," we face a rising tidal wave of lawsuits in our country so great "that no mind could form a complete picture of all this parti-colored mass of faces, movements, words, misfortunes, true sayings and lies, all racing by like a river in flood."

Mediation and other alternative dispute resolution measures are an open door offering us an escape from this litigation madness. It is an invitation to see conflicts resolved quietly and peacefully between neighbors, rather than as adversarial lawsuits. Mediation is a way of reason, empowering us to make choices for ourselves and our families rather than having decisions imposed upon us by attorneys and courts. It is a viable alternative to using the courtroom as a battlefield. It returns power to where it rightfully belongs, to "we, the people."

Mediation draws its ideas and concepts from many fields. Psychology contributes the dynamics of dealing with defense mechanisms, anger and motivation. Psychiatry helps us understand the physiology of stress and the fight-or-flight experience. Sociology enlightens us as to how individuals and groups interact and form communication networks. Management and organizational theorists give us practical ways to negotiate and maintain order for the greater good of everyone concerned while pursuing common goals and objectives. The law provides the processes and procedures of mediation. But the Gentle Man from Galilee and His teachings in the Bible give us the reasons and the motivation to make everything work together as it should. "These diverse ideas are integrated by their use for a common purpose, the resolution (or management) of disagreement. Conflict management is therefore a practical art rather than a theoretical science." [3]

There will be skeptics and those who scoff at alternative dispute resolution. But it is an idea whose time has come . . . again. Jesus, the ultimate conflict resolver, told us almost two thousand years ago that this was the best way to resolve disputes. The One who mastered the art of conflict resolution tells us the responsibility for healing conflicts falls directly on our shoulders (Matt. 5:23–24; 18:15–17). Not lawyers. Not judges. Us—you and me. "We, the people," are to take the initiative in going to meet with our neighbor *face-to-face*, whether we wrong others or others wrong us. We are to talk *to* those in conflict with us—not *about* them.

Most importantly, we are to show love (Mark 10:21). This means being concerned about the spiritual well-being of others (1 Cor. 13:1, 4–7). It means being willing to lay down our lives for others (John 10:17–18; 15:13). We are not to seek vengeance for wrongs suffered (Matt. 5:38–48; 27:12–14). In love, we are to exercise mercy (Matt. 5:7), compassion (Luke 7:13; 15:20), and forgiveness (Luke 17:3–4) in intimate, interpersonal contact with our adversaries. No one fulfills this by sending threatening messages to opponents through lawyers and the courts. Love means being humble and "quick to listen, slow to speak, and slow to become angry" (Jas. 1:19). It means becoming a bridge to the Lord rather than being a wedge between people and God.

Disputes and irritations give us opportunities to make something beautiful happen, as expressed so well in this anonymous poem, "The Oyster":

There once was an oyster whose story I tell,
Who found that sand had got under his shell;
Just one little grain, but it gave him much pain,
For oysters have feelings although they're so plain.
Now, did he berate the working of Fate
Which had led him to such a deplorable state?
Did he curse out the Government, call for an election?
No; as he lay on the shelf, he said to himself,
"If I cannot remove it, I'll try to improve it."
So the years rolled by as the years always do,
And he came to his ultimate destiny-stew.
And this small grain of sand which had bothered him so,
Was a beautiful pearl, all richly aglow.
Now this tale has a moral—for isn't it grand
What an oyster can do with a morsel of sand;
What couldn't we do if we'd only begin
With all of the things that get under our skin.
—Anonymous[4]

———

Conflicts are good for us. They remind us of godly perspectives, just like the passerby who once saw some men building a stone church. One of the men was chiseling a triangular piece of rock. "What are you going to do with that?" asked the traveler. "Do you see that little opening way up there near the spire?" said one worker, pointing his finger. "Well, I'm shaping this down here so it will fit in up there." Our short time on this earth is a prelude to heaven. How we fulfill the greatest commandments of God right now prepares us for what He has prepared for us in glory. Life shapes us down here so we will fit in better up there.

Dr. Martin Luther King Jr. once explained, "Cowardice asks the question, 'Is it safe?' Expediency asks the question, 'Is it politic?' Vanity asks the question, 'Is it popular?' But conscience must ask the question, 'Is it right?'" Now, as our great country faces the severe challenge of overwhelming litigation from "We, the people," will you and I be the ones to move beyond cowardice, expedience, and vanity to do what is right and pure and true and honorable as Jesus taught us—even if we must do so alone?

Anne Alexander once said, "The circumstances of life, the events of life, and the people around me in life, do not make me what I am, but reveal what I am." What will a serious commitment to resolving conflicts in mediation reveal about us? Will we rise to our apologies when we wrong others? Will we do whatever it takes to reconcile relationships? Will we persevere in seeking dispute resolution and reconciliation? Do we understand the critical difference between not giving up versus not giving in? Will we walk in the way of Jesus to peacefully and sacrificially resolve our conflicts or just stand in the way? Will we have the faith necessary to transform our world? Will we have a passion so strong in our hearts that it is our constant nature to unite rather than divide people?

Resolving conflicts for the sake of our relationship with God and with each other is not easy. It will take our time, our resources, and our resolve to make it work. Commitment like this is rarely ever convenient. But, as Christians, Christ calls us to commit ourselves to this primary task. And "If it is to be, it begins with me."

Centuries have rolled by since Jesus told us to "love the Lord your God with all your heart, mind, soul and strength, and to love your neighbor as yourself" (Mark 12:28–34). In that time, as evangelist Terry Rush points out, "We are failing to be positioned on the cross. Near the cross? Yes. Upon it—not as often." Today we need to become cross-bearers once again, even if it brings trouble, persecution and hardship. More Christians should be like teabags—best when placed in hot water! Now is the time—for ourselves, our great country, and our great God—that we should take up our crosses daily and follow Jesus (Luke 9:23–25; 14:25–27).

To paraphrase Winston Churchill, mediation "is not the end. It is not even the beginning of the end. But it is, perhaps, the end of the beginning." This new wine seeks hearts like new wineskins. Let's become neighbors to each other in America once again.

Come, let us reason together. Be part of the solution. Give peace a chance.

Appendix

MEDIATION RESOURCES

This list of resources provides information about groups and organizations you can call or write to help you cope with your separation or divorce. Consult your local directory for organizations in your area.

This list does not include every organization that deals with the various aspects of mediation. Inclusion on this list does not constitute endorsement of the organization by the author or publisher of this book. Neither the author nor the publisher exercises any control over the work performed or materials provided by any group or organization on this list or any fees that may be charged.

Academy of Family Mediators (AFM)
1500 S. Highway 100, Suite 355
Golden Valley, MN 55416
(612) 525-8670
Fax: (612) 525-8725
(Founded in 1980, this organization has 2,200 member attorneys, mental health professionals, and others trained in family mediation in twenty-five state groups. Provides referral service and certifies training programs.)

American Arbitration Association (AAA)
140 West 51st Street
New York, NY 10020-1203
(212) 484-4000
Fax: (212) 765-4874
(Founded in 1926. Has 8,500 members. Publishes Dispute Resolution Journal and numerous other pamphlets, journals, and information.)

American Bar Association—Alternative Dispute Resolution Committee
750 North Lake Shore Drive
Chicago, IL 60611-4497
(312) 988-5584
Fax: (312) 988-6281
(Affiliated with the American Bar Association. Networks lawyers interested in family mediation.)

American Bar Association Standing Committee on Dispute Resolution
1800 M Street, N.W., Suite 2005
Washington, DC 20036
(202) 331-2258
Fax: (202) 331-2220
(Groups over 5,000 attorneys, judges, law professors, and other legal professionals and laypersons serving as an information clearinghouse on dispute resolution. Conducts workshops at legal conferences. Encourages participation of state and local bar associations in dispute resolution activities.)

American Center For Law and Justice
P.O. Box 64429
Virginia Beach, VA 23467
(804) 579-2489
Fax: (804) 579-2836
(Religious, non-profit public interest law firm and educational organization dedicated to pro-liberty, pro-life and pro-family causes. Supports those involved in defending religious and civil liberties of Americans.)

Association of Christian Conciliation Services
1537 Avenue D, Suite 352
Billings, MT 59102
(406) 256-1583
Fax: (406) 256-0001

Association of Family and Conciliation Courts
329 Wilson Street
Madison, WI 53703-3612
(608) 251-4001
Fax: (608) 251-2231
(An interdisciplinary association of judges, lawyers, mediators, and mental health professionals dedicated to family law services as a complement to the judicial process. Provides newsletters and other resources.)

Center For Dispute Settlement (CDS)
1666 Connecticut Avenue, N.W., Suite 501
Washington, DC 20009
(202) 265-9572
(Founded in 1971, this private, nonprofit corporation designs, implements and evaluates programs applying mediation and other dispute resolution measures. Manages complaint center and provides service for mediation of disputes.)

Center For Public Resources, Inc.
366 Madison Avenue
New York, NY 10017
(212) 949-6490
Fax: (212) 949-8859
(Organization of over 600 major corporations, law firms and legal academics working to resolve significant corporate and public disputes by mediation and other alternatives to litigation. CPR national, regional, and specialized panels number over 500 distinguished lawyers and former judges.)

Christian Legal Fellowship
P.O. Box 160
Etobicoke, Ontario M9C 4V2
(416) 629-2245
(This is a Canadian organization fulfilling the same sort of function as the Christian Legal Society.)

Christian Legal Society
4208 Evergreen Lane, Suite 222
Annandale, VA 22003
(703) 642-1070
Fax: (703) 642-1075
(This is a professional society of over 4,000 Christian lawyers, judges, law professors, and law students across America who exercise their Christian faith in the practice of law in association with pastors and concerned laypeople.)

Childfind of America, Inc.
ATTN. Mediation Consultant
P.O. Box 277
New Paltz, NY 12561-9277
(800) 292-9688 or (800) 426-5678

Community Associations Institute
1630 Duke Street
Alexandria, VA 22314
(703) 548-8600
Fax: (703) 684-1581 or (703) 836-6907
(Provides materials for resolving condominium and cooperative apartment development disputes.)

Community Dispute Services (CDS)
140 W. 51st Street
New York, NY 10020
(212) 484-4000
(Founded in 1968 and operating in thirty-five regional offices, this service, formerly known as the National Center for Dispute Settlement and now affiliated with the American Arbitration Association, adapts traditional dispute settling techniques like mediation to meet community and institutional needs. Maintains a Community Disputes Settlement Panel of third-party, neutral persons.)

Conflict Resolution Center International (CRCI)
2205 E. Carson Street
Pittsburgh, PA 15203-2107
(412) 481-5559
Fax: (412) 481-5601
(Founded in 1982, supports mediators and other conflict resolvers who attempt to settle interracial, tribal, religious, ethnic, and other intercommunal disputes.)

Divorce and Family Mediators
37 Arch Street
Greenwich, CT 06830
(203) 622-5900
Fax: (203) 622-8298

Divorce Mediation Research Project
1720 Emerson Street
Denver, CO 80218
(303) 447-8116
(Publishers of Directory of Mediation Services.)

Endispute, Inc.
1201 Connecticut Avenue, N.W., Suite 501
Washington, DC 20036
(202) 429-8782
Fax: (202) 728-2920
(Founded in 1982 by Washington, DC lawyer Jonathan Marks, and Boston University Law Professor Eric Green. Provides 78 mediators, split between ex-judges and lawyers in 10 locations in six states. Recently merged with *Judicial Arbitration & Mediation Services, Inc.*)

Family Center for Mediation and Counseling Services
3514 Players Mill Road
Kensington, MD 20895
(301) 946-3400
Fax: (301) 946-3400

Florida Dispute Resolution Center
Supreme Court Building
Tallahassee, FL 32399-1905
(904) 921-2910
(Works closely with the Florida State Courts Administrator in overseeing statewide public mediation and ADR measures.)

Institute For Christian Conciliation
1537 Avenue D, Suite 352
Billings, MT 59102
(406) 256-1583
Fax: (406) 256-0001
(Founded in 1982 to equip and assist Christians to respond to conflict biblically. Provides conflict counseling, mediation and arbitration services to help resolve lawsuits, family conflicts, business disputes and church divisions. Ken Sande, author of The Peacemaker, is Executive Director.)

Institute For Mediation and Conflict Resolution (IMCR)
425 W. 144th Street, 4th Floor
P.O. Box 15
New York, NY 10031
(212) 690-5700
Fax: (212) 690-5707
(Founded in 1969, this agency is supported by foundation grants and contracts and provides assistance to community disputants in resolving differences on a voluntary basis.)

Inter-American Commercial Arbitration Commission
OAS Administration Building
19th & Constitution Avenue, N.W., Room 211
Washington, DC 20006
(202) 458-3249
Fax: (202) 458-3293
(Founded in 1934, this commission promotes multi-national cooperation in dispute resolution of international trade controversies in 32 North and South American countries.)

International Council For Dispute Resolution (ICDR)
C/O The IRC Group
1835 K Street, Suite 600
Washington, DC 20006-1203
(202) 775-9172
Fax: (202) 223-4335
(Founded in 1985, this is a consulting firm of former American and foreign ambassadors aiding corporations needing assistance in international disputes.)

Judicate, Inc.
1500 Walnut Street, Suite 1300
Philadelphia, PA 19102
(800) 473-6544
Fax: (205) 546-8567
(Provides approximately 700 ex-judge mediators nationwide.)

Judicial Arbitration & Mediation Services, Inc. (JAMS)
500 N. State College Boulevard, Suite 600
Orange, CA 92668
(714) 939-1300
Fax: (714) 939-8718
(Founded in 1979 by former California state court judge H. Warren Knight. Provides 250 ex-judges as mediators in 22 locations in five states.

Martindale-Hubbell Publishing Company
121 Chanlon Road
New Providence, NJ 07974
(800) 526-4902
Fax: (908) 464-3553
(Publishes *Law Directory* and *Dispute Resolution Directory* providing state-by-state listings of attorneys and other professionals engaged in mediation and other alternative dispute resolution services.)

National Academy of Conciliators (NAC)
1111 W. Mockingbird Lane, Suite 300
Dallas, TX 75247
(214) 638-5633
Fax: (214) 638-4052
(Founded in 1979.)

National Association For Mediation In Education (NAME)
University of Massachusetts
205 Hampshire House
Amherst, MA 01003
(413) 545-2462
Fax: (413) 545-4802
(Founded in 1984, with membership of 1,000, this organization assists those interested in teaching grade school and university students conflict resolution skills. Acts as a national clearinghouse for information on mediation.)

National Center For Mediation Education (NCME)
2083 West Street, Suite 3C
Annapolis, MD 21401
(301) 261-8445 or (800) 781-7500
(Founded in 1984, a center for training mediators in separation or divorce cases.)

National Institute for Dispute Resolution (NIDR)
1901 L Street, N.W., Suite 600
Washington, DC 20036
(202) 466-4764
Fax: (202) 466-4769
(Founded in 1981, promotes use of mediation as an alternative to litigation.)

Peace Education Foundation
2627 Biscayne Boulevard
Miami, FL 33137
(305) 576-5075
Fax: (305) 576-3106
(Provides mediation training for public schools; publishes Win Win! magazine.)

Rutherford Institute
P.O. Box 7482
Charlottesville, VA 22906
(804) 978-3888
Fax: (804) 978-1789
(Organization providing legal services protecting American religious freedoms.)

Society of Professionals in Dispute Resolution (SPIDR)
815 15th Street, N.W., Suite 530
Washington, DC 20005-2201
(202) 783-7277
Fax: (202) 783-7281
(Founded in 1972, this is an international organization to advance and represent the interests of mediators and other third party neutrals. Membership in 1994 exceeded 3,000.)

U.S. Arbitration & Mediation, Inc.
4300 Two Union Square
Union Street
Seattle, WA 98101-2327
(206) 467-0794
Fax: (206) 467-7810
(Provides more than 400 attorney-mediators in 44 U.S. franchises.)

SUGGESTED READING

Adams, Jay E. *Handbook of Church Discipline*. Grand Rapids: Zondervan Publishing House, 1986.

Buzzard, Lynn R., and Thomas S. Brandon Jr. *Church Discipline and the Courts*. Wheaton, Ill. Tyndale House Publishers, Inc., 1987.

Dobson, Dr. James. *Love Must Be Tough*. Waco, Tex. Word, Inc., 1983.

Fenton, Horace L. Jr. *When Christians Clash*. Downers Grove, Ill. InterVarsity Press, 1987.

Fisher, Roger, and William Ury. *Getting to Yes*. 2nd ed. New York: Penguin Books, 1991.

Flynn, Leslie B. *When the Saints Come Storming In*. Wheaton, Ill. Victor Books, 1988.

Jones, G. Brian, and Linda Phillips-Jones. *A Fight to the Better End*. Wheaton, Ill. Victor Books, 1989.

Kniskern, Joseph Warren. *When the Vow Breaks: A Survival and Recovery Guide for Christians Facing Divorce*. Nashville: Broadman & Holman Publishers, 1993.

Lovenheim, Peter. *Mediate, Don't Litigate*. New York: McGraw-Hill Publishing Company, 1989.

Mains, Karen Burton. *The Key to a Loving Heart*. Elgin, Ill. David C. Cook Publishers, 1979.

Sande, Ken. *The Peacemaker: A Biblical Guide to Resolving Personal Conflict*. Grand Rapids: Baker Book House, 1991.

Talley, Jim. *Reconcilable Differences*. New York: Thomas Nelson, Inc., 1985.

White, John and Ken Blue. *Healing the Wounded*. Downers Grove, Ill. InterVarsity Press, 1985.

NOTES

Introduction
1. R. William Ide III, "Rebuilding the Public's Trust", *ABA Journal* (September 1993): 8.
2. Isaiah 1:18.

Chapter 1
1. Paraphrasing Thomas Wolfe, *Of Time and the River*, (1935) book 2:14:155.
2. President John F. Kennedy, Inaugural Address, January 20, 1961. These are two of seven inscriptions carved on the walls at the gravesite of John F. Kennedy, Arlington National Cemetery.
3. Joseph Story, *Commentaries on the Constitution of the United States*, 2d ed., vol. 2, cha 45, 617 (1851). (This passage was not in the first edition, but appeared in all later editions.)
4. Carl Sandburg, interview with Frederick Van Ryn, *This Week Magazine*, January 4, 1953, 11.
5. Carl Sandburg, *Remembrance Rock*, epilogue, chap. 2, 1001 (1948).
6. By laws I refer to: (1) constitutional law, being the general principles of the U.S. Constitution and related state constitutions; (2) statutes enacted by U.S. Congress and the state legislatures which tell us what a person legally can do or not do (within constitutional guidelines); (3) regulations, being orders issued by public administrative agencies responsible for supervising and controlling matters affecting the general public welfare; (4) ordinances, being local laws enacted by city councils and municipal governments protecting the health, safety and welfare of the public in accordance with applicable state law; and (5) court decisions, being case law opinions of the various courts that interpret existing law and bind people in the court's territory or jurisdiction.
7. America has two court systems, federal and state, organized similarly with a supreme court on the highest level and a number of subordinate courts on the levels below. For most decisions not involving trade, patents, or federal tax matters, a case usually begins in the Federal District Court (provided that the dispute involves citizens of different states and the amount is more than $50,000, or a federal law question exists), with appeals going to various Courts of Appeal, and finally up to the U. S. Supreme Court, which reviews selected Federal Court decisions, Federal law or constitutional questions, and state law diversity. On the State level, there are various local courts or small claims courts (with a number of different names varying from State to State) to handle small disputes of local citizens, trial courts, circuit courts or superior courts to handle larger disputes of State citizens (and appeals from the local courts), then a level (in some states) of appellate courts or state district courts of appeal to review appeals from lower courts, and finally the State Supreme Court, also hearing appeals from the lower courts. In some State cases involving a Federal statute or constitutional right, an appeal from the State Supreme Court can be made to the U.S. Supreme Court for a final decision.

8. President Abraham Lincoln, address at Civil War battlefield, Gettysburg, Pennsylvania, 1863.

9. President Abraham Lincoln, in a proclamation appointing a National Fast Day, March 30, 1963—*The Collected Works of Abraham Lincoln*, Roy Basler, ed., vol. 6, 156 (1953).

10. Judge Thomas M. Reaveley, "Ultimate Concord, the Convention and Us," *Florida Bar Journal* (July/August, 1988): 52.

11. Charles R. Swindoll, *Dropping Your Guard: The Value of Open Relationships* (Waco, Tex.: Word Books, 1983), 23, quoting Bruce Larson, *There's a Lot More to Health Than Not Being Sick* (Waco, Tex: Word Books 1981), 59-60.

12. *Columbus Dispatch*, 8 September 1992), 7A.

13. The *Miami Herald*, 27 October 1993, 5A.

14. Terence Moran, "Stop Blaming Lawyers For Life," The *Daily Business Review*, Friday, 21 June 1991, pp. 5A–6A.

Chapter 2

1. Fear of divorce in a declining economy influences many people to forego marriage. Are people becoming more cynical about marriage? Data from the Census Bureau through 1991 confirms that the number of marriages has been declining. The proportion of Americans who married in 1991 was lower than any year since 1965. In 1960, there were 73.5 marriages for every 1,000 unmarried women. By 1987, that figure dropped to an all-time low of 55.7 marriages. Men in the 35-to-39 age group who had never married increased to 17.6% in 1991, up from 7.8% in 1980. The percentage of never-married women in the same age group increased from 6.2% in 1980 to 11.7% in 1991.

2. *When The Vow Breaks: A Survival and Recovery Guide For Christians Facing Divorce* (Nashville, TN: Broadman & Holman Publishers, 1993). If you are facing a separation or divorce, you will find this book to be very encouraging and enlightening. While not being a book that promotes divorce, it is a guide to help couples in crisis deal with their situations responsibly and lovingly in limiting the damage of divorce while leaving the door open for reconciliation if reasonably possible.

3. That Court finally made a decision in December, 1991.

4. *Schutz* v. *Schutz*, 581 So.2d 1290 (Fla. 1991). We will review more issues involving custody and support of children during a separation or divorce in chap. 3.

5. The District of Columbia and eight other states have adopted a short separation period as a no-fault ground for dissolution.

6. "Keeping The Knot Tied," *ABA Law Journal*, March, 1994, 105.

7. One such example is found in §§61.075 and 61.08, Florida Statutes.

8. Prior to a domestic violence prevention pilot program in 1991, only 30 percent of the victims sought relief through Dade County, Florida courts. During the program, those pressing charges in court increased to 68 percent. Reason? The courts took Florida's domestic violence laws seriously. Coordinators earnestly organized the domestic violence section of the Family Law Division and put it into action. A hot line was available 24 hours a day. Safe Space shelters offered alternate living arrangements for those needing to escape violence. A circuit court judge was available on weekends, nights and holidays to help abuse victims get restraining orders for protection. Counselors, health specialists, and members of victim's advocate groups comforted victims throughout the proceedings. Drug and alcohol referrals were made. Support groups provided forums for victims to comfort each other. Spouse batterers were ordered into a 26-week domestic intervention program to stop them from becoming more violent. Due to the outstanding success of the pilot program, victims now feel safer in reporting incidents of violence with confidence that their complaints will be taken seriously and acted upon promptly.

9. Christians know that this is not the way God looks at marriages (See Matt. 19:1–11; 1 Corinthians 7). It is the way the civil laws are evolving, however.

10. The manner in which courts divide property under American law is heavily influenced by English Common Law. In England, the national church had exclusive jurisdiction over the regulation of marriage after the Norman Conquest. The Common

Law viewed women as legal dependents of their husbands and restricted in their ability to own property. Women received alimony in ecclesiastical courts as compensation for the inability to hold separate property. Almost all Common Law states distributed property by title, beginning in the 19th Century. Therefore, since women were restricted in owning property, and property was distributed by title in divorce, women understandably came up short. More recent equitable distribution provisions of the No-Fault laws changed this, however. It allows property to be redistributed notwithstanding who owns the title (although title ownership is still a factor to be considered).

11. The laws of each state can vary considerably. This is especially true if spouses are domiciled in a community property state (Arizona, California, Idaho, Louisiana, Nevada, New Mexico, Texas, Washington or Wisconsin). In community property states, for example, each spouse acquires an automatic one-half interest in all property and income of the marriage. By contrast, in non-community property states each spouse has an interest in the marital property, but when considering this interest for equitable distribution it may not automatically equate to a one-half interest.

12. Courts usually divide marital assets between the spouses, while separately awarding non-marital assets to one spouse or the other.

13. For example, if one spouse is in more financial need than the other, the court may award more property toward the support of the needy spouse. Child custody issues also can affect property distributions, such as awarding the home to the parent having primary custody. If one spouse has clearly worked harder in making a marital asset more valuable, that also affects the distribution percentages.

14. Karen S. Peterson, "Lost Love Can Turn Jekylls Into Hydes," *USA Today*, 21 August 1992, p. 2D.

15. This misconduct could also adversely affect that spouse's consideration as a custodial parent of any children.

16. Child support awards are more generous. The court takes into account what is reasonably necessary to provide for the child's needs, frequently until he or she legally becomes an adult (18 to 21 years old, depending upon the state).

17. Other reforms being considered include requiring mandatory security deposits from those not making prompt support payments. Support payments may soon become credit card debts, with all financing charges imposed on the paying spouse. Courts will advise credit bureaus of delinquent spouses. Informal administrative hearings to enforce support, as alternatives to court hearings, will speed up enforcement. Ask your attorney to advise you of the remedies available to you in your state.

18. Nancy S. Palmer, Esq., "Chair's Comments," *Family Law Commentator* (September 1993): 3.

19. *Katz* v. *Katz*, 505 So.2d 25, 26 (Fla. 3d DCA 1987).

20. *Tomaino* v. *Tomaino*, 629 So.2d 874 (Fla. 4th DCA 1993).

21. *Florida Bar News*, 1 April 1994, pp. 20.

22. *Miami Daily Business Review*, 16 November 1993, pp.A1, A14.

23. "Florida Supreme Court Gender Bias Study," *Florida Law Review*, vol. 42 (1990), xvii-xx.

24. Dr. Charles Swindoll, *Better Families*, vol. 18:5, May 1994, 1.

25. As quoted in *Sermons Illustrated*, October, 1992, Card 8.

Chapter 3

1. Quoted by Judge Hugh S. Glickstein in his article, "1992: A Year to Rediscover the Best Interests of the Child," *Florida Bar Journal* (February 1992): 70.

2. Of course, it must be said that the absence of conflict may be just as damaging to children if it results in apathy, disdain and boredom. The point is that if a child does not see a loving, cooperative parenting relationship within an intact and involved family unit, there will be problems even before a separation or divorce occurs.

3. Patty Shillington and Phil Long, "Girl sues for Right to Leave Parents," *Miami Herald*, 5 March 1993, p. 1A, 6A.

4. Phil Long and Patty Shillington, "Daughter Wins Right to Lawyer in Custody Fight," *Miami Herald*, 27 March 1993, p. 1A.

5. Phil Long, "Judge Gives Kimberly Her Wish," *Miami Herald*, 19 August 1993, pp. 1A, 12A.

6. Phil Long and Patty Shillington, "Biology vs. Psychology: Defining The American Family," *Miami Herald*, 11 August 1993,p. 8A.

7. This is also fruitful ground for the child to use manipulation in holding out for greater privileges. Kids will test the boundaries of parents to see what they can get away with. Each parent needs to respect reasonable limits for the child to provide synergy among everyone concerned during visitation.

8. In recent years, some states have moved away from use of the term *custody* in describing which parent is the custodial parent or non-custodial parent. One reason for this is that the term incorrectly implies that one parent has possessory rights or may make parenting decisions to the exclusion of the other parent. Consequently, some state legislatures are using the more neutral terminology of *primary residential parent* and

9. The Shared Parental Responsibility Doctrine is generally defined as "a court-ordered relationship in which both parents retain full parental rights and responsibilities with respect to their child, and in which both parents confer with each other so that major decisions affecting the welfare of the child will be determined jointly." Section 61.046 (11), Florida Statutes.

10. Assuming that the court considers the child to have intelligence, understanding, and experience to express a reasonable preference.

11. Since 1973 the number of single fathers with custody of young children has changed dramatically. In a U.S. government study completed by Daniel Meyer (University of Wisconsin) and Steven Garashy (Iowa State), in the 1980s single-father families grew at a faster rate than any other family type—including those headed by single mothers. Even so, life can be more difficult for single fathers. While admirers praise a man for being a caring father, they will still think that he receives help with the children from others. Single fathers feel more limitations in finding groups with whom they can connect. In addition, according to Meyer and Garashy, few single fathers receive child support awards from courts. In part, their study found, this could be due to single fathers generally being better off economically than single mothers. To assist the needs of single fathers, various loosely knit organizations have sprung up around the country such as Fathers for Equal Rights. Also, many organizations offer a staff of lawyers, social workers and other specialists to fathers struggling with custody issues.

12. When a sexual abuse charge was raised in the past, evaluators were impressed by any detail provided by a child. But now that significant detail of sexual matters is readily accessible to children through the media, and one can never discount the "coaching" a child receives from a desperate parent, more sophisticated methods of detection are being used. Ironically, if such fabricated charges are found meritless by the court, the accusing parent may lose custody of the child. See, e.g., *Pallay* v. *Pallay*, 605 So.2d 582 (Fla. 4th DCA 1992).

13. This occurs when a parent intentionally programs a child to poison his or her mind against the non-custodial parent rather than facilitating the relationship, often referred to as Parental Alienation Syndrome. The *Schutz* case, discussed earlier in this chapter, is a vivid example of how this process of alienation destroys a parent-child relationship.

14. Fortunately, enforcement of kidnapping laws is available throughout the United States under the Uniform Child Custody Jurisdiction Act (adopted in some form in all states), which allows for transfer of witnesses, social service investigative reports and other evidence from state to state if necessary. The Federal Parental Kidnapping Prevention Act, which includes administration of a parent-locator service to track down kidnapping parents and enforcement by the U.S. Department of Justice, is also available. In international abductions, the Hague Convention on the Civil Aspects of International Child Abduction may apply. Under the convention, the removal of a child from one country to another is wrongful when it breaches the custody rights being exercised by a person under the law of the state where the child was habitually resident (determined by geography and passage of time) immediately before the removal.

15. 18 to 21 years, depending upon the state. However, this may be different if the child is mentally retarded or impaired or otherwise dependent upon the parent obligated to pay child support.

16. This is another area where compromise between the parents is vital. If support includes payment for college, courts usually limit it to four years of undergraduate studies, or similar trade school training.

17. It may be possible to qualify for Aid to Families with Dependent Children (AFDC) benefits to help provide for children.

18. U.S.C. §652(a)(8) (1988). This commission met six times between September 1991 and February 1992 before adopting extensive recommendations designed to improve enforcement of interstate child support obligations. The report introduced into Congress is called "Supporting Our Children: A Blueprint for Reform (1992)."

19. The commission urged Congress to require that all new employees disclose on their tax forms whether they must pay child support. If so, the commission recommended that employers withhold child support payments from the paychecks of affected employees. Some critics believe that this is an invasion of privacy of parents who do pay child support in a timely manner.

20. Under the Revised Uniform Reciprocal Enforcement of Support Act, a spouse who is owed support must rely on a state attorney in the state where the delinquent spouse resides to pursue his or her action. It is not uncommon for dispassionate prosecutors to bargain away the interests of the spouse who is owed support or to pursue the claim less zealously than other pending matters. The spouse in need is then faced with having to hire a local attorney to pursue the claim—an additional financial burden that may be impossible to meet. Under child support reforms being considered, this would change. The spouse not receiving support could pursue an action in his or her own state and force the delinquent spouse to defend against prosecution there.

Chapter 4

1. Consequently, many bankers jokingly refer to church debts as "evergreen loans"—they rarely get paid off on time and frequently require forbearances, advances, and other concessions.

2. The right of an individual to be free from invasion of privacy is a relatively recent addition to America law. Rather than evolving from English Common Law (such as an action for libel), invasion of privacy can be traced directly to a phrase coined by the late Thomas M. Cooley in his 1880 treatise, *The Law of Torts*: "The right to one's person may be said to be a right of complete immunity: to be let alone." [Emphasis added]. Samuel D. Warren, together with Louis D. Brandeis who was later to become a revered U.S. Supreme Court Justice, later applied this phrase to existing legal principles and developed the concept of "the right of privacy" in an 1890 Harvard Law Review article.

By recognition of this right, the United States Supreme Court gradually established a fundamental constitutional right of privacy in a number of specific circumstances based upon the First, Fourth, Ninth and Fourteenth Amendments to the U.S. Constitution in instances where there is governmental intrusion into one's personal privacy. Many states have enacted privacy amendments to their state constitutions for other governmental interference of this type. However, general recognition of a right to privacy from governmental intrusion has also led individuals to seek relief from civil courts for invasion of their privacy by other individuals. This type of action also allows for jury trials and potential claims for compensatory and punitive damages, as occurred in the *Collinsville* case under review.

Privacy can be categorized into four different kinds of interests which may be the subject of invasion by others:

A. *Intrusion upon a person's seclusion or solitude* such as entering a house or apartment without permission of the occupant, or taking photographs of a person or his or her property in a private place;

B. *Appropriation of a person's name or likeness* such as unauthorized use of a person's name or photograph in an advertisement, or unauthorized broadcasts or photographs of a performance requiring paid admission;

C. *Public disclosure of embarrassing private facts* such as details about a person's sexual relationships, contents of personal letters, facts about an individual's hygiene, or other intensely personal matters; and

D. *Publicity which places a person in a false light* such as inventing quotes or fictionalizing actual events.

The *Collinsville* case appears to hinge on the first and third forms of privacy invasion described above.

Guinn had to prove that the church's actions were highly offensive to a reasonable person and that the personal matters discussed were not of legitimate concern to the public. She also had to prove that she did not consent to publication of facts by the church elders regarding her private life.

3. *Guinn* v. *Church of Christ of Collinsville*, 775 2d 766 (Okl. 1989).

4. Dissent by Justice Hodges in *Guinn* v. *Church of Christ of Collinsville*, 775 2d at 795, citing *Serbian Orthodox Diocese* v. *Milojevich*, 426 U.S. 696, 96 S.Ct. 2372, 49 L.Ed.2d 151 (1976) and other case authorities. In the famous Serbian case, a defrocked bishop sued his church, claiming that the defrockment was wrongful and arbitary under the internal doctrines of the church. He sought a court declaration that he should remain in control of the diocesan property. The Supreme Court held that a dispute involving defrockment of a bishop was primarily of a doctrinal nature, and the question of who was entitled to the property followed the other dispute as merely a secondary issue. Members of a church are bound by the policy of the church, even if undemocratically made and whether or not rational or in accordance with due process principles. The Court based its holding on its long held position that secular courts not interfere with a church's religious determinations concerning questions of discipline, faith or ecclesiastical law.

5. *Paul* v. *Watchtower Bible & Tract Society of New York*, 819 F.2d 875, (9th Cir. 1987), cert. denied 484 U.S. 926, 108 S.Ct. 289, 98 L.Ed.2d 249 (1987).

6. Civil courts do have the authority to resolve property disputes between rival factions of a church without violating the First Amendment. *Jones* v. *Wolf*, 443 U.S. 595, 602, 99 S.Ct. 3020, 3024, 61 L.Ed.2d 775 (1979). A civil court may review the legalities of a church meeting and determine who is a legitimate member of church for the purpose of controlling church property. *Bouldin* v. *Alexander*, 89 U.S. (15 Wall.) 131, 140, 21 L.Ed. 69 (1872); *Reid* v. *Gholson*, 229 Va. 179, 327 S.E.2d 107, 113 (1985) cert. denied, 474 U.S. 824, 106 S.Ct. 80, 88 L.Ed.2d 65 (1985).

7. *Fowler* v. *Bailey*, 844 2d 141, 145-146 (Okl. 1992).

8. *Nally* v. *Grace Community Church of the Valley*, 204 Cal. Rptr. 303, 320 (1984).

9. *Nally* v. *Grace Community Church of the Valley*, 194 Cal.Ap 3d 1147, 240 Cal.Rptr. 215 (Cal.Ap 2 Dist. 1987).

10. *Nally* v. *Grace Community Church of the Valley*, 763 2d 948 (Cal. 1988).

11. *Nally* v. *Grace Community Church of the Valley*, 763 2d 948, 960 (Cal. 1988).

12. *Nally* v. *Grace Community Church of the Valley*, 763 2d 948 (Cal. 1988), cert. denied 490 U.S. 1007, 109 S.Ct. 1644, 104 L.Ed.2d 159 (1989).

13. *Schmidt* v. *Bishop*, 779 F.Sup 321 (S.D.N.Y. 1991); *Bladen* v. *First Presbyterian Church*, 857 2d 789 (Okl. 1993); *Byrd* v. *Faber*, 57 Ohio St.3d 56, 565 N.E.2d 584 (1991); *Hester* v. *Barnett*, 723 S.W.2d 544 (Mo.Ap 1987).

14. *Schmidt* v. *Bishop*, 779 F.Sup 321, 328 (S.D.N.Y. 1991).

15. *Destefano* v. *Grabrian*, 763 2d 275 (Colo. 1988).

16. *Destefano* v. *Grabrian*, 763 2d 275, 284, 287 (Colo. 1988).

17. *Destefano* v. *Grabrian*, 763 2d 275, 281 (Colo. 1988), citing *Lund* v. *Caple*, 675 2d 226, 231 (Wash. 1984).

18. *Strock* v. *Pressnell*, 527 N.E.2d 1235, 1240, N. 5 (Ohio 1988).

19. *Strock* v. *Pressnell*, 527 N.E.2d 1235, 1245, N. 10 (Ohio 1988).

20. See *Cox* v. *Thee Evergreen Church*, 836 S.W.2d 167 (Tex. 1992); *Davis* v. *Church of Jesus Christ of Latter Day Saints*, 244 Mont. 61, 796 2d 181 (1990); *Heath* v. *First Baptist Church*, 341 So.2d 265 (Fla. Ap) cert. denied, 348 So.2d 946 (Fla. 1977); *Fintak* v. *Catholic Bishop of Chicago*, 366 N.E.2d 480 (Ill. 1977).

21. *United States* v. *Ballard*, 322 U.S. 78, 64 S.Ct. 882, 88 L.Ed. 1148 (1944); *U.S.* v. *Bakker*, 925 F.2d 728 (4th Cir. 1991).

22. *Nelson* v. *Dodge*, 76 R.I. 1, 68 A.2d 51 (1949).
23. *Davis* v. *Black*, 70 Ohio Ap 3d 359, 591 N.E.2d 11 (1991); *Broderick* v. *King's Way Assembly of God Church*, 808 2d 1211 (Alaska 1991); *Byrd* v. *Farber*, 57 Ohio St.3d 56, 565 N.E.2d 584 (1991); *J.* v. *Victory Tabernacle Baptist Church*, 236 Va. 206, 372 S.E.2d 391 (Va. 1988); *Mutual Service Casualty Ins. Co.* v. *Puhl*, 354 N.W.2d 900 (Minn. 1984). The tragic Wayside Baptist Church case points up how cases like these can threaten to destroy an entire congregation. That Miami, Florida congregation hired a youth minister who subsequently sexually abused a number of teenage boys. A Dade County court found the Church guilty of negligence in hiring the minister, currently serving a 15-year sentence for sexual battery, and entered judgment on a jury verdict for $4.2 million dollars. The Church's attorney said the Church could be forced into bankruptcy since it carried insurance of only $1-million. "Church Loses Motion To Overturn $4.2M Verdict," Dana Phillips, *South Florida Business Journal*, May 6-12, 1994, 22.
24. *Bass* v. *Aetna Insurance Co.*, 370 So.2d 511 (La. 1979).
25. *Dayton Christian Schools* v. *Ohio Civil Rights Commission*, 578 F.Sup 1004, 1011 (Ohio W.D. 1984).
26. *Dayton Christian Schools, Inc.* v. *Ohio Civil Rights Commission*, 766 F.2d 932 (6th Cir. 1985).
27. *Ohio Civil Rights Commission* v. *Dayton Christian Schools*, 477 U.S. 619, 106 S.Ct. 2718, 91 L.Ed.2d 512 (1986).
28. The Supreme Court's reason for making this decision rested on the landmark case of *Younger* v. *Harris*, 401 U.S. 37, 91 S.Ct. 746, 27 L.Ed.2d 669 (1971). The legal principle at work here is that Federal Courts will abstain and not intervene into matters still under review by state agencies. It is called the "Abstention Doctrine."
29. *Ohio Civil Rights Commission* v. *Dayton Christian Schools*, 106 S.Ct. at 2723.

Chapter 5

1. *Sermons Illustrated*, December 1994, card 23.
2. Samuel B. Casey, executive director, Christian Legal Society, letter to members, November 30, 1994.
3. Mark Curriden, "Defenders of the Faith," *ABA Law Journal* (December 1994):, 87.
4. John Lofton, "Nothing To Celebrate In Perversion Of Rights," *USA Today*, 3 July 1991, p. 10A.
5. M. Stanton Evans, "The Supreme Court Is Wrong About Religion," *Reader's Digest* (December 1994) p. 87.
6. 406 U.S. 205, 92 S.Ct. 1526, 32 L.Ed.2d 15 (1972).
7. 455 U.S. 252, 102 S.Ct. 1051, 71 L.Ed.2d 127 (1982).
8. Religious intolerance brewed in Great Britain and most of Europe. It arose from the uneasy alliance between government and particular churches established by law and recognized as the sole repository of religious truth. The British Parliament granted that authority to the Church of England as the established church. The goal was to cause the people, through persuasion or coercion if necessary, to accept and practice the social, political, and religious orders sanctioned by church and state. Those who spoke against the government or its officers were punished for seditious libel. Those who spoke against the established church were guilty of blasphemous libel. Citizens were compelled to pay tithes or taxes to support the established church, and forced to attend its worship services. Dissenters had to pay money to support religious opinions they did not agree with, listen to sermons and doctrines they rejected, and were denied the right to hold public office. They suffered severe civil and religious consequences, sometimes to the point of having their marriages annulled and children declared illegitimate.
9. As quoted by the late North Carolina Senator and constitutional law expert Sam J. Ervin, Jr. in an article, "Why I Believe in the FIRST Amendment," *Liberty* (November/December 1985): 12.

10. With later adoption of the Fourteenth Amendment and its Due Process Clause in July 1868, the First Amendment now shields and protects religious liberties of citizens from both federal and state governmental interference.

11. *Epperson* v. *Arkansas*, 393 U.S. 97, 103-104, 89 S.Ct. 266, 270, 21 L. Ed.2d 228 (1968).

12. *Zorach* v. *Clauson*, 343 U.S. 306, 313-14 (1952). "The government may (and sometimes must) accommodate religious practices and . . . may do so without violating the Establishment Clause." *Hobbie* v. *Unemployment Appeals Commission of Florida*, 480 U.S. 136, 144-145, 107 S.Ct. 1046, 1051, 94 L.Ed.2d 190 (1987).

13. Joseph Story, *Story's Commentaries on the Constitution of the United States*, vol. 2, 630 (5th ed. 1891).

14. *United States* v. *Lee*, 455 U.S. 252, 102 S.Ct. 1051, 71 L.Ed.2d 127 (1982); *Hernandez* v. *Commissioner*, 490 U.S. 680, 109 S.Ct. 2136, 104 L.Ed.2d 766 (1989). Similar governmental interests were protected in *Gillette* v. *United States*, 401 U.S. 437, 91 S.Ct. 828, 28 L.Ed.2d 168 (1971) where the Supreme Court sustained the military selective service system against the claim that it violated the Free Exercise Clause by conscripting persons who opposed the Vietnam War on religious grounds.

15. For example, in *Reynolds* v. *United States*, 98 U.S. 145, 25 L.Ed. 244 (1879), the Supreme Court considered the practice of polygamy in the Mormon Church. In a unanimous decision, the Court noted that polygamy was offensive in Anglo-American and European nations, and there were explicit criminal statutes forbidding the practice, including one enacted by Congress. In that case, the Court determined that the anti-polygamy law did not violate the First Amendment rights of the Mormon Church and its religious practices.

16. Quote by Thomas Jefferson in response to an address given by a committee of the Danbury Baptist Association (January 1, 1802), reprinted in *Writings of Thomas Jefferson* 113 (H. Washington ed. 1861). Interestingly enough, although few would dispute that Jefferson was not knowledgeable and competent to comment on the First Amendment, he was in France at the time the First Amendment was drafted and passed. Even so, Jefferson and James Madison were instrumental in having Jefferson's Bill for Establishing Religious Freedom, which proposed complete separation of church and state, passed by the Virginia Legislature in November 1785 and enacted into law as the Virginia Statute for Religious Liberty. Madison then used the Virginia Statute in drafting the First Amendment concepts and securing approval of Congress in 1791.

17. *Engel* v. *Vitale*, 370 U.S. 421, 431-32, 82 S.Ct. 1261, 1267, 8 L.Ed.2d 601 (1962)—being the first "school prayer" case decided by the Supreme Court.

18. *Marsh* v. *Chambers*, 463 U.S. 783, 103 S.Ct. 3330, 77 L.Ed.2d 1019 (1983).

19. 36 U.S.C. §172 (1954). The House report on the legislation amending the Pledge states that the purpose of the amendment was to affirm the principle that "our people and our Government [are dependent] upon the moral directions of the Creator." H.R.Re No. 1693, 83rd Cong., 2d Sess. 2, reprinted in 1954 *U.S. Code Cong. & Admin. News* 2339, 2340.

20. *Church of Holy Trinity* v. *U.S.*, 143 U.S. 457, 471 (1892).

21. *Zorach* v. *Clauson*, 343 U.S. 306, 313 (1952).

22. U.S. Supreme Court Justice O'Connor, Concurring opinion in *Wallace* v. *Jaffree*, 472, U.S. 38, 105 S.Ct. 2479, 2497, 86 L.Ed.2d 29 (1985).

23. *Lee* v. *Weisman*, U.S. , 112 S.Ct. 2649, 120 L.Ed.2d 467 (1992). This case has stilled a great deal of controversy. Litigation and legislation over prayer in public schools has exploded since this case was decided, creating a split among various federal courts. The conflict centers on students accusing schools of unconstitutionally interfering with their First Amendment right of religious expression, and those who see any prayer in schools as an improper and illegal government endorsement of religion. One key difference is who leads the prayer. After the Weisman decision, the 5th U.S. Circuit Court of Appeals upheld a resolution allowing high school seniors to choose a volunteer to deliver an invocation and benediction at their graduation ceremonies that was "nonsectarian and nonproselytizing in nature." *Jones* v. *Clear Creek Independent School District*, 977 F.2d 963 (1992). That Court reasoned that any taint of governmental entanglement is removed by allowing the students themselves to control the prayer,

rather than the school having a teacher or outside clergy engage in prayer at student exercises. Also, the Court believed that graduating high school seniors were less impressionable in their religious beliefs than younger students. However, the 3rd and 9th U.S. Circuit Courts of Appeal rejected the Jones rationale in 1993 cases involving student-led prayers. See, e.g., *Harris* v. *Joint School District No. 241*, 821 F. Sup 638 (D. Idaho 1993) and subsequent appeal to 9th U.S. Circuit Court of Appeals. One would expect the 1995 Republican-controlled Congress to introduce a constitutional amendment allowing for individual and group prayer in public schools to resolve much of this confusion.

24. *Wallace v. Jaffree*, 472 U.S. 38, 105 S.Ct. 2479, 86 L.Ed.2d 29 (1985). The Court struck down an Alabama effort to "legislate" prayer into public schools, but properly noted the obvious in saying that any period of silence during a typical school day could be used by every student for meditation or voluntary prayer if one chooses. Justice O'Connor concurred in this decision, but made this special note: "A state sponsored moment of silence in the public schools is different from state sponsored vocal prayer or Bible reading. First, a moment of silence is not inherently religious. Silence, unlike prayer or Bible reading, need not be associated with a religious exercise. Second, a pupil who participates in a moment of silence need not compromise his or her beliefs. During a moment of silence, a student who objects to the prayer is left to his or her own thoughts, and is not compelled to listen to the prayers or thoughts of others. For these simple reasons, a moment of silence does not stand or fall under the Establishment Clause according to how the Court regards vocal prayer or Bible reading. . . . It is difficult to discern a serious threat to religious liberty from a room of silent, thoughtful schoolchildren." In a dissenting opinion, Chief Justice Burger also noted: "Some who trouble to read the opinions in this case will find it ironic—perhaps even bizarre—that on the very day we heard arguments in this case, the Court's session opened with an invocation for Divine protection. Across the park a few hundred yards away, the House of Representatives and the Senate regularly open each session with a prayer. These legislative prayers are not just one minute in duration, but are extended, thoughtful invocations and prayers for Divine guidance. They are given, as they have been since 1789, by clergy appointed as official Chaplains and paid from the Treasury of the United States. Congress has also provided chapels in the Capitol, at public expense, where Members and others may pause for prayer, meditation—or a moment of silence. Inevitably some wag is bound to say that the Court's holding today reflects a belief that the historic practice of the Congress and this Court is justified because members of the Judiciary and Congress are more in need of Divine guidance than are schoolchildren."

25. *Stone* v. *Graham*, 449 U.S. 39, 101 S.Ct. 192, 66 L.Ed.2d 199 (1980). A divided Court (5-4 decision) struck down a Kentucky state law requiring posting of a privately purchased copy of the Ten Commandments on a wall of every public school classroom in the state. The Court indicated, however, that the Ten Commandments and the Bible might be integrated into a school curriculum study of history, civilization, ethics or comparative religion without being unconstitutional.

26. *Epperson* v. *Arkansas*, 393 U.S. 97, 89 S.Ct. 266, 21 L.Ed.2d 228 (1968). However, in *Edwards* v. *Aguillard*, 482 U.S. 578, where the Court struck down a Louisiana statute requiring equal time for teaching evolutionism and creationism, the Court nevertheless stated that schools may teach alternative theories of origin other than evolution—including evidence disproving evolution and showing a design model.

27. *School District of Abington Township* v. *Schempp*, 374 U.S. 203, 83 S.Ct. 1560, 10 L.Ed.2d 844 (1963).

28. *Engel* v. *Vitale*, 370 U.S. 421, 82 S.Ct. 1261, 8 L.Ed.2d 601 (1962).

29. *Illinois ex rel. McCollum* v. *Board of Education*, 333 U.S. 203, 210-211, 68 S.Ct. 461, 464-465, 92 L.Ed. 649 (1948).

30. *Washegesic* v. *Bloomingdale Public Schools*, 813 F. Supp 559 (W.D. Mich. 1993). After losing an appeal to the Federal Court of Appeals, the "Head of Christ" was removed from the school in February 1995. An appeal is being made to the U. S. Supreme Court.

31. Peter J. Riga, "A Secular Portrayal of Christ?" *The National Law Journal*, January 24, 1994, 15.

32. So named after the Supreme Court's landmark decision in *Lemon* v. *Kurtzman*, 403 U.S. 602, 91 S.Ct. 2105, 29 L.Ed.2d 745 (1971).

33. One of the most recent examples of this appears in the conflicting opinions of the Supreme Court justices in *Board of Education of Kiryas Joel Village School District* v. *Grumet*, U.S. , 62 U.S.L.W. 4665, June 27, 1994, in which the Justices ruled 6-3 that a New York law creating a school district for the benefit of a village of Satmar Hasidim (practitioners of a strict form of Judaism) violated the neutrality required by the First Amendment Establishment Clause.

34. ___U. S.___, 113 S.Ct. 2462, 125 L.Ed.2d 1 (1993).

35. ___U. S.___, 113 S.Ct. 2141, 124 L.Ed.2d 352 (1993).

36. ___U. S.___, 113 S.Ct. 2217, 124 L.Ed.2d 472 (1993).

37. Santeria evolved from East African religious practices, transplanted with the slave trade to Cuba, and mixed with Roman Catholicism and native practices. Santeria members offer sacrifices of chickens, pigeons, goats, sheep, etc. by cutting the carotid artery in order to nourish and demonstrate devotion to spirits called orishas. After completing the sacrifice, the animals are often cooked and eaten by the members.

38. 494 U.S. 872, 110 S.Ct. 1595, 108 L.Ed.2d 876 (1990).

39. Religious Freedom Restoration Act of 1993, Pub.L. 103-141, 107 Stat. 1488, 42 U.S.C. §2000bb.

40. Actually, the *Smith* case is still valid caselaw precedent. RFRA does not technically reverse the Court's decision since that is not within the power and authority of Congress. However it does provide that any laws of general application may not substantially burden a person's exercise of religion except if the government demonstrates that the application of the burden: (1) is in furtherance of a compelling governmental interest; and (2) is the least restrictive means of furthering that compelling governmental interest. Therefore, the Act does reverse the effect of *Smith* by establishing a new right of action in favor of aggrieved religious individuals to require the government to demonstrate that it has a compelling governmental interest in enforcing any law hindering a religious practice.

41. Concurring opinion of Justice O'Connor in *Board of Education of Kiryas Joel Village School District* v. *Grumet*, U.S. , 62 U.S.L.W. 4665, 4673–4674, June 27, 1994.

42. *Bob Jones University* v. *United States*, 461 U.S. 574, 103 S.Ct. 2017, 76 L.Ed.2d 157 (1983).

43. Section 501 (c) (3) of the Internal Revenue Code.

44. Daniel J. Little, "Thus Saith The IRS," *Liberty*, March.April 1994, 18–22.

45. Sam J. Ervin, Jr., "Why I Believe in the FIRST Amendment," *Liberty*, November/December, 1985, 10.

46. In *Walz* v. *Tax Commissioner*, 397 U.S. 664, 694, 90 S.Ct. 1409, 1424, 25 L.Ed.2d 697 (1970), the Court upheld a tax exemption for a religious organization noting that nontaxation permitted a lower degree of entanglement between government and religion. The Court stated that it was critical to avoid contexts where any "governmental evaluation" of religious practices, "state investigation into church operations," or any involvement of government in "difficult classifications of what is or is not religious."

47. U.S. Supreme Court Chief Justice Burger dissenting opinion in *Wallace* v. *Jaffree*, 105 S.Ct. 2479, 2508 (1985), quoting Horace, Epistles, Book III (Ars Poetica), Line 139.

48. *Thomas* v. *Review Board, Indiana Employment Security Division*, 450 U.S. 707, 716, 101 S.Ct. 1425, 1431, 67 L.Ed.2d 624 (1981); *Presbyterian Church* v. *Hull Church*, 393 U.S. 440, 450, 89 S.Ct. 601, 606–607, 21 L.Ed.2d 658 (1969); *Jones* v. *Wolf*, 443 U.S. 595, 602-606, 99 S.Ct. 3020, 3024–3027, 61 L.Ed.2d 775 (1979); *United States* v. *Ballard*, 322 U.S. 78, 85–87, 64 S.Ct. 882, 885-887, 88 L.Ed. 1148 (1944).

49. See, e.g., *DeMarco* v. *Holy Cross High School*, 797 F. Sup 1142, 1151–1152 (E.D.N.Y. 1992), reversed 4 F.3d 166 (2nd Cir. 1993), where the District Court and Court of Appeals disagreed as to evaluation of the value and truthfulness of religious doctrine and whether a challenged action or practice conforms to a religious purpose; *Church of Scientology* v. *City of Clearwater*, 756 F. Sup 1498, 1509–1512 (M.D. Fla.

1991) ("zone of interests" requirement for standing to raise a First Amendment challenge under 42 U.S.C. §1983), affirmed in part, vacated in part, and reversed in part, 2 F.3d 1514 (11th Cir. 1993) where the Court of Appeals found error with the District Court's investigation into whether Scientology was, in fact, a religion stating, "The City could not . . . [contend] that the tenets of Scientology are fantastic or false and by arguing, as a consequence, that its collection of funds under the cloak of religion is therefore fraudulent. The First Amendment precludes civil authorities from evaluating the truth or falsity of religious beliefs."

 50. *Jaffree* v. *Board of School Commissioners of Mobile County*, 554 F.Sup 1104, 1128 (S.D. Ala. 1983). In 1985, when the U.S. Supreme Court reviewed this case, the Court made specific reference to this amazing quote, which was clearly contrary to that Court's decisions and the plain meaning of the First Amendment.

 51. Lynn Buzzard & Thomas S. Brandon, Jr., *Church Discipline and the Courts*, (Wheaton, Ill: Tyndale House Publishers, Inc. 1986), 218-219.

 52. Judge Edith H. Jones, "How Infirm A Foundation," *Christian Legal Society Quarterly*, Spring, 1993, 5.

Chapter 6

 1. Submittal by Charles H. Harp II, "War Stories," *ABA Journal*, June, 1985, 148.

 2. Submittal by Myron Shwartz and Judge Tommy Thompson, "War Stories," *ABA Journal*, May 1, 1988, 174.

 3. Cartoon by Stromoski, *Omni*, December, 1994, 94.

 4. Terence Mann, "Stop Blaming Lawyers For Life," *The Review*, June 21, 1991, 5A.

 5. Matthew A. Hodel, "No Hollow Hearts", *ABA Journal*, October, 1991, 68.

 6. Thom Weidlich, "A Cynical Age Sees Few Heroes In Its Lawyers," *The National Law Journal*, November 29, 1993, 24, 26.

 7. David Margolick, "Hollywood's Love-Hate Affair With Lawyers," The *Miami Herald*, July 5, 1993, 1C, 2C.

 8. You can determine whether an attorney has the minimum level of competence by receiving knowledgeable referrals; checking out references; calling the State Bar Association to find out if the lawyer is a member in good standing, whether there have been any disciplinary complaints made in the last five years, and whether he or she is certified to practice in the area of your legal conflict; and by researching the attorney's background and ratings in the Martindale Hubbell Law Directory.

 9. Abraham Lincoln echoed these thoughts by once advising his fellow lawyers: "Resolve to be honest at all events; and if, in your own judgment, you cannot be an honest lawyer, resolve to be honest without being a lawyer. Choose some other occupation, rather than one in the choosing of which you do, in advance, consent to be a knave."

 10. *Christian Legal Society Quarterly*, Fall 1991, 15.

 11. Creed of Professionalism adopted by the Board of Governors for the Florida Bar on May 16, 1990.

 12. The rules of evidence in many courts allow for exclusion of certain relevant facts because considering the same would result in unfair prejudice to one or more parties, confusion of the issues, mislead the jury, or because presentation of the evidence would only result in undue delay, waste of time or be duplicative of matters already considered. The principle at work here is to exclude relevant evidence in order to protect the judicial process from bias or prejudice. Cherished values such as protecting legally privileged information in the interest of preserving confidential exchanges (lawyers, clergy, doctors, etc.) and honoring personal privacy, dignity, security, autonomy often must take precedence over the naked truth in a particular case. But, as we shall see, the end result is that decisions are being made in court without all the relevant facts being on the table for consideration.

 13. Franklin Delano Strier, "Through A Juror's Eyes," *ABA Journal*, October 1, 1988, 80.

 14. The *Florida Bar News*, November 1, 1992, 2.

15. David Landis, "Attorney Angst," *USA Today,* March 5, 1992, 1D.
16. *Washington State Physicians Insurance Co.* v. *Fisons,* 858 2d 1054 (Wash. 1993).
17. *In the Estate of Lewis E. Wadsworth,* So. 2d , 15 FLW D1511, D1512 (Fla. 5th DCA 1990).
18. Judge Thomas M. Reavley, "Ultimate Concord, the Convention and Us," The *Florida Bar Journal,* July/August, 1988, 52.
19. Arnold H. Rutkin, Editorial, *Family Advocate,* American Bar Association, Vol. 16, No. 3, 1994, 4.
20. Gary Blankenship, "More Lean Times Ahead For Lawyers," The *Florida Bar Journal,* September 15, 1994, 1.
21. Thom Weidlich, "In World Legal Bills, U.S. Wins On Hours," *The National Law Journal,* October 17, 1994, A5, citing an International Financial Law Review 1000 report by London-based Euromoney Publications, Inc. based on a survey of 24 countries. American lawyers averaged 2,500 billable hours per year, while United Kingdom lawyers ranked second at 2,250.
22. In a 1994 independent study, commissioned by Lexis-Nexis, 250 managing partners and administrators of American law firms with more than 10 lawyers confirmed that there is a definite move away from traditional, open-ended, hourly billing in the 1990s to a variety of alternative billing methods such as project billing, flat fee billing, task-based billing, and use of blended or average hourly rates and discounted hourly rates. However, these measures have served to increase law firm profits above those received from normal hourly rates. "Poll Finds New Billing Practices Make Some Firms More Profitable," The *Florida Bar News,* December 15, 1994, 9.
23. James Fox Miller, "The Curse of the Legal Profession," The *Florida Bar Journal,* February, 1991, 9.
24. Cited in "That's Outrageous!" *Reader's Digest,* June 1993, 133.
25. Mark Hansen, "Suicide Suit Dismissed," *ABA Journal,* July 1994, 25.

Chapter 7

1. Matthew A. Hodel, "No Hollow Hearts," *ABA Journal,* October, 1991, 68.
2. Patricia A. Seitz, "Tales of Peanut Butter and Jelly," The *Florida Bar Journal,* October, 1993, 6.
3. Bob Cohn, "The Lawsuit Cha-Cha," *Newsweek,* August 26, 1991, 58.
4. Cited in "That's Outrageous!" *Reader's Digest,* October, 1994, 97.
5. Cited in "That's Outrageous!" *Reader's Digest,* June, 1994, 65.
6. Cited in "That's Outrageous!" *Reader's Digest,* July, 1993, 136.
7. Roger Conner, "Have Too Many Americans Lost Their Sense of Accountability?" *The PriceCostco Connection,* December 1994, 13.
8. "Members Speak on Accountability," *The PriceCostco Connection,* December 1994, 13.
9. Martin J. Campbell, Letter to Editor, The *Florida Bar Journal,* October 1993, 4.
10. Gary A. Grasso, "Defensive Lawyering: How To Keep Your Clients From Suing You," *ABA Journal,* October 1989, 100.
11. "News Of the Weird," *New Times,* December 1–7, 1994, 8.
12. 791 F.2d 1191 (5th Cir. 1986).
13. See Matthew 24:41–46 (explaining final judgment procedures)." Id. at 1199, n.2.
14. For these individuals filled up with arrogance and pride, any reading of Romans 13:1–7 regarding obedience by the populace to governmental authorities (and judges) must also be made in conjunction with other passages such as Romans 12:9–21 preceding that passage, and also the principles of Romans 2:1–11, 21–24.
15. Don Van Natta, Jr., Jeff Leen and Manny Garcia, "Tough Judge Gets Harsh Verdict," The *Miami Herald,* November 27, 1994, 1A, 22A.
16. The Federal Jury Selection and Service Act of 1968 (28 U.S.C. §§ 1861-1875 (1979)) does, however, allow for disqualification of potential jurors who are not U.S. citizens; unable to speak, read, write and understand English; charged with or convicted

of a felony; or have physical or mental disabilities which make it impossible to serve properly as jurors.

17. Pub.L. 95-572, §6 (a) (1), November 2, 1978, 92 Stat. 2456.

18. John D. McKinnon, "Can O.J. Find A Fair Jury?" The *Miami Herald*, August 21, 1994, 5M.

19. Mark Curriden, "Small-Town Justice," *ABA Journal*, November, 1994, 69.

20. In *Batson* v. *Kentucky*, 476 U.S. 79 (1986), the U.S. Supreme Court ruled that the use of peremptory challenges to disqualify potential jurors on the basis of race violated constitutional equal protection rights under the Fourteenth Amendment. But how is such discrimination proven when no reasons need be given in using such challenges? Continued use of peremptory challenges almost encourages lawyers to use deception in still seeking the same discriminatory ends.

21. The U.S. Supreme Court, in *J.E.B.* v. *T.B.*, U.S. , S.Ct. 92-1239 (April 19, 1994) where a defendant male in a paternity case brought by the State of Alabama argued that the State used nine peremptory challenges in a discriminatory fashion to remove all males from the jury, ruled 6-3 that gender based peremptory challenges are unconstitutional under the Equal Protection Clause of the Fourteenth Amendment to the U.S. Constitution.

22. Jeff Barge, "Reformers Target Jury Lists," *ABA Journal*, January, 1995, 26.

23. Judges in many states do have discretion to allow for juror questions under controlled circumstances. This usually involves a juror writing down a question after the lawyers have completed their questioning of a witness and giving it to the judge to review in terms of its legal acceptability. After discussing the questions privately with the attorneys and there is no objection, the judge, not the juror, will ask the permissible questions of the witness. This procedure avoids many of the concerns raised by juror questions.

24. For many years after adoption of the Constitution, juries and judges worked on a level plane in interpreting the law. But, in the 1895 decision of Sparf & Hansen v. U.S., 156 U.S. 51, the U.S. Supreme Court ruled that jurors in federal trials could not decide questions of law. (Most states also followed this holding.) Therefore, the Court held, trial judges must instruct jurors on the applicable law so they could render a proper verdict. Many judges worked with attorneys in preparing a standard set of jury instructions for various types of cases, still in wide use today.

25. Christine Evans and Don Van Natta, Jr., "The Verdict on Juries: Only Human," The *Miami Herald*, Sunday, May 2, 1993, 1A, 24A.

26. J. Frank, *Law and the Modern Mind*, 174 (1930).

27. As quoted by Franklin Delano Strier, "Through the Juror's Eyes," *ABA Journal*, October 1, 1988, 81.

28. Walter K. Olson, "System Overload," *ABA Journal*, October, 1991, 70.

29. Stephanie B. Goldberg, "The Ide Agenda," *ABA Journal*, October, 1993, 123.

Chapter 8

1. Charles Dickens, *A Tale of Two Cities* 1 (1859).

2. Bob Cohn, "The Lawsuit Cha-Cha," *Newsweek*, August 26, 1991, 58, 59.

3. Tom Fiedler, "Congress May Curtail the Liability Lottery," The *Miami Herald*, April 24, 1994, 5C.

4. The annual study of State Court Caseload Statistics is a joint project of the Conference of State Court Administrators, theState Justice Institute, and the National Center for State Courts. The Court Statistics Project of the NCSC compiles and reports comparable court caseload data from the 50 states, the District of Columbia, and Puerto Rico.

5. Of the 100.5 million trial court cases, 18.4 million were civil cases (10 percent tort cases); 13 million, criminal cases; 1.5 million juvenile cases; and 67.5 million, traffic or other ordinance violation cases.

6. The breakdown was 19 million new civil cases; 12.4 million criminal cases; 1.6 million juvenile cases; and 60.1 million traffic or other ordinance violation cases.

7. Appeals offer litigants an opportunity to reverse or change an unfavorable trial court decision by convincing an appellate court that the trial court judgment contained

a reversible error by allowing inadmissible testimony, giving improper jury instructions, misinterpreting state law, etc.

8. Cited in "State Court Caseload Statistics: Annual Report 1991—A Commentary on State Court Caseloads and Trends in 1991", National Center for State Courts, February, 1993.

9. These new case filings include 19.7 million new civil cases, up 3 percent from 1991; 13.2 new criminal cases, up four percent from the prior year; and 1.7 million new juvenile cases.

10. Randall Samborn, "Accelerating Caseloads Threaten To Swamp State Courts," The National Law Journal, May 9, 1994, A11.

11. "Bankruptcy Explosion," USA Today, December 17, 1990, 1B, citing New Generation Investment Inc. Bankruptcy Datasource.

12. Robert Kuntz, "Money Woes Deepen For Federal Courts," Miami Review, March 1, 1993, 1, 10.

13. Henry J. Reske, "Judges Irked By Tough-on-Crime Laws," ABA Journal, October 1994, 18.

14. J. Clifford Wallace, "Tackling The Caseload Crisis," ABA Journal, June 1994, 88.

15. Sanford Jaffe, "ADR: The Quiet Revolution in the Courts," Legal Times, September 6, 1993, 28.

16. David O. Stewart, "Quiet Times," ABA Journal, October 1994, 40.

17. "Prisoner Population Explosion," USA Today, July 21, 1992, 1A.

18. As quoted in ABA Journal, September, 1994, 40–41.

19. As cited in "That's Outrageous!" Reader's Digest, August, 1994, 96.

20. Henry J. Reske, "Keeping A Trim Federal Judiciary," ABA Journal, December 1993, 26.

21. Henry J. Reske, "Judges Irked By Tough-on-Crime Laws," ABA Journal, October 1994, 18.

22. Ibid.

23. Henry J. Reske, "Keeping Pace With Judicial Vacancies: Senior Judges and the Clinton Administration Struggle to Fill in the Gaps," ABA Journal, July 1994, 34. By the time of the Senate's mid-October, 1994 recess, however, the number of vacancies declined to 59. Henry J. Reske, "Judicial Vacancies Declining," ABA Journal, January 1995, 24.

24. Robert Kuntz, "Money Woes Deepen for Federal Courts," Miami Review, March 1, 1993, 10.

25. J. Clifford Wallace, Chief Judge, 9th Circuit U.S. Court of Appeals, "Tackling the Caseload Crisis: Legislators and Judges Should Weigh the Impact of Federalizing Crimes," ABA Journal, June 1994, 88.

26. Henry J. Reske, "Keeping Pace With Judicial Vacancies: Senior Judges and the Clinton Administration Struggle to Fill in the Gaps," ABA Journal, July, 1994, 34.

27. Henry J. Reske, "Judges Irked By Tough-on-Crime Laws," ABA Journal, October, 1994, 18.

28. James Podgers, "Chasing The Ideal: As More Americans Find Themselves Priced Out of the System, The Struggle Goes On To Fulfill The Promise of Equal Justice For All," ABA Journal, August, 1994, 57.

29. David Lyons, "Judges To Ease Caseload," The Miami Herald, July 27, 1993, 1B, 2B.

30. Don DeBenedictis, "Struggling Toward Recovery: Courts Hope That Belt-Tightening Lessons From Recession Will Help Them Make It Through The '90s," ABA Journal, August, 1994, 55.

31. Robert Kuntz, "Money Woes Deepen For Federal Courts," Miami Review, March 1, 1993, 1.

32. David Lyons, "Cash Squeeze May Postpone Civil Jury Trials," The Miami Herald, April 3, 1993, 2B.

33. David Lyons, "Lack Of Money For Jurors Delays Trial," The Miami Herald, June 22, 1993, 2B.

34. J. Michael McWilliams, "Dwindling Judicial Resources," *ABA Journal*, July, 1993, 8.

35. Don DeBenedictis, "Struggling Toward Recovery: Courts Hope That Belt-Tightening Lessons From Recession Will Help Them Make It Through The '90s," *ABA Journal*, August, 1994, 51.

36. Manny Garcia and Don Van Natta, Jr., "Grand Jury: Justice System Broken," The *Miami Herald*, May 12, 1994, 1B.

37. Jeff Schweers, "Requests For New Judges May Be Low," The *Florida Bar News*, November 15, 1993, 1.

38. Gary Blankenship, "Judiciary Grows Slowly Compared to the Rest of State Government," The *Florida Bar News*, January 1, 1995, 1, 14.

39. Mark Curriden, "Cash Crunch Delaying Litigation," *ABA Journal*, May 1994, 41.

40. Don DeBenedictis, "Struggling Toward Recovery: Courts Hope That Belt-Tightening Lessons From Recession Will Help Them Make It Through The '90s," *ABA Journal*, August,1994, 51. Fortunately, although the Connecticut courts remain under-funded, management measures made court operations more efficient, and the 1995 appropriation for the justice system increased to $162 million—up from the $126 million in 1991 (although there is no money allocated for salary increases to judges).

41. Jeffrey Schweers, "Marriage License Increase To Benefit Family Courts," The *Florida Bar News*, April 30, 1994, 28.

42. *Seitz v. Surfside, Inc.*, 517 So.2d 49 (Fla. 3d DCA 1987).

43. *The Village of King's Creek Condominium Association, Inc.* v. *Goldberg*, 596 So. 2d 1195 (Fla. 3d DCA 1992).

44. "McDonald's Settles Hot-Coffee Lawsuit," The *Miami Herald*, December 2, 1994, C1.

45. Cited in "That's Outrageous!" *Reader's Digest*, October, 1993, 84.

46. Joan Fleischman, "Violent Funeral Caused Anguish, Family Contends," The *Miami Herald*, December 26, 1994, B1.

47. Nancy Klingener, "Puppy Love: It Costs One Pet Owner $2,567," The *Miami Herald*, November 2, 1993, 5B.

48. Kenneth Budd, "Community Associations Around the Nation Are Saying . . . Give Mediation A Chance," *Common Ground*, January/February, 1992, 26.

49. Cited in *Sermons Illustrated*, June 1993, card 13.

50. *Bass v. Carlson*, 419 So.2d 410 (Fla. 2d DCA 1983).

51. Abraham Lincoln, "Government Cannot Endure Half Slave And Half Free," Republican State Convention, Springfield, Illinois, June 16, 1858.

52. Gary Fields, "Who's Minding The Kids?" *USA Today*, May 20, 1994, 1A.

53. Walter Russell Mead, "Economic Growth . . . Shrinking Paychecks," The *Miami Herald*, September 11, 1994, 1M.

54. As quoted by Henry J. Reske, "Paying The Price In Court: Breakdowns In Society Have Legal Impact On Children," *ABA Journal*, July 1994, 86.

55. "Violent Homes Called Key To Juvenile Crime," The *Miami Herald*, October 18, 1993.

56. Ronnie Green, "A Cry For Help Goes Unheeded," The *Miami Herald*, September 20, 1993, 1A.

57. Rorie Sherman, "Juvenile Judges Say: Time To Get Tough," The *National Law Journal*, August 8, 1994, A1.

58. Florida Bar President Patricia A. Seitz, "Which Do We Want: Guardrails or Ambulances?" The *Florida Bar Journal*, March 1994, 8.

59. Florida Bar President Patricia A. Seitz, "Tales of Peanut Butter and Jelly," The *Florida Bar Journal*, October 1993, 6, 8.

60. Doreen Weisenhaus, "Addressing Overload," The *National Law Journal*, May 9, 1994, A20.

61. Stuart M. Gerson, "Beyond Both Side's Tort-Reform Canards," *Legal Times*, May 11, 1992, 29.

Part Two Introduction

1. Justice Warren Burger, "Annual Report on the State of the Judiciary," *American Bar Association Journal* (March 1982), 68—as cited in Ken Sande's excellent book, *The Peacemaker* (Grand Rapids, Mich.:Baker Book House 1991), 38.

2. Justice Antonin Scalia, "Teaching About The Law," *Christian Legal Society Quarterly*, vol. 7, no. 4 (Fall 1987), 8-9—also cited by Ken Sande, *The Peacemaker* (Grand Rapids, Mich.:Baker Book House 1991), 38.

Chapter 9

1. John C. Susko, "Family Law Attorneys—Don't Ignore Mediation, Live With It and Improve It," The *Florida Bar Journal*, December 1987, 65.

2. R. William Ide III, "Summoning Our Resolve: Alternative Dispute Resolution Aims For Settlement Without Litigation," *ABA Journal*, October 1993, 8.

3. Bernard J. D'Avella, Jr., "The Ups and Downs of Alternative Dispute Resolution," *Legal Times*, September 6, 1993, 23.

4. Benjamin Sells, "Give Peace, Alternative Dispute Resolution A Chance," *Florida Bar News*, 15 June 1994, p. 23.

5. Arbitration was the first form of non-judicial dispute resolution. It can be legally binding or non-binding, but is most commonly practiced where one or more neutral experts consider the issues in dispute and render a binding decision based upon their knowledge and expertise within a particular discipline. An arbitration award has the force and effect of a legal judgment once confirmed by a court. Mini-trials is an adversarial exchange of information and negotiations between designated representatives of each disputing party before a presiding neutral third party advisor (many times a real judge or magistrate) and a jury. Evidence is presented by all disputing parties. The jury renders a non-binding decision, which serves as a reasonable prediction of how a civil court jury might decide in a case, thereby allowing the parties to settle without the time and expense of a full-scale trial. Neutral evaluation involves each party submitting a written brief of facts and argument to a neutral evaluator, followed up by a "working session" during which the parties and their legal counsel present summary arguments. The evaluator then assesses the strengths and weaknesses of each advocated position and renders a non-binding evaluation of the case issues.

6. 28 U.S.C. 471 et seq..

7. Margaret L. Shaw, "Courts Point Justice In A New Direction," The *National Law Journal*, April 11, 1994, C1.]

8. §44.1011 (2), Florida Statutes (1993).

9. See, e.g., §44.1011 (1), Florida Statutes (1993).

10. There is an interesting hybrid use of mediation and arbitration which is becoming very popular in recent years called "med-arb," short for "mediation-arbitration." Simply put, the parties initially try to resolve their dispute through mediation. If they cannot (or will not) agree on a settlement, the mediator then changes hats and becomes an arbitrator in rendering a decision for the parties. The Christian Conciliation Association and other organizations use this form of dispute resolution with good results.

11. Biblical mediation does involve a minimal amount of counseling the parties to a dispute, however. For this reason, I favor use of private mediation with a "team approach" by using a knowledgeable lawyer and counseling therapist working in tandem as mediators.

12. Engaging attorneys in the mediation process brings with it a number of adversarial concerns, as pointed out earlier in this chapter.

13. University of San Francisco Law Professor Joshua D. Rosenberg, "Court Studies Confirm That Mandatory Mediation Works," The *National Law Journal*, April 11, 1994, C7 (and citations noted in that article).

14. Professors Frank E.A. Sander and Stephen B. Goldberg, "When You Are Considering Ways To Keep A Client Out Of Court, The Challenge Is In Making The Right Choice," *ABA Journal*, November 1993, 67-68. Readers will find the goals and settlement impediments tables in this article very enlightening and helpful.

Chapter 10

1. Although we will review the following keys to conflict resolution as vehicles for biblical mediation, some dispute resolution measures discussed below may be closer to arbitration procedures rather than mediation. In 1 Corinthians 6:1-8, for example, it appears that Paul contemplates that one or more disputing Christians consent to be bound by the decision of a neutral Christian or group of Christians. Arbitration brings disputing parties before an uninvolved third party for the imposition of a decision. Mediation, in contrast, brings in a third party to assist the disputing parties to reach a mutually satisfactory resolution themselves. But the Scriptures are not definitive on this matter. They seem to support arbitration or mediation, as the parties involved freely decide for themselves depending upon the situation and factors involved. We will use the perspective of mediation, however, since arbitration through an imposed decision may not heal a broken relationship, while mediation allows the parties to work through their personal and legal difficulties in a more constructive manner.

2. *Raca* is an Aramaic word of utter contempt, akin to the Hebrew word for "empty" and signifying that one is intellectually "empty-headed," such as Abimelech's hirelings in Judges 9:4 and the "vain" man in James 2:20. *Vine's Expository Dictionary of Biblical Words* (Nashville, Tenn: Thomas Nelson Publishers 1984), 504.

3. Some might protest that this means sinful anger is just as wrong as murder. That might well be true. John equates hatred among Christians with murder. (1 John 3:15)

4. The root word is *tis,* meaning "anything" and appears 452 times in the New Testament, including Rom. 14:14; 1 Cor. 2:2, 10:19; 2 Cor. 2:10, 2 Cor. 3:5; Phil. 3:15; Jas. 1:7; 1 John 5:14.

5. The root word for "listen" in Matthew 18:15–16 is *akouo,* meaning "to hear something, and by hearing to learn, comprehend and understand." It appears 437 times in the New Testament, including John 5:24, 8:43, 47, 10:3, 8, 16, 27, 12:47; Acts 2:37; Rom. 10:14. The root word for "refuses to listen" in Matthew 18:17 is *parakouo,* meaning "to hear casually, carelessly, or as an aside and ignoring the advice or be unwilling to obey or respect what is being said." This form of the word appears only 2 times in the New Testament, both being in Matthew 18:17, although the same concept, in a different context, can be seen in the way Jesus ignored men from the house of Jairus in Mark 5:36.

6. This may be the reason why Jesus emphasized that is important to go to the offender and "show him his fault."

7. Samuel E. Ericsson, "How Dare You Sue One Another!" *Implications* (Annandale, VA:Christian Legal Society 1987), 3.

8. The only time a Christian may properly disobey the church is when its instructions conflict, clearly and unmistakably, with the Scriptures (Matt. 23:1-3; Acts 4:18–20, 5:27–32). A similar distinction is made when there is a conflict between God's law and civil laws of humankind. In both cases, a Christian's obligation is to obey God and the Scriptures as the ultimate authority. Therefore, when anyone is rejecting God's Word as part of being rebellious, that person is clearly in the wrong and in need of spiritual discipline.

9. However, the *Collinsville* case, reviewed in chapter 4, warns us that there are limits to any such privilege in instances where an individual voluntarily withdraws from church membership.

10. In verse 1, the words, "has his father's wife" in Greek mean "to have or use a woman (unlawfully) as a wife." (John the Baptist used similar terms to challenge Herod that it was unlawful to have his brother Philip's wife (Matthew 14:4; Mark 6:18).) The woman referred to was probably: (1) the Christian's stepmother, or Paul would have referred to her as the man's mother; and (2) not a Christian, or Paul would have spoken against her as well as the Christian man.

11. Verses 2 and 3 are very strong words! They express the depth of Paul's disgust with the circumstance, and the incredible apathy of the Corinthians in tolerating this situation. This man brought reproach upon the church, and polluted his own body—the temple of God (1 Corinthians 3:17, 6:19).

12. Some erroneously believe that tough love is contradictory with unconditional love. They argue that unconditional love does not set up limits of what is acceptable about another person's conduct. They view such limits as conditions in an effort to try and control the love object. They believe that unconditional love requires one to love others no matter what they do, and without trying to change them. Not so! There is a difference between unconditional love for a person, and unconditional acceptance of what they do. The former is biblical and loving, but the latter is not biblical at all. Unconditional love does not mean "anything goes." God loves the whole world—Christians and pagans alike—but only those who choose to believe in Christ will have eternal life (John 3:16). The Bible has numerous examples of loving the sinner, but hating the sin. Tough love says: "I love you unconditionally as a person. But I cannot accept your conduct to the extent it adversely affects my life or harms yourself or others." Unconditional love for people, and using tough love to set limits on acceptable conduct, are not contradictory at all but very consistent with helping any person see a need for personal repentance.

13. Paul undoubtedly desired to restore the man's heart to God. To do this, he allowed the man to suffer the consequences of his actions. By putting the man out of the life and fellowship within the Lord's church, and into the world controlled by Satan (Col. 1:13; 1 Tim. 1:20; 1 John 5:19), Paul hoped he would come to his senses. Like the lost son, perhaps he would see his need and return once again to his family in Christ.

14. This passage in 1 Corinthians 6 pertains only to disputes between Christians. It is written by the apostle Paul to Christians in Corinth who were in doubt as to how to resolve civil law disputes while being faithful to Christ. Some believe this passage applies to lawsuits between Christians and unbelievers, but this is clearly contrary to the text written to Christians and specifically referring to believers (v. 5). A corollary concern is whether this passage allows for lawsuits between faithful Christians and those who have been disfellowshipped pursuant to Matthew 18:15–17 and who are now treated as unbelievers. Many commentators believe that it does. Still others believe this passage forbids any lawsuits between people who merely profess to be Christians. This is a closer and more controversial call since it puts one into the position of having to judge the heart of another person. Although every case must be evaluated on its own merits since some people can masquerade as Christians (2 Cor. 11:13–15), I believe that the situation where an individual claims to be a Christian is likely to be covered by this passage because it is so difficult to know one's heart. In all events, the passage clearly forbids faithful Christians to sue other faithful Christians since such a lawsuit is an act of disobedience and poor witness to unbelievers.

15. The root word is *krino*, meaning "to contend with one another as warriors or combatants in a dispute or suit at law." The word appears 114 times in the New Testament, including Matt. 5:40.

16. The root word is *adikeo*, meaning "to suffer or receive wrong, hurt, damage, harm." It is used 27 times in the New Testament, including 1 Cor. 6:8; 2 Cor. 7:2; and Col. 3:25.

17. Certainly, repentance must be present. Also, in some marriage relationships conditions are not only appropriate but absolutely necessary. For example, an alcoholic spouse may return home saying, "I repent of drinking. Will you forgive me?" This mirrors the lost son's actions. But if the same spouse comes home saying those words while drunk and holding a bottle of liquor in front of the children, who would say it is wrong to throw the person out the door? See our discussion on tough love earlier in this chapter, and how it works with unconditional love.

18. I am indebted to Ancil Jenkins, Minister at the Sunset Church of Christ in Miami, Florida, for opening my eyes to much of the meaning behind this passage. He has graciously allowed me to share with you some of his observations in our discussion of these verses.

19. A tunic is the outside coat or outer garment similar to a poncho with a hole in the middle for one's head to go through. It kept one protected during the day, and warm at night. It was so precious that the Law of Moses did not allow one's tunic to be offered up as a pledge for a loan unless the one receiving it gave it back at the end of each day so the person could sleep with it

20. This illustration really focuses on the importance of elevating spiritual issues above property disputes, and to avoid further damage to the one being wronged. It does not necessarily mean, for example, that a Christian is always to give anyone who sues, or wants to sue, any or all of his or her property. 1 Corinthians 6:1–8 provides for alternative dispute resolution measures, as we have seen. But even that passage says it is better for Christians to concede disputes before going to law against other Christians because of the greater evils this presents.

21. Thomas Strahan, "Should A Christian Assert His Legal Rights?" *The Word and the Law, A Biblical Studies Guide*, (Oak Park, Ill: Christian Legal Society, 1977) Vol. 1, 64.

22. The Law of Moses provided that the first-born son was to receive two-thirds of the inheritance and the younger son one-third (Deut. 21:15–17). It is likely that the one complaining here might be the younger son who wanted more than his share of the inheritance.

Chapter 11

1. Chris Lehmann, "In God They Still Trust, But In Court They Argue," The *National Law Journal*, September 19, 1994, A20.

2. These states include Arizona, California, Colorado, Florida, Georgia, Hawaii, Illinois, Indiana, Maine, Nebraska, New Hampshire, New Jersey, North Carolina, Ohio, Oregon, Tennessee, Texas, Virginia, and Wisconsin. Sharon Press, "Building and Maintaining a Statewide Mediation Program: A View From the Field," 81 *Kentucky Law Journal*, 1029 (1992–93).

3. Robert Moberly, "The Florida Mandatory Mediation Experiment: Ethical Standards for Court-Appointed Mediators," 21 *Florida State Law Review*, 3 (Winter 1994), citing Florida Dispute Resolution Center, Florida Mediation/Arbitration Programs: A Compendium (1992).

4. Alison Gerenser and Megan Kelly, "Family Mediation: An Alternative to Litigation," The *Florida Bar Journal*, November 1994, 49.

5. *Sterling Village Condominium, Inc.* v. *Breitenbach*, 251 So. 2d 685 (Fla. 4th DCA 1971), in which the court ruled that removal of screening around a condominium porch and replacement with glass jalousies was prohibited.

6. Kenneth Budd, "Community Associations Around the Nation Are Saying . . . Give Mediation A Chance," *Common Ground*, January/February 1992, 28.

7. The *Florida Bar News*, June 15, 1993, 25.

8. "Survey Highlights ADR's Advantages," *Corporate Legal Times*, May 1993, 44, citing a March 1993 article appearing in the Wall Street Journal.

9. William H. Schroder, Jr., "Private ADR May Offer Increased Confidentiality," The *National Law Journal*, July 25, 1994, C14.

10. Dwight Golann, "Consumer Financial Services Litigation: Major Judgments and ADR Responses," *The Business Lawyer*, May 1993, 1143-1145.

11. Hal Davis, "Banks Follow Brokerages: Arbitrate Yes, Litigate No," The *National Law Journal*, September 12, 1994, B3. The Bank of America's decision to use ADR was upheld by a California state court in the 1992 case, *Badie* v. *Bank of America*, No. 944916—believed to be the first ruling in America upholding an ADR bank policy.

12. As cited by Richard C. Reuben, "Decision Gives Banking ADR A Boost," *ABA Journal*, December 1994, 32.

13. The American Arbitration Association is a nonprofit organization established in 1926 with its headquarters in New York City and regional offices in 35 cities across the U.S.

14. As noted by Keith W. Hunter and James K. Hoenig, "Dispute Resolution in Construction and Real Estate," *Real Estate Review*, Spring 1993, 80.

15. In 1975-81, the first Dispute Resolution Board was used in connection with completion of the Colorado Department of Transportation's Eisenhower Tunnel project, according to authors and AAA representatives Keith W. Hunter and James K. Hoenig.

16. Support for use of ADR in these and other federal agencies came through the enactment of the Administrative Dispute Resolution Act (Pub. L. No. 101–552), the

Negotiated Rule Making Act of 1990 (Pub. L. No. 101-648), and the Judicial Improvements Act (Pub. L. No. 101-650).

17. Cathy A. Costantino and Martha W. McClellan, "Scoring With ADR: The FDIC and RTC," *Probate & Property*, July/August 1993, 52.

18. Daniel W. O'Connell, Esq., "Growth Management Conflict Resolution In Florida," *Growth Management Studies Newsletter*, vol. 4, no. 1, September 1988, 2.

19. Robert Turk, Esq., "Mediation Can Avoid Lengthy Trials," *South Florida Business Journal*, Business Strategies, June 3-9, 1994, 24 A.

20. Clyde A. Szuch and Elizabeth J. Sher, "Demographics of Legal Profession Make ADR Inevitable," *Corporate Legal Times*, May 1993, 44.

21. "Academy of Matrimonial Lawyers' New Code of Conduct Promotes ADR," 2 *World Arbitration And Mediation Report*, 259 (1991).

22. Rosalind Resnick, "Hard-hit Accountants Offer To Mediate Claims," The *Miami Herald*, Business Monday Section, January 18, 1993, 11.

23. By 1992, Peace Foundation materials were sent to more than 13,000 schools, churches and private individuals nationwide, including school systems in New York City, St. Louis, Denver, Buffalo, Los Angeles and Philadelphia.

24. Cristina I. Pravia, "Stay Cool: Organization Launches Magazine to Help Students Resolve Conflicts," The *Miami Herald*, June 20, 1993, 32.

25. Jon O'Neill, "The Peacemakers: Can We Talk? Kid Counselors Take on Conflicts That Make School a Dangerous Place," The *Miami Herald*, December 18, 1992, 3E.

26. "Rewarding Government That Really Works," *Parade Magazine*, December 25, 1994, 7.

27. Esther Shein, "Mediation Resolves Conflicts in Schools," The *Boston Globe*, October 3, 1993, A 12.

28. My divorce settlement occurred only after my ex-wife refused to participate in church mediation based upon the principles of 1 Corinthians 6:1–8, but was ordered by the court to participate in civil law mediation. Fortunately this allowed us to talk without interference of attorneys and quickly resolve our property matters.

29. The *Florida Bar News*, March 1, 1994, 51.

30. Jessica Pearson and Nancy Thoennes, "Mediating and Litigating Custody Disputes: A Longitudinal Evaluation," 17 *Family Law Quarterly*, 497 (Winter 1984), 505.

31. "Pro Se Family Mediation Project," *Florida Dispute Resolution Center Newsletter*, Spring 1994, 11.

32. Chesterfield Smith, "Viewpoint: How To Curtail Lawyer Bashing," The *Florida Bar News*, July 1, 1994, 2.

33. Bernard J. D'Avella Jr., "The Ups and Downs of Alternative Dispute Resolution: Giving Up the Thrill of Battle," *Legal Times*, September 6, 1993, 25.

34. Kenneth Budd, "Community Associations Around the Nation Are Saying . . . Give Mediation A Chance," *Common Ground*, January/February, 1992, 25.

35. James Podgers, "Chasing The Ideal: As More Americans Find Themselves Priced Out of the System, The Struggle Goes On To Fulfill The Promise of Equal Justice For All," *ABA Journal*, August 1994, 61.

36. "Rewarding Government That Really Works," *Parade Magazine*, December 25, 1994, 7.

37. Roger I. Abrams, "What Have We Done To Ourselves?" The *Florida Bar Journal*, February 1990, 27.

38. As quoted by Adrienne Drell, "Chilling Out," *ABA Journal*, October 1994, 72.

39. Chief Justice Warren Burger, in an address on April 13, 1993 at the Robert Taylor Memorial Lecture at the University of Tennessee, "Burger Laments the Shysters of the Bar," *Legal Times*, May 3, 1993, 11.

40. Anthony T. Kronman, *The Lost Lawyer: Failing Ideals of the Legal Profession* (Cambridge, Mass.: Harvard University Press 1993).

41. Adrienne Drell, "Chilling Out," *ABA Journal*, October 1994, 72.

42. Chesterfield Smith, "Viewpoint: How To Curtail Lawyer Bashing," The *Florida Bar News*, July 1, 1994, 2.

43. As quoted by R. William Ide III, "The Will To Make A Difference," *ABA Journal*, July 1994, 8.

44. R. William Ide III, "The Will To Make A Difference," *ABA Journal*, July 1994, 8.

45. Ken Sande, "Finding Gold in a Trash Can," *Connections*, vol. 1, no. 3, December 1994, 6.

46. As quoted by R. William Ide III, "The Will To Make A Difference," *ABA Journal*, July 1994, 8.

Epilogue

1. Quoted by Bruce W. Flower, "Law in the Schools: Attitudes, Goals, and Methods," *Florida Bar Journal* (October 1993): 38.

2. As cited in *Sermons Illustrated*, October 1992, card 25.

3. W. C. Hill, "Conflict Management," *Baker Encyclopedia of Psychology*, (Grand Rapids, Mich: Baker Book House, 1985), 215.

4. Quoted in *Sermons Illustrated*, May 1987, item 24.

Index